Fragmenting Reality

Mind, Meaning and Metaphysics

Series Editors:
Johannes L. Brandl, University of Salzburg, Austria
Christopher Gauker, University of Salzburg, Austria
Max Kölbel, University of Vienna, Austria
Mark Textor, King's College London, UK

The *Mind, Meaning and Metaphysics* series publishes cutting-edge research in philosophy of mind, philosophy of language, metaphysics and epistemology. The basic questions in this area are wide-ranging and complex: What is thinking and how does it manage to represent the world? How does language facilitate interpersonal cooperation and shape our thinking? What are the fundamental building blocks of reality, and how do we come to know what reality is?

These are long-standing philosophical questions but new and exciting answers continue to be invented, in part due to the input of the empirical sciences. Volumes in the series address such questions, with a view to both contemporary debates and the history of philosophy. Each volume reflects the state of the art in theoretical philosophy, but also makes a significant original contribution to it.

Editorial Board:
Annalisa Coliva, University of California, Irvine, USA
Paul Egré, Institut Jean-Nicod, France
Olav Gjelsvik, University of Oslo, Norway
Thomas Grundmann, University of Cologne, Germany
Katherine Hawley, University of St. Andrews, United Kingdom
Øystein Linnebo, University of Oslo, Norway
Teresa Marques, University of Barcelona, Spain
Anna-Sophia Maurin, University of Gothenburg, Sweden
Bence Nanay, University of Antwerp, Belgium
Martine Nida-Rümelin, University of Freiburg, Switzerland
Jaroslav Peregrin, Czech Academy of Sciences, Czech Republic
Tobias Rosefeldt, Humboldt University of Berlin, Germany
Anders Schoubye, University of Edinburgh, United Kingdom
Camilla Serck-Hanssen, University of Oslo, Norway
Emily Thomas, Durham University, United Kingdom
Amie Lynn Thomasson, Dartmouth College, USA
Giuliano Torrengo, University of Milan, Italy
Barbara Vetter, Humboldt University of Berlin, Germany
Heinrich Wansing, Ruhr University of Bochum, Germany

Titles in the series include:
Knowledge and the Philosophy of Number, by Keith Hossack
Names and Context, by Dolf Rami
The Metaphysics of Contingency, by Ferenc Huoranszki
Fragmenting Reality, by Samuele Iaquinto and Giuliano Torrengo

Fragmenting Reality

An Essay on Passage, Causality and Time Travel

Samuele Iaquinto and Giuliano Torrengo

BLOOMSBURY ACADEMIC
LONDON • NEW YORK • OXFORD • NEW DELHI • SYDNEY

BLOOMSBURY ACADEMIC
Bloomsbury Publishing Plc
50 Bedford Square, London, WC1B 3DP, UK
1385 Broadway, New York, NY 10018, USA
29 Earlsfort Terrace, Dublin 2, Ireland

BLOOMSBURY, BLOOMSBURY ACADEMIC and the Diana logo are trademarks of
Bloomsbury Publishing Plc

First published in Great Britain 2022
This paperback edition published 2024

Copyright © Samuele Iaquinto and Giuliano Torrengo, 2023

Samuele Iaquinto and Giuliano Torrengo have asserted their right under the Copyright, Designs and Patents Act, 1988, to be identified as Authors of this work.

For legal purposes the Acknowledgements on p. vii constitute an extension of this copyright page.

Cover design by Louise Dugdale
Cover image © hanakaz/iStock

All rights reserved. No part of this publication may be reproduced or transmitted in any form or by any means, electronic or mechanical, including photocopying, recording, or any information storage or retrieval system, without prior permission in writing from the publishers.

Bloomsbury Publishing Plc does not have any control over, or responsibility for, any third-party websites referred to or in this book. All internet addresses given in this book were correct at the time of going to press. The author and publisher regret any inconvenience caused if addresses have changed or sites have ceased to exist, but can accept no responsibility for any such changes.

A catalogue record for this book is available from the British Library.

A catalog record for this book is available from the Library of Congress.

ISBN: HB: 978-1-3502-3532-8
       PB: 978-1-3502-3535-9
       ePDF: 978-1-3502-3533-5
       eBook: 978-1-3502-3534-2

Series: Mind, Meaning and Metaphysics

Typeset by RefineCatch Limited, Bungay, Suffolk

To find out more about our authors and books visit www.bloomsbury.com and sign up for our newsletters.

To Lucrezia
S.I.

To Muffin. And Peaches, Petunia, Bimbo and Beep Beep
G.T.

Contents

Figures	viii
Preface	ix
Introduction: From global coherence to fragmented time	1
1 Flow Fragmentalism	19
2 Open Future	69
3 Causation	97
4 Relativity	117
5 Time Travel	133
Notes	159
References	179
Index	189

Figures

1	The temporal dimension as seen from a 'god's eye' view.	79
2	h_1 'passes through' $F_1 = \langle i_1, h_1 \rangle$, while h_2 'passes through' $F_2 = \langle i_1, h_2 \rangle$.	82
3	Three nodes.	83
4	A branching succession of fragments with respect to F_0.	88
5	Reality is constituted only by facts in h_1.	91
6	Twin paradox scenario.	128
7	An 'expanded' representation of fragments though a system of (perspective, location) coordinates, and its 'compressed' version as a sequence of fragments.	137
8	Novikovian time travel.	138
9	Non-Novikovian time travel. First attempt.	141
10	The problem with the first attempt: incoherent fragments.	142
11	The tracking role solution.	147
12	MOV and changing the past.	151
13	Vacillating past.	153
14	Vacillator's truth-conditions.	155
15	Whither the in-between past?	156

Preface

> [T]here is nothing in all the world that keeps its form. All things are in a state of flux, and everything is brought into being with a changing nature. Time itself flows on in constant motion, just like a river.
>
> Ovid, *Metamorphoses*, Book XV

Things change. Time flows. Many cultural, philosophical, and religious traditions agree on this. And perhaps as many others disagree. The two authors of this book, if confronted with their deepest beliefs, find themselves on opposite sides of the barricade. However, in this book they have joined forces to elaborate a view in which a realist stance towards the passage of time is vindicated to the best of their efforts, and yet almost none of the usual assumptions about it are uphold. The outcome is a view that should be of interest not only to philosophers, but also to scholars in physics, psychology and linguistics, and whoever is curious about the nature of time.

Most of the material presented here has been written from scratch, but some parts are based on previously published papers (both jointly and individually). The Introduction is wholly new. Chapter 1 is based on our 2019 paper 'Flow Fragmentalism', *Theoria* 85: 185–201. Section 1.1 contains significant new material (section 1.1.4.6 is partly based on Iaquinto's 2020 paper 'Modal Fragmentalism', *The Philosophical Quarterly*, 70: 570–87). Sections 1.2 and 1.3 are largely new (section 1.2.3.1 is adapted from Iaquinto's 2019 paper 'Fragmentalist Presentist Perdurantism', *Philosophia* 47: 693–703). Chapter 2 draws on our 2020 paper 'The Invisible Thin Red Line', *Pacific Philosophical Quarterly*, 101: 354–82. There is extensive new material both in section 2.1 and in section 2.2. Chapters 3, 4 and 5 are entirely new. We wish to thank the editors and publishers concerned for permission to reuse our papers in a revised form.

Our works have been presented in a number of conferences and workshops in Germany, Italy, Japan, Romania, Switzerland and the USA. We would like to thank Giacomo Andreoletti, Maria Balcells, Sara Bernstein, David Braddon-Mitchell, Claudio Calosi, Fabrice Correia, Damiano Costa, Vincenzo Crupi, Ciro De Florio, Natalja Deng, Nikk Effingham, Aldo Frigerio, Akiko Frischhut, Christopher Gauker, Alessandro Giordani, Andrea Iacona, David Ingram, Martin

Lipman, Roberto Loss, Cristian Mariani, Giovanni Merlo, Ulrich Meyer, Kristie Miller, Peter Øhrstrøm, Sven Rosenkranz, Giuseppe Spolaore, Jan Sprenger, Jonathan Tallant, Achille Varzi and two anonymous referees of Bloomsbury for their helpful comments. Samuele Iaquinto would like to acknowledge the support of the Italian Ministry of Education, University and Research (PRIN Project 'Logic and Cognition: Theory, Experiments, and Applications', 2019–21). Giuliano Torrengo acknowledges the support of the Spanish Ministry of Science and Innovation (Project CHRONOS: PID2019-108762GB-I00, Project RYC-2017-22480), and the Department of Philosophy 'Piero Martinetti' of the University of Milan (under the Project 'Departments of Excellence 2018–2022', awarded by the Italian Ministry of Education, University and Research).

Finally, we would like to ask you not to be too demanding with each and every page that follows. After all, any work that should not have been just an article will contain well-wrought pieces, incomplete but possibly suggestive and inspiring sketches, and clever tricks to distract the reader when the remaining dust is pushed under the carpet.

Introduction: From global coherence to fragmented time

Fragmentalism describes the world as irreducibly fragmented in structure, so calling into question one of the pillars of traditional metaphysics, that is, the idea that reality is a *unitary* place. Each 'fragment' of reality is internally coherent, but nothing prevents different fragments from containing facts that are incompatible with one another. The view was originally introduced by Kit Fine (2005, 2006) as a non-standard version of the A-theory able to overcome some of the problems afflicting traditional dynamic approaches, like presentism, the growing block view and the moving spotlight theory. In recent years, the view has been gaining more and more attention,[1] the debate mostly focusing on how to pin down Fine's original insight. Part of the debate has been devoted to the idea – originally advocated by Fine – that fragmentalism is more promising than standard tense realism in offering an A-theoretic interpretation of the Special Theory of Relativity.[2] Fragmentalism has also been finding applications in fields of studies other than time. For instance, it has been recently argued that fragmentalism has the tools to deliver a new realist account of the quantum state.[3] Another example is the view called Modal Fragmentalism, which extends the idea that reality is irreducibly fragmented to the modal case.[4]

In this book, we develop a fragmentalist theory of time, which we call *Flow Fragmentalism*, and then explore its ramifications in a number of philosophical topics. In Chapter 1, after presenting the view, we argue that it offers an explanation of the passage of time that is unavailable to standard tense realism, and it is thus more effective than the latter in vindicating the inherent dynamism of reality. Chapter 2 presents a branching-time version of Flow Fragmentalism, in which a genuine form of openness of the future is vindicated. We argue that the view retains all the benefits of what we call ontological and topological openness. In Chapter 3, we provide a fragmentalist theory of causation, comparing and contrasting it with Humean reductionism about laws of nature.

Chapter 4 develops a relativistic version of Flow Fragmentalism and then discusses its advantages over Fine's version. Chapter 5 concludes the book by discussing how to understand time travel within the flow fragmentalist framework. Before entering the details of Flow Fragmentalism, in this introduction we spend some words on our methodological approach (section 0.1), we set the background of the debate on the nature of passage, motivating our general preference for the fragmentalist position (sections 0.2, 0.3 and 0.4), and finally we discuss some crucial assumptions of fragmentalism, and the way we interpret them (section 0.5).

0.1 Methodological remarks

This book is about the nature of time, and the discipline it belongs to is analytic metaphysics, broadly conceived. The methodological approach we will be following is one in which we directly appeal to the idea of reality being in a certain way, or things being really so and so. In this way, when discussing the nature of an alleged aspect of reality X (such as the passage of time, our main topic), we can distinguish *realist* and *anti-realist* positions concerning X, depending on whether they take reality to encompass X. The theories that we will discuss (and the one we will defend) are meant to be *metaphysically cogent* descriptions (at some level of abstraction) of reality. The aim is to 'carve nature at its joints', and not merely to describe reality in a manner that is adequate for some practical purpose. If a theory succeeds in allowing for formulations of metaphysically cogent descriptions of X, we say that it *captures* the target X. In order to formulate the theory that we defend, we will specify its *official idiom*, and give extensive glosses on the notions used in it, and the theses in the official idiom that constitute our official theory.[5] Although in the official idiom we do not have explicit mentions of facts, we will often recur, for ease of exposition, to expressions of the form 'the fact that *so and so*',[6] and talk of reality being constituted by facts, or of certain facts obtaining (as we will see in section 1.1.2, the distinction between constitution and obtainment is particularly important for the theory of time that we are going to develop).

Metaphysical theories that try to capture a certain alleged aspect of reality X can be used to formulate not only descriptions, but also hypotheses that aim at providing *explanations* concerning the nature of X. We will assume that there are explanatory relations between facts, and that certain facts may be explanatorily more basic than others, with respect to the target explanandum. For a theory to capture *X* is to possess the necessary resources to adequately encode the notion of *X* and express theses about *X*. For a theory to explain *X* (to a certain extent) is to provide hypotheses about *X* that are explanatory. What it takes for a hypothesis to be explanatory depends on the aim of the inquiry. Roughly, in a metaphysical inquiry such as the one that we pursue here, an explanatory hypothesis tells us what the nature of *X* is, and it is directed at answering questions such as what and how something is, rather than why something happened, and does not necessarily, or characteristically involve causal links. We stay neutral on whether there is a specific kind of 'metaphysical explanation' carried out by pointing out *grounding* relations between facts. At the same time, we do not wish to overstate the specificity of the explanations we will discuss and defend. Although we will not explicitly use any empirical data to support our various hypotheses, we believe that metaphysics is (or should be) an *empirically oriented* enterprise, possibly in a continuum with more hard-core empirical disciplines.

0.2 The debate on the nature of passage

Time is a difficult philosophical topic, with a notoriously elusive nature. One reason why time is so baffling is that there are several aspects of what we think of the world (and of our experience of it) which qualify as temporal. The phrase 'the nature of time' is thus potentially ambiguous. A further, perhaps deeper reason is that, even once we have disambiguated what we mean with the expression, it may remain unclear which kind of explanation one should provide. For the purpose of this book, we will proceed as follows. We stipulate – somewhat arbitrarily – that the passage of time is a subject matter central to a discourse about time in general, and call what we aim at accounting for *ordinary passage*. To a first approximation, with this expression we intend whatever we refer to when we say things like 'Two seconds have passed since the cat went out', 'Your son is already eighteen? Time passes, doesn't it?' and 'She passed her time in New York working hard'. The notion is vague, but it constitutes a starting point to understand the core claims of the realist and the anti-realist with respect to the passage of time. Roughly, the two parties disagree on whether the notion of ordinary passage is metaphysically cogent, and it thus deserves to show up in an account of how reality is like.

The realist answers positively to the question. A tradition that begins at least with the work of Arthur N. Prior has it that the ordinary passage is *robust passage*, namely the objective, mind-independent change in what is present. In this tradition – with which we will be mostly concerned in this book – presentness, and tenses in general, play a key role in accounting for the nature of passage.[7] The anti-realist answers negatively, or at least she maintains that only the minimal core of the ordinary notion is metaphysically cogent. According to the main anti-realist tradition, which traces back at least to the early Bertrand Russell, ordinary passage is *anaemic passage*.[8] Roughly, the thesis here is that ordinary passage merely requires that a relation of *earlier/later than* between events or moments obtains; tenses, presentness, and other purported features of reality belong entirely to the representational sphere.[9]

In this book, we will *not* be concerned with reasons for preferring realism over anti-realism or the other way around. We will rather assume realism, and look into its various manifestations, arguing for a specific version of it, Flow Fragmentalism. Realism in the Priorian tradition of robust passage has been elaborated in many forms in the context of what we call – following a suggestion by Kit Fine (2005) – the *standard framework* of the debate on the nature of passage. As we will see, the accounts in the standard framework manage (to which degree of success is matter of debate) to *capture* the idea of robust passage. The various standard versions of presentism, growing block, moving spotlight have the theoretical means to express that an objective, mind independent change in what is present happens. Roughly, they encode in the notion of real tense the idea of robust passage. However, they arguably lack the means to *explain* what makes it the case that the passage of time happens. We do not find in them any hypothesis telling us what passage consists of. The *non-standard* versions of realism have more theoretical means at their disposal, and in the course of the book we will argue that Flow Fragmentalism allows us to use the non-standard tools to provide an explanation of the passage of time that has also various other theoretical virtues that make it preferable to other realists options.[10]

0.3 The standard framework

Among the many naïve ideas or intuitions involving time, there are two that are interesting as a starting point for understanding the view of temporal reality that we will investigate in this essay.[11] The first is that the present time, the time that you are experiencing now, is *somehow privileged*. Maybe it feels different, maybe we tend to think of it as different, or maybe it is different indeed and we can deduce that effortlessly from ordinary observations. The second idea pulls us in the opposite direction: all times are alike, each – to paraphrase a famous aphorism

– prevents things from happening all at once. There is no principled way to distinguish 12.00 on the 3rd of February 2049 from 15.15 on the 17th of March 1953. Maybe what happens, respectively, at those times, makes it the case that they are very different, qualitatively speaking. But *as times*, they are like any other time you may wish to pick as a further example; either with a date expression, a description, or with an indexical such as 'now' or 'three minutes ago'.

Among the many metaphysical views that populate the philosophical debate on the nature of passage, the traditional (in the analytic tradition) opposition between the so-called A-theory and B-theory of time reflects this opposition of intuitions. The A-theory respects the intuition that the present time is privileged, and downplays the intuition according to which all times are on a par; while the B-theory respects the intuition that all times are born equal, and downplays the idea that the present time is privileged. A traditional way to flesh out the A-theory vs. B-theory debate is in terms of the opposition between tense realism and tense anti-realism.[12] Roughly, for the A-theorist, tensed expressions and attributes such as 'past', 'present' and 'future' capture some substantive aspect of reality, where 'substantive', as a first approximation, stands for 'non-representational' and 'mind-independent'. Therefore, the difference between the present and other times is metaphysically significant, and the present is indeed special in its unique status. Consequently, the intuition that all times are on a par should be downplayed; for instance, it can be understood as another way to say that all times either were or will be present at a certain point, and in this are similar to the present. To the contrary, for the B-theorist, we should not take the intuition of specialness as having serious metaphysical consequences. When we say or think of this or that time that it is present (and others are past and future), we fail to attribute a substantive property to a time. Tensed expressions are mere means to refer to times in a manner that is sensitive to the context that we happen to inhabit. The intuition of the privilege of the present should be understood as reflecting a *false belief* that we have about the temporary specialness of each of the times through which our conscious life unfolds. And the belief is false because no time is absolutely special, *not even for a brief moment*; rather, each one is special *relative* to itself – which is a very diluted form of specialness to enjoy.[13]

The appeal to tense realism and anti-realism facilitates us to disentangle two ingredients that are conceptually meshed into the notion of privilege or specialness:

(1) The metaphysical substantivity of the present
(2) The uniqueness of the present

The time we ordinarily refer to as 'the present' or 'now' may have a substantive metaphysical status, but that does not guarantee that it is the *only* time that has such a status. After all, it is plausible to maintain that the time in question has a substantive metaphysical status in virtue of its *intrinsic* properties. If so, the fact that it has a substantive metaphysical status cannot depend on the fact that *other* times do not have it.[14] It is thus important to understand that although in the standard framework (1) and (2) go always together, they could, in principle, part company (as they will in the non-standard framework). Traditional versions of A-theory – presentism, growing block, moving spotlight – converge on attributing to the present both substantiveness and uniqueness, but may disagree on how to construe them. For instance, usually presentists interpret substantiveness as existence: the present is privileged in virtue of being the only time that exists.[15] For the growing-blockers existence is not enough for being privileged, since both present and past times exist, the fact that the present is the last arrived is what makes the present special.[16]

The reason why in the standard framework (1) and (2) go always together is that the standard framework is committed to what we call *strong global coherence of reality*,[17] according to which (i) there is only one reality, and (ii) each part of it coheres with every other part. If strong global coherence holds, either one time is in the relevant sense privileged or none is; there is no in-between option. Imagine two times, t (12.00 on the 3rd of February 2049, say) and t' (15.15 on the 17th of March 1953, say) being both present in an absolute and objective sense. If t is present, since $t' < t$, then t' is (absolutely and objectively) past. But by assumption t' is also present. If reality is strongly coherent, t' cannot be also past, since neither there is 'another reality' in which it could be past, nor it is both present and past in the only coherent reality there is.[18] By *reductio* (and given that an analogous rationale holds for any pair $t \neq t'$), we are left with two options: one present or none.[19]

Furthermore, in the standard framework, the privilege of the present is linked with a third conceptual ingredient of the (purported) nature of time, which is crucial for what it interests us here.

(3) The robustness of the passage of time

If the present is distinct from the other times in a substantive sense, then *what* is present changes as time goes by. And if change in what is present happens, then there is what we have called *robust passage*. Since the privilege of the present is a necessary condition for robust passage, any position that downplays the specialness intuition and takes seriously the egalitarian one is bound to an *anaemic* view of passage. According to the latter, the temporal relations of *earlier* and *later*, which are the basic tools of the B-theorist, capture all there is to temporal passage.

To sum up, in the standard framework, the privilege of the present and the robustness of passage 'align', so that a realist stance with respect to the present and its unicity corresponds, or leads to, a realist stance with respect to the passage of time, and vice versa.[20] This means that the standard framework is not the friendliest environment for the idea that both intuitions, that is, the egalitarian intuition of the specialness one, deserve a shot at metaphysical significance. Such an idea characterizes fragmentalism as a theory of time, and – as we will see – it is important for empowering tense realism with crucial explanatory tools.[21]

0.3.1 Classic moving spotlight theory

One step towards a realist account of the passage of time that, to a certain extent, accommodates both the idea of the privilege of the present and that of the equality of all times is the moving spotlight theory.[22] We will dwell a bit on it to better motivate the need to move from a standard to a non-standard framework to fulfil the aim of providing an explanation of the passage of time. The view is a standard form of A-theory, since it maintains that there is an objective privilege of the present time over the others; roughly, the present time is the only one that is present *simpliciter*, or absolutely, and not merely relative to itself, as every time is. But unlike presentism and growing block view, it treats all times in the same way when it comes to existence. In other words, the moving spotlight combines an eternalist *ontology* typical of the B-theory, with an A-theoretic *metaphysics* (or 'ideology', or 'doctrine'), according to which *presentness* is a substantive property, but the non-present times partake of existence nonetheless. In this and the next section, we will go through two realist accounts of the passage of time that are based on what we call, respectively, classic and articulated moving spotlight theory. This will allow us to focus on the three ingredients – the substantivity and uniqueness of presentness on the one side, and the robustness of the flow on the other – which, as we saw, go hand in hand in the standard framework, but which part company in the non-standard one. We will thus begin to spell out the claim that standard theories can capture robust passage, but only non-standard ones have the means to explain it.

There are various forms of moving spotlight theory. The simplest one, which is sometimes called the classic moving spotlight theory (C-MST, for short)[23] is the one in which the mitigation of the tension between the thesis of the privileged present and the idea of equality of all times is carried out in the most crude way. The egalitarian intuition is respected (as long as it is respected) entirely by means of the thesis that all times are equal in ontological status, while the specialness intuition is respected entirely by the thesis that one and only one time instantiates a substantive property of *presentness*.

In C-MST, times are tenselessly 'lined up' by the temporal relation of *earlier* and *later*, but they also have a tensed aspect in virtue of the A-properties – namely properties such as *being present*, or *being n units in the past/in the future* – that they instantiate. More precisely, the facts about the earlier and later relation are *independent* of the facts about presentness, and while the facts about the temporal order are tenseless and thus obtain at any time, the facts about A-properties are tensed and thus obtain only temporarily. But what are times in C-MST? A lot of issues about the nature of times are orthogonal to what we are interested here. For instance, whether they are reducible to concrete events, or are like 'containers' for events. The minimal assumption we need is that in C-MST times play the role of *temporal locations*, in the sense that they can be used as semantic parameters relative to which (or 'at which') entities are *located* and have *properties*. If an apple that is green on Monday has become red on Friday, we can say that (assuming $t = 12.00$ am on Monday and $t' = 12.00$ am on Friday) the apple is located both at t and at t', and it is green at t, but red at t'.[24]

Robust passage in C-MST is construed as the movement of the present across temporal locations in the temporal dimension. Of course, when we talk about 'movement' here we are using a metaphor. Literally speaking, a movement is a change in *spatial* locations across time; and the present does not move in that sense (nor 'time' in any sense does). The water in a river, or the leaves floating on its surface move or pass by the bystander on the bank. Time may be *like* a river, but it does not move or pass in the same literal sense of the water or the leaves.[25] The metaphorical aspect of the movement of the present lies in the fact that we treat the temporal dimension as it were composed by spatial rather than temporal locations. The non-metaphorical aspect lies in the fact that the change in question is taken to be tensed, or 'robust', as opposed to the mere at-at kind of change that we find in B-theories. Let us go through this a bit slower.

At least since Prior, it is customary for realists to construe the metaphor of passage, or flow of time as a *sui generis* change. One that requires *merely* that Priorian Flow below be satisfied.

Priorian Flow It was the case that *p*, and is not now the case that *p*.[26]

Where *p* can contain (metric) tensed expressions of any sort. For instance, *p* can be something like 'Pepa was born 30 years ago'. The idea is that to say that time passes is to say that past events and present ones become more and more temporally distant from one another: Pepa's birth recedes more and more into the past, while Pepa becomes more and more distant from her birth.[27] In the context of C-MST, Priorian Flow is satisfied *solely* in virtue of the change of temporal location of the present; that is, the change in which time exemplifies it. We interpret C-MST as entailing that robust passage is a form of change that is (a) 'pure', non-qualitative, and (b) tensed, or robust. As for (a), what we mean by 'non-qualitative' can be understood if we think that there is a difference between the change that Pepa undergoes by having more wrinkles on her face, and the change that Pepa undergoes *merely* by getting more and more distant from her birth. The first is a qualitative kind of change, the second is not. The change that a time undergoes from being non-present to being present is pure, non-qualitative in this sense.[28]

As for (b), the difference between tensed, or robust change and tenseless or at-at change is usually discussed in the context of the debate on the nature of ordinary, qualitative change – as in an apple turning from green to red. From the point of view of the B-theorist, qualitative change is just *at-at* change. That is to say, there is nothing over and above the qualitative change of an entity x from being F to being G than the fact that at t, x is F, and at a later time t', x is G (where being F is incompatible with being G). Having incompatible properties at different times is all it takes to change. From the point of view of the A-theorist, qualitative change is a form of *tensed* change. If x changes from being F to being G, it has to be that at a certain point x is *presently* F (although it *will be* G) in some absolute sense, and then later x is *presently* G (and it *was* F) in some absolute sense. Qualitative change is robust change and it requires something more than the facts underlying at-at change, it requires the robust passage of time.

C-MST interprets ordinary qualitative change as *at-at* change, and the passage of time as *tensed* (and pure) change.[29,30] The theory differs from an egalitarian B-theoretic view merely because, *on top of* the at-at qualitative change, we find also absolute non-qualitative change in what time exemplifies the property of being present. In this view, whether a qualitative property is possessed by an object is *only* a time-relative matter, whereas whether a time possesses presentness is an absolute, non-time relative matter of fact.

Note that even though the only thing that changes in an absolute manner in this theory is the position of presentness along the B-theoretic temporal series, it is still true that it is the *whole temporal dimension* that changes. We have something that changes *locally*, namely what time instantiates presentness, but we also have a *global* change in the whole temporal dimension. Think of the analogy with what happens when an alcohol or mercury-in-glass thermometer changes from 35 to 35.1 degrees. The change happened locally, around the sign '35', but *in virtue* of such a local change the whole thermometer underwent a change. The sign '39', for instance, changed from being more to less distant from where the level of the alcohol (or the mercury) is. Of course, such a global change is rather shallow from a metaphysical point of view.

Indeed, if what changes in the times in the past and in the future is merely the *relative temporal distance* from the present, then all but the times in the vicinity of the present undergo a mere Cambridge change.[31] Yet one may try to construe this picture in a more substantive way by insisting that it is not merely the distance from the present that changes, but also the tense aspect of *each* time. By 'moving' from being at a temporal distance of n units from the present, to being at a $m > n$ temporal distance from the present, a time t undergoes a substantive change in which A-properties it instantiates *simpliciter*: t shifts from *being n time units in the past* to *being m time units in the past*; and analogously does any other past time (*mutatis mutandis* for the future ones).

If you don't think that the novelty introduced by this interpretation marks a significant difference with the more austere one, you are not alone. It seems quite clear to us that even if A-properties like *being n units of time in the past* (or *being past*, for what matters) are properties that times have *simpliciter*, that is, in a non-time relative manner, they are also properties that, in this picture, are had *derivatively*. And the problem, *nota bene*, is not the fact that times have them derivatively per se, but the fact that it is *entirely* in virtue of their relative distance from the present that times have them. If the picture is that of an ordered temporal dimension *upon which* a moving spot of light shines, then there is no reason to think that the property of *being n units in the past* is explanatorily more fundamental than *being at a distance of n units of time from the present*. Quite to the contrary, since in C-MST the temporal order is given by facts concerning the relation of before and after that are independent of facts about the instantiation of presentness, it is the latter relation that must be more fundamental, on pain of contradiction. In this picture, it is the fact that the 11.00 o'clock on a given day bears the relation of being one hour apart (in the future direction) to noon on that same day, together with the fact that now it is noon, what explains the fact that 11.00 is now one hour in the past. If it were the other way around, the facts about temporal distances between times would *not* be *in*dependent of the facts about A-properties, contrary to what is assumed in C-MST.

0.3.2 Articulated moving spotlight theory

An account of robust passage as robust pure change is not the only one possible in the context of the standard moving spotlight view. In non-classical (but still standard) forms of the view we find attempts to interpret robust passage as a qualitative form of change that involves the whole temporal dimension. We will use the label 'A-MSTs' for those more articulated versions. Roughly, A-MSTs take the global change in the temporal dimension more seriously, as a change that happens in virtue of some intrinsic change in the entities that occupy them. In Williamson's (2002) version, things existing at various temporal locations can lose and gain properties such as *being concrete* or *being conscious*. Cameron (2015) speaks of the change of the age of the entities located in the past and the future as what alters their qualitative nature. Correia and Rosenkranz (2012) maintain that the facts along the temporal dimension change their tense aspect (i.e. they 'become older') while maintaining their numerical identity as time goes by.[32] In general, in A-MSTs robust passage requires intrinsic qualitative changes across the temporal dimension, rather than pure change in A-properties.

This feature of A-MSTs complicates the picture of temporal reality more than one may think at first sight. Come back to the idea, which we have just expressed, of having variation along the *temporal* dimension as *time* goes by. What does it mean that something located at 22.50 on 8 December 1980 (John Lennon at the moment he was shot dead, say) changes intrinsically as you are reading these lines and the present 'moves on'? We can easily see what a change in the tense aspect of a certain past event (or of the time at which the event happens or an entity is located) is: the assassination changes from being a certain amount of time in the past to being a bit more into the past. And one can see what intrinsic change of an entity persisting through time is: John Lennon has the property of non-being shot at a previous time, and then he has the property of being shot at 22.50. But talk of an intrinsic change that something located at a specific time t undergoes – John Lennon located at 22.50 on 8 December 1980 – is a weird hybrid.

What we need to do to shed some clarity on the issue is to distinguish between two roles that times can have with respect to change. Times can have the role of temporal *locations*, as we have seen, but they can also have the role of temporal *perspectives*, or viewpoints.[33] To a first approximation, objects have different qualitative aspects with respect to the different temporal locations that they occupy; remember the example of the apple, which is green at t and red at t'. Temporal locations, in turn, have different tense aspects (that is, A-properties) relative to different temporal perspectives. For instance the time *t* at which the apple is green is present from the perspective of *t*, but past from the perspective of *t'*, the location at which the apple is red. But, according to A-MSTs, there is also (and perhaps primarily) variation in how an object qualitatively is at a particular location from various perspectives. For instance, from the perspective of *t'* the apple is *not* green at *t*, rather, it *was* green at *t*. More incisively, perhaps, from the perspective of 22.50 on 8 December 1980, John Lennon is alive and conscious at 22.50 on 8 December 1980. But from the perspective of 9 December 1980, John Lennon is not alive and conscious on 22.50 on 8 December 1980, rather he *was* so.

Now, A-MSTs capture robust passage in terms of the qualitative robust change that involves the entities that are located at the various temporal locations along the whole temporal dimension. This may be an improvement on C-MST, but it is doubtful that A-MSTs is in a different spot (no pun intended) than C-MST when it comes to explain the passage of time. As long as A-MSTs remain within the standard framework, they are committed to the *unicity* of the present. According to them, there is *one* privileged temporal perspective, and how things (along the temporal dimension) are from the privileged perspective is how things are *simpliciter*.[34] Robust passage involves a 'wide' form of robust change, as it were, but still a unique present. Acknowledging the perspective role of times, in itself, does not mean taking on board the idea that *all* perspectives are on a par, which is what would allow us to express hypotheses about the links between distinct perspectives. As we will argue, only by appealing to such links a theory can explain, and not merely capture, the passage. Let us then drop strong global coherence and enter the non-standard framework.

0.4 The non-standard framework

A first problem with the accounts of the passage of time that can be elaborated within the standard framework has received certain attention in the literature.[35] The problem is the following. There is an explanatory gap between the hypothesis that there is one privileged present time and the explanandum that time passes or flows. Consider our ordinary understanding of space. We can think of the space around us in a way that is structurally similar to time, that is, as a dimension in which things happen. Depending on the locations (in space) where things happen, they stand at various distances to one another. And yet it makes sense to say of time that flows, or passes, but we would not say the same of space. Why? Is it because we think that there is a metaphysically privileged location in time, the present, and a privileged perspective from it? That is very doubtful, since it does not seem that a metaphysically privileged *spatial* position and perspective would make space dynamic.[36] Think of an Aristotelian world, in which space has a metaphysically privileged *centre*, and there are absolute, non-relative matters of fact with respect to whether something is going towards it or away from it. Does it make sense to say that in the Aristotelian universe space flows? No. The reason why an objective present 'sits well' in the standard realist picture is not because it explains the passage of time. Rather, it sits well because it forces us to *add* into the picture the idea that the present 'moves along' the temporal dimension, since a picture with a stuck objective present would be *in*adequate for time. In other terms, in the standard framework the passage of time is a primitive.

However, our criticism is *not* that taking the passage of time as a primitive is theoretically faulty. The point is, rather, that if we aim at explaining and not merely capturing the passage of time, the standard picture, in which the privilege of the present time is confined to *one* temporal perspective, has too little theoretical tools. To put it bluntly, if reality is constituted only by the present perspective, and we ask what makes it the case that there is a robust change along the temporal dimension, it looks like we are bound to answer that the present 'moves' itself in a way that reminds of what R.E. Raspe, in his novel, says of Baron Munchausen, who pulled himself out of a swamp by his own hair.[37]

While the standard framework is characterized by strong global coherence, the non-standard framework is characterized by its failure. Again following Fine (2005), we will distinguish two approaches to non-standard tense realism: *external relativism* and *fragmentalism*. As we said in section 0.3, strong global coherence is composed by two tenets: (i) the unicity of reality (there is only one reality), and (ii) its coherence (each part of it coheres with every other part). According to external relativism, unicity fails, but coherence holds. Reality is not unique, because to each temporal perspective there corresponds a reality constituted by the tensed facts that are oriented towards the temporal location that in that perspective is present. One way to develop the idea is to understand the constitution of reality by tensed facts as irreducibly relative to times.

To understand the point, a comparison with *internal* relativism may be useful. A tense *anti*-realist may be an internal relativist. In that case, she can accept that tensed facts constitute reality, but only relative to times, and – crucially – derivatively. For instance, she can maintain that relative to a temporal location t (during the third century BC, presumably), the tensed fact that *Socrates is sitting* constitutes reality; and this is the case because the tenseless fact that *Socrates is sitting at t* constitutes reality in an absolute, non-time relative manner. In this view, at the bottom level, the one involving tenseless facts, the 'relativization' to times is internal to the facts themselves and does not concern the relation of constitution. To the contrary, according to external relativism, the explanatorily fundamental level involves tensed facts, which constitute reality relative to times in a way that is not further explainable. If the fact that *Socrates is sitting* constitutes reality relative to, or from the perspective of *t*, this is not in virtue of some further fact constituting reality in an absolute manner. The relativization remains external and concerns the relation of constitution irreducibly. Notice that constitution is relativized to times in their role as perspectives, rather than as locations (as it is in internal relativism). More precisely, the external relativist identifies temporal perspectives with distinct realities, and takes such an identification as primitive. In this picture 'to constitute reality relative to *t*' means to constitute a certain reality, one that we can label 'the perspective from *t*'.

Relativizing constitution is losing the unicity of reality, while preserving its coherence. To the contrary, according to fragmentalism, the coherence of reality fails, but its unicity holds. While external relativism takes temporal perspectives as primitive and 'pluralizes' reality by relativizing constitution, fragmentalism identifies the perspectives of the relativist, which in this context are more aptly called fragments, with collections of tensed facts.[38] In this picture, reality is one, and constitution is absolute, but it is not globally coherent or, to use Kit Fine's words, 'of a piece' (2005: 263). However, coherence is maintained locally, at the level of fragments.[39] Although all facts constitute reality absolutely, it is not the case that they all *obtain together*; only the facts that cohere with one another obtain together, or co-obtain. Note that the fragmentalist must take as primitive either (local) coherence or co-obtainment; after all, if fragments are identical to maximally coherent collections of facts, she cannot – on pain of circularity – explain coherence and co-obtainment merely as belonging to the same collection.

Trading off primitive perspectives for primitive coherence has its payoff, if we consider the respective capacity of the two approaches to go beyond an account of passage as articulated in the standard framework. The external relativist has multiplied the dynamic reality of the standard account. Within each reality, the flow along the temporal dimension is captured from a particular perspective, but the facts in one perspective cannot be explanatorily relevant for the facts in another perspective, since there is not *one* temporal dimension all the perspectives are about. Indeed, the unicity of reality is prevented by the way strong global coherence fails in external relativism. The situation is different in fragmentalism, according to which there is a unique temporal dimension, and the various fragments contain the facts that (incoherently) constitute it. Although such facts cannot obtain together, they can be explanatorily relevant to one another, since they are about the *same* temporal dimension. Fragmentalism is thus more apt to provide an articulated explanation of the passage of time. It does not merely encompass more than the perspective from the present, but it also has the resources to 'put together' the extra tools.

The rest of this book is dedicated to developing and defending our preferred version of fragmentalism, Flow Fragmentalism and the account of the passage of time that can be built from it. Before moving to Chapter 1, we present three core assumptions of fragmentalism, which will be discussed in more detail in the next chapters.

0.5 Assumptions

The first assumption is that, as we have just seen, fragmentalism is not a form of relativism. There are never many realities in the fragmentalist picture, but always *one* reality that comes in pieces. There are at least two ways to spell out this idea. One is by introducing a fundamental relation of co-obtainment. Talk of co-obtainment is *absolute* and not relative to fragments, times, temporal standpoints, or what have you. By individuating classes of facts that obtain together one with another, we can then *label* fragments, and say that 'in' one of them such and such is the case, while in another fragment different things go on. Alternatively, and this is the way we prefer, one can adopt a pluralist approach to fundamentality, and maintain that there are two equally fundamental jargons here: constitution, which is an absolute matter, and obtainment, which is a fragment relative matter. According to this approach, talking of facts obtaining within a fragment is just as explanatorily primitive as talking of the same facts constituting absolutely reality.

Secondly, fragmentalism is *not* an invitation to believe that there are *true contradictions* (cf. Fine 2005: 282). Even if reality lacks global coherence, incompatible facts – the fact that Petunia the guinea pig is sleeping, and the fact that Petunia is awake, for instance – never 'obtain together' within the same fragment. There is no obvious reason, thus, to take the sentence 'Petunia is both sleeping and awake' as an accurate or true representation of reality. Does that mean that fragmentalism rejects the idea of *dialetheias*, propositions that are both true and false? It depends. To give an idea of what we will articulate more accurately in the next chapters, one can concede that from the case just described we can indeed infer both that Petunia is awake, and that Petunia is not awake. However, we cannot put together those two facts and conclude that Petunia is both awake and not awake. Conjunction, in a fragmented universe, simply does not behave like that.[40] Following this route leads us to dialetheias, since as soon as we accept that the truth of a negated sentence entails the falsity of the non-negated one, we will have that sentences such as 'Petunia is awake' are both true and false. However, no sentence of the form 'Petunia is both awake and not awake' is ever true. There are other routes here one can follow, as we will see, but in accordance to the assumption just stated, none of them entails that there are true contradictions.[41]

The third and last assumption is that a global point of view, the perspective *sub species aeternitatis* is not a metaphysically cogent description of how things really are. The point is more subtle and somewhat vaguer than the former two, and a comparison with external relativism may be useful to grasp it. As Fine (2005: 281) points out, 'both [the relativist and the fragmentalist] are concerned, in their own ways, to deny the existence of a single coherent reality. But the relativist denies that it is single, while the fragmentalist denies that is coherent.' Now, denying the existence of something that is *both* unique and coherent is compatible with accepting the existence of something, a über-reality as Fine calls it, that is either not unique but coherent (as for the relativist), or it is unique but not coherent (as for the fragmentalist). Fine does not go much further into the issue, but he points out that the über-reality of the relativist is neither a further perspective, nor something upon which all other limited perspectives are like viewpoints, and that the über-reality of the fragmentalist is neither a further all-encompassing fragment, nor a hidden entity that manifests itself only in distinct fragments (cf. Fine 2005: 282–3).

As it will be clearer in the rest of the book, we interpret this assumption in a quite radical way. Roughly, we take the absence of a globally coherent reality to rule out the existence of cross-fragment facts. In certain cases we can talk of facts belonging to different fragments 'in one go', as when we claim that there are explanatory links between them, but the truth of such claims is always accounted for in terms of facts that are 'entirely contained', as it were, into distinct fragments. However, we acknowledge that less radical readings of the assumption are legitimate. Lipman (2018), for instance, seems to abide by it only in the sense that facts belonging to different fragments cannot co-obtain, but they may enter other relations, for instance the relation of *passing into* (see section 1.3.2). That is, according to him there are not cross-fragment facts involving co-obtainment, but there can be cross-fragment facts of other kinds. In contrast, we will argue explicitly in favour of the interpretation according to which there are no irreducible cross-fragment facts of any sort.

1

Flow Fragmentalism

In the Introduction, we saw that the main difference between the standard versions of tense realism and the non-standard ones is the idea that there is a unique privileged present. The difference will be understood in the rest of the book in terms of whether we abide by a principle of Neutrality among temporal perspectives. The standard views reject the principle, while the non-standard ones endorse it. Once Neutrality is on board, we can no longer think of reality as a single globally coherent place. However, there are various ways to recover a local notion of coherence. Flow Fragmentalism, the view we advocate, is a way to articulate the idea that there is a single reality that is fragmented in locally coherent units. For the purpose of this chapter, we will make two simplifications, which will be dropped later on (respectively, in Chapter 2 and Chapter 4). First, that the coherent units, the fragments, encode the temporal viewpoint on a temporal dimension that is *linear*. That is, we will not take into account the indeterminacy or 'openness' of the future. Secondly, fragments are centred on what can be roughly thought of as 'Newtonian' times, that is, spatially maximal aggregates of simultaneous events. That is, no relativistic consideration about simultaneity and temporal order will be taken into account.

Like Gaul, the chapter is divided in three. The first part (section 1.1) gives the outline of our position and states its central theses (given the simplifications mentioned above). The second part dwells on some main objections and gives replies (section 1.2), and the third and last part considers other versions of fragmentalism and compares them with Flow Fragmentalism (section 1.3).

1.1 Flow Fragmentalism

1.1.1 Standard vs. non-standard tense realism

Following Fine (2005: 270–3), we characterize *Standard Tense Realism* as the idea that tensed facts constitute, in an absolute sense, a single coherent reality, i.e. as the conjunction of the following four claims:

Realism Reality is constituted by tensed facts.

Absolutism Constitution of reality is not irreducibly relative, i.e. its relative constitution must be explained in terms of its absolute constitution.

Coherence Reality is not irreducibly incoherent, i.e. its constitution by incompatible facts must be explained in terms of its constitution by compatible facts.

Presentness Only tensed facts obtaining at present constitute reality.[1]

The first three theses – Realism, Absolutism, Coherence – lead to contradictions that have the flavour of McTaggart (1908)'s paradox. It is easy to see how. Assuming that there is some qualitative variation through time, if we let facts obtaining at any two different times constitute reality, it may happen that incompatible tensed facts constitute reality. For instance, suppose that Socrates is sitting during the whole morning, but then he goes for a walk with Thrasymachus in the afternoon. If Absolutism holds, both the fact that *Socrates is sitting* and the fact that *Socrates is standing* constitute reality absolutely speaking (that is, not relative to a time). But if Coherence holds too, reality cannot be constituted by incompatible facts, such as the fact that *Socrates is sitting* and the fact that *Socrates is standing*.[2] Presentness allows someone who accepts Realism to accept both Coherence and Absolutism, precisely by assigning a privilege to the facts that presently obtain, and thus ruling out that facts that obtain at different times (and may be incompatible with one another) constitute reality. If Socrates is presently sitting, and later on he will be standing, it is not the case that the fact that *Socrates is sitting* and the fact that *Socrates is standing* both constitute reality; since only the first one constitutes reality.

Non-standard forms of tense realism reject Presentness, and embrace the idea that all times are on a par when it comes to what facts constitute reality, by endorsing the principle of Neutrality below.

Neutrality With respect to what facts constitute reality, no time is privileged.[3]

As a consequence, non-standard forms of tense realism have to reject either Absolutism or Coherence. External Relativism is the rejection of Absolutism: constitution of reality is an irreducibly relative matter (Fine 2005: 278). There is a whole plethora of *perspectives* relative to which different facts constitute reality. In each perspective we find the tensed facts which obtain at a time, and which constitute reality relative to such a time. Crucially, as underlined in section 0.4, there is no overarching perspective encompassing all perspectives. That is to say that there is no *single* reality constituted by all the tensed facts.

Fragmentalism keeps Absolutism but rejects Coherence. As anticipated on page 14, the idea is that reality is constituted by tensed facts that obtain at different times in an absolute sense; hence it is constituted by incompatible facts, *even though* it is not the case that incompatible facts obtain together. According to Fragmentalism, reality is not 'of a piece', but it is rather constituted by different fragments, that is, maximal collections of tensed facts (Fine 2005: 281). Each fragment is internally coherent, but the whole of reality is not. Hence, although the fragmentalist gives up the idea of a reality that is coherent as a whole, she is not compelled to endorse the conclusion that incompatible facts can obtain together. For instance, if Socrates is now sitting and then standing, both the fact that *Socrates is sitting* and the fact that *Socrates is standing* constitute reality in an absolute sense. However, the fact that *Socrates is standing* obtains in a fragment of reality different from the one in which the fact that *Socrates is sitting* obtains. We will return on this point in a moment.

1.1.2 Pluralism

According to the fragmentalist variety of non-standard theories, facts that obtain at times different from the present constitute reality in the same sense as facts that obtain at the present time (i.e. absolutely). However, as we have just underlined, within each fragment not all such facts obtain, otherwise fragments wouldn't be internally coherent. In other terms, not all facts that constitute reality obtain in all fragments. There are different ways to spell out this idea. The gist of all of them is that we need a principled way to block the inference from the premise that certain incompatible facts constitute reality, to the conclusion that they also obtain together.

The way in which Flow Fragmentalism captures the idea is the following. We will exploit expressions such as 'within a fragment *F*', 'within some fragment', 'within all fragments' to work as operators that qualify claims about what facts *obtain*, as distinct from claims about what facts *constitute* reality, which will be unprefixed. In our regimented language, thus, *no* fact obtains *simpliciter*, although facts constitute reality absolutely speaking (and hence *simpliciter*). While for the standard tense realist (who rejects Neutrality and accepts Presentness) obtainment *in the present* is obtainment *simpliciter*,[4] for the flow fragmentalist there is no obtainment *simpliciter*, but only *within a fragment*. Yet constitution is absolute (contrary to what the external relativist maintains). Thus, in our take on the position, fragmentalism requires a form of double talk: the absolute talk of constitution and the irreducibly relative talk of obtainment.

It is important to stress that the latter does not represent merely a 'coherence' constraint on how we can *describe* the reality constituted by incoherent facts. Rather, the distinction between (absolute) *constitution* and (irreducibly relative) *obtainment* is between two *ways* facts relate to reality in the fragmentalist's picture, none of which can be explained in terms of the other. Flow Fragmentalism is thus a form of pluralism, not in the sense that it accepts incompatible metaphysical theories as equally valid, in their own respective ways, but in the sense that it comes with two distinct metaphysical commitments with respect to how facts relate to reality. Neither of them is explanatorily more fundamental, and both are equally metaphysically perspicuous, in their own ways.

Although there is no 'real definition' of the one in terms of the other, there are inferential connections between them. In particular, the following principle holds.

Obtainment-Constitution A tensed fact obtains in some fragment *iff* it constitutes reality.

The principle guarantees that there are no 'free floating' facts, neither in the sense that there are facts that obtain within some fragment, but do not constitute reality, nor in the sense that there are facts that constitute reality, but do not obtain in some fragment or another. To stress the point again, the biconditional should not be read as expressing a duality between the two notions, as if they were two faces of the same medal: obtainment and constitution are two ways of relating to reality which are irreducible to one another. The inferential connection expressed by Obtainment-Constitution holds because there is a single reality constituted by *all* tensed facts, and obtainment is the way those facts arrange themselves along the temporal dimension.

This commitment to two basic ways facts relate to reality is undoubtedly a cost in terms of ideology for Flow Fragmentalism.[5] However, it allows us to take co-obtainment as derivative on relativized obtainment, according to the definition below.

Co-obtainment The fact that ϕ and the fact that ψ co-obtain $=_{df}$ For some fragment F, ϕ obtains within F and ψ obtains within F.

As in other forms of fragmentalism, reality as a whole is incoherent (Coherence does not hold), but there are no instances of two incompatible facts obtaining together. Along the temporal dimension, reality is coherently fragmented in coherent perspectives – *viz.* divided into fragments constituted by facts that cohere with one another. However, unlike other forms of fragmentalism (such as

Lipman's or Loss', which will be discussed in more detail shortly), Flow Fragmentalism requires a way to *explicitly* state what facts obtain within each fragment, and takes this way of talking as more fundamental than talk of obtaining together.

1.1.3 The official idiom

Bearing these remarks in mind, we will now formulate Flow Fragmentalism in its *official idiom*, which does not require commitment to the existence of facts as a distinct ontological category.[6] We begin with a propositional tensed language $\mathcal{L}$ containing atomic sentences $p, q, \ldots$, two tense operators WAS and WILL, and two connectives $\neg$ and $\wedge$. We call a sentence of $\mathcal{L}$ *simple* if and only if it is atomic (that is, it formalizes present tense sentences like 'Socrates is standing') or it is formed by an atomic sentence and tense operators (that is, it formalizes sentences like 'Socrates was standing' or 'Socrates will be sitting'). Simple sentences can be thought of as expressing the facts that constitute reality. By resorting to $\mathcal{L}$, in the official idiom, rather than stating that *the fact that p* constitutes reality, we simply state that *p*. Given the fragmented nature of reality at the level of constitution, nothing about the relations between the various facts that constitute reality can be said by recurring to $\mathcal{L}$ alone. For instance if Socrates sits, we can state:

(1) Socrates is sitting

and if he stands a moment after, we can state:

(2) Socrates is standing

but from (1) and (2), we cannot infer that Socrates is both sitting and standing. And in general, the inferential rule of conjunction introduction (adjunction) will *not* hold: $\phi, \psi \nvDash \phi \wedge \psi$. However, if Socrates talks while he sits, then we can say that he is sitting and talking. In order to articulate this idea, we will resort to a richer language $\mathcal{L}^{+\odot}$, which contains not only (the fragment $\mathcal{L}$ of) the language of tensed propositional calculus, but also operators that allow us to state what is the case *relative to a fragment*. The idea is to index each fragment with a number, and to introduce a family of operators of the form $\ulcorner \odot_{F_x} \urcorner$, which informally read as 'within the fragment F_1', 'within the fragment F_2', ... We can thus *explicitly* state not only what facts constitute reality (absolutely speaking), but also which facts obtain relative to specific fragments. The official idiom of Flow Fragmentalism will contain – in its semi-formal version – not only statements such as (1) and (2) but also such as:

(3) $\odot_{F_n}$ Socrates is sitting
(4) $\odot_{F_m}$ Socrates is standing
(5) $\odot_{F_n}$ Socrates is sitting and talking

Within the scope of such operators, the ordinary rules of sentential calculus hold. For instance, we will have the corresponding 'uniformly prefixed' version of adjunction.

$$\odot_{F_x} \phi, \odot_{F_x} \psi \vDash \odot_{F_x} (\phi \wedge \psi)$$

Besides, since (by Obtainment-Constitution) if a fact obtains relative to a fragment, then it constitutes reality, one can safely move from a prefixed sentence to the sentence within its scope.

$$\odot_{F_x} \phi \vDash \phi$$

Therefore, while from (3) and (4) we cannot infer that Socrates is both sitting and standing (adjunction does not hold unrestrictedly), from (5) we can infer that he is both sitting and talking.

It is important to stress the difference between what is expressed by *simple* sentences, and what we could call *complex* sentences, namely the ones that contain '$\odot_{F_x}$', or the connectives '¬' and '∧'. Both can be metaphysically cogent, when true, but there is a difference in the way they can be so. The idea can be put informally and roughly as follows: simple sentences express facts (successfully, when true), complex sentences say something *about* the facts (successfully, when true). A conjunction $\phi \wedge \psi$ does not express a conjunctive fact. Indeed, there are *no* conjunctive facts in our view. What $\phi \wedge \psi$ expresses is that the fact that ϕ and the fact that ψ obtain together. Analogously, a negation ¬ϕ does not express a negative fact. There are *no* negative facts in our view.[7] What ¬ϕ expresses is that there is at least one fragment where the fact that ϕ does not obtain. And crucially, as there are no conjunctive or negative facts, there are no 'within facts'. A sentence such as $\odot_{F_x} \phi$ does *not* express the 'second-order' fact that *within the fragment F_x, the fact that ϕ obtains*. There is no such fact. It says something *about* the fact that ϕ, namely that it obtains within the fragment F_x; it does not express a further fact that somehow 'contains' it. Of course, in a sense also a simple sentence ϕ says something about a fact: it says that the fact that ϕ constitutes reality. But this is so only because expressing (verbally) a fact, and stating that that fact constitutes reality is one and the same thing. Analogously, there is a sense in which also sentences like *WAS*ϕ or *WILL*ϕ say something about a fact: they say that the fact that ϕ obtained in the past or that it will obtain in the future. But again, this is so only because expressing the fact that *WAS*ϕ/*WILL*ϕ, and stating that the fact that ϕ constituted/will constitute reality is one and the same thing. So, even if all sentences of $\mathcal{L}^{+\odot}$ in some sense say something about the facts, not all sentences of $\mathcal{L}^{+\odot}$ express facts, for the complex ones do not.

Since our official idiom does not commit us to the existence of facts, properly speaking this difference cannot be understood in terms of what facts exist. Rather, it is again the duality of constitution and obtainment that surfaces here. Constitution is the 'unadorned' way things are the case, as it were, while obtainment relative to a fragment tells us how what is the case organizes into fragments. The connectives allow us to articulate such a fragmentation. Roughly, a conjunction $\phi \land \psi$ says that there is at least one fragment in which both it is the case that ϕ and it is the case that ψ, while a negation $\neg \phi$ says that there is at least one fragment in which it is not the case that ϕ. We will provide more formal details in the rest of the chapter (especially in section 1.1.4.5), and in the next one (especially in section 2.3). For now, it is important to stress that the distinction between constitution and obtainment is reflected in the distinction between simple and complex sentences in the official idiom.

1.1.4 The passage of time

Now, how does Flow Fragmentalism account for the idea that the passage of time is a robust feature of reality, and not something that is merely due to the representational capacities of conscious beings such as ourselves? In this section, we will spell out the flow fragmentalist theory of passage in detail and confront it with alternative realist views.

1.1.4.1 *Capturing and explaining the passage*

In the standard framework, the core idea is to consider as primitive that the world goes from one present state to another. This fact is encoded in the idea of *real tense*, whether we express it through primitive tense operators, or through attribution of 'pure' tensed properties to times – i.e. A-properties such as *being past*, *being present* and *being future*.[8] Such a treatment of the passage of time as brute has been criticized for being suspicious. Is the mere attribution of A-properties, or the resort to primitive tense operators *alone*, sufficient for accounting for robust passage? Roughly, the problem for the standard realist is to avoid ending up upholding a position that is equivalent to a 'stuck' or 'frozen' present metaphysics. The introduction of an objective intrinsic property – presentness – seems to leave an explanatory gap, as it were, between a metaphysically cogent description of how reality presently is, and how it constantly changes.[9] Indeed, certain philosophers suspect that the standard realist account of passage is no less 'anaemic' than the temporal succession that we find in the universe of the tense anti-realist. These include tense realists such as Fine, who writes:

> For the fact that time flows is a tenseless fact about time; it is not one that holds at one time rather than another. But the proposed [by the standard tense realist] explanation is tensed; it states of each of a number of times that it is *present* or was *past* or will be *future*. But if we try to convert it into a tenseless explanation, we end up with a triviality. We must say something like: it is always the case that some time is present, that all earlier times were present and all later times will be present. And this is something that even the anti-realist can accept.
>
> Fine 2005: 287

As we have anticipated in section 0.2, we are happy to grant that standard forms of tense realism *capture* passage. However, we agree with what we take to be the general spirit of the criticism. If our resources are limited to *one* temporal perspective – being it the present or five minutes ago – an *explanation* of how reality changes from one state into another is hard to come by. Of course, one may always resist the idea that we *need* an explanation here. After all, if passage is taken as primitive, what else can be added? There are two subtle dialectical points here that we wish to make.

First, the fact that something is taken as primitive does not rule out that we cannot provide some explanatory discourse about it. Consider, for example, *identity*. A primitivist about identity is not forced to maintain that the axioms and inferential rules of first order logic with identity do not have any (relevant) explanatory role. A primitivist cannot say that they provide a *real definition* of identity (not even in the second order formulation), but they surely can say that they provide us with an explanation of the *behaviour* of identity in broader contexts – those, for instance, involving predication. Something along this line can be true of the passage of time. Even if one takes it as a primitive captured by the notion of real tense, that does not mean that showing how real tenses behave is not explanatory of passage itself.

Second, although we stressed that capturing and explaining are two different intellectual enterprises, there may be an interplay between the two here. After all, the line between criticizing a realist position because it fails to capture passage by its primitives, and criticizing it because the posit of primitives is not enough to explain passage may be very thin. Even the staunchest critic could agree that it is not incoherent to *stipulate* that there is robust passage in the tense realist picture while insisting that it is nonetheless a very shallow way to even just capture passage. Fine seems to have something like that in mind when he comments:

> We naturally *read more* into the realist's tense-logical pronouncements than they actually convey. But his conception of temporal reality, once it is seen *for what it is*, is as static or block-like as the anti-realist's, the only difference lying in the fact that his block has a privileged centre. Even if presentness is allowed to shed its light upon the world, there is nothing in his metaphysics to prevent that light being 'frozen' on a particular moment of time.
>
> Fine 2005: 287, emphasis ours

Why do we *tend* to read more? And what is the 'more' that we bestow upon the standard realist story? Fine seems to say that tensed notions invite to think of reality as dynamic, but standard tense realism does not *authorize* us to take this invite seriously.[10] Once the standard picture is seen 'for what it is', we see that it merely postulates that there is robust passage. But then again, why is postulating not enough, why are we not authorized to take seriously, on a metaphysical level, such a postulation?

Philosophers who are not convinced by the 'stuck present' objection to standard tense realism, have sometimes replied with something like a shrug. For instance, Deasy says:

> A-theorists... can distinguish their views from the 'frozen' A-theory by pointing out that on their views, there are instants that were and will be present. If there are instants that were and will be present, then the present instant is not always present.
>
> Deasy 2018: 284

By talking of 'shrug' here we do not intend to imply that the argumentations against the problem of the frozen present have been shallow or that they have not been properly articulated. Deasy (2018), for instance, goes into a great deal of details to spell out the distinction between a frozen present scenario and an un-frozen one depending on various conceptions of tensed reality.[11] What we mean is that, at bottom, the standard realist reply is that to consider tenses as dynamic is coherent, and it is not otherwise problematic to maintain that such a thesis is metaphysically cogent. As we said, the dialectic here is subtle. We do not want to take a 'thorough' stance on either side. Our point is that granting that there is something like capturing passage through a primitive in the theory (even if it turns out that this is 'not enough' for theorizing on the passage, in some sense), a position that beside capturing also provides an explanation of the primitive notion, by showing how it behaves in larger, relevant contexts, has more theoretical virtues than one that merely captures passage. And this is exactly what happens in Flow Fragmentalism, passage is primitive and captured by tenses, but it is also explained by the links between tensed facts that obtain within different fragments. But before going into the details of how we propose to carry out the explanatory part of the story, we need to consider two alternative options: a position that promises to come with more explanatory import, while at the same time staying within a standard framework, and a non-standard position that is realist but in which passage is not primitive.

1.1.4.2 Cameron's age properties

In section 0.3.2, we have already argued that the 'articulated' versions of standard moving spotlight theory (A-MST) do not substantially differ from the classical ones when it comes to explaining the passage of time. Both the classical and the articulated views capture passage by encoding it in a primitive of the theory. The difference is that in the simple view passage is 'pure change' in the position of the present, while in the articulated view, passage is intrinsic qualitative change in the entities across the temporal dimension. Now, given that we have not dwelled on the details in the Introduction, one may wonder whether, at least in some of its manifestations, the articulated theory may do a better job at completing the standard picture with an explanation of how passage comes about. Cameron (2015) is one obvious candidate. Our point in this section will be that no matter the theoretical virtues of Cameron's position with respect to other standard views, it still just captures passage, rather than providing an explanation of how it comes about.

Let us begin by noticing that Cameron acknowledges that taking tenses as primitive does the job of capturing passage in a standard framework:

> One option [to solve the stuck present problem] is to say that there are a bunch of brute tensed facts concerning other times having been/going to be present. We can then say that it is true that t was/will be present if and only if reality contains the brute tensed fact that t was/will be present. . . . t's being present is simply a way reality was/will be, it is not a way reality is, even atemporally speaking.
>
> Cameron 2015: 209

However, as it is clear from passages shortly after the one just quoted, Cameron is not happy with this solution because he thinks that it is ad hoc, in that it introduces a costly ideology to the sole effect of solving the frozen present problem.[12] The ad-hocness charge can be seen as a way to articulate the point (that we attributed to Fine) that standard tense realism does not authorize the introduction of a robust passage into the picture. It does not so, because the stipulation that reality is dynamic is done *merely* in order to differentiate the view from a stuck present picture.

What is, then, Cameron's alternative to introduce robust passage into the picture? His idea relies on two explanatory tools. The first is to attribute temporal *distributional properties* to the entities that exist in the temporal dimension: '[a] temporal distributional property says how a thing is across time' (p. 173). Consider an entity x that exists throughout a period $t_0 - t_n$ and changes its qualitative properties – let us assume that x changes many colours as time goes by. In Cameron's picture, what is fundamental is not that at t_0, x is red, at t_1 is blue, and so on. Rather, at the fundamental level x exemplifies *one* distributional property, that of *being at t_0 red, then blue, etc*. It is *in virtue* of x's exemplifying this distributional property that x has, derivatively, different qualitative properties at different temporal locations. What is meant here by 'fundamental level' is that it is in the essence of things to have certain distributional properties. It is a matter of fact intrinsic to them, and not explainable in further terms (for instance, the fact that they have different properties at different times). The second explanatory tool is to attribute, in an absolute, non-time relative manner, *age properties* to the entities that are located in the temporal dimension. Cameron's age properties are not restricted to what are ordinarily called 'ages' of people and things in general. Ordinary ages are restricted to things that presently exist: Angela Merkel has a certain age, Petunia the guinea pig has a certain age, the computers in our offices have their ages. In Cameron's view, also things that are entirely located in the past or in the future have ages. Cleopatra has now a certain age, as it has a certain age the first human being stepping on Mars even if they are not yet born (and of course, assuming that humanity will at a certain point set foot on Mars). Besides, the age of (past, present and future) things constantly *changes*. Petunia is now two years old, but she will be three next year, and Cleopatra is several centuries old now, but in one year's time she will be one year older. Also, age properties are possessed essentially by things. The fact that an entity x has a certain age is a fact that is intrinsic to x and no further explainable in further terms (for instance, the temporal distance from the objective present of x's initial moment of existence).

From both the fact that things have temporal distributional properties, and the fact that their ages constantly change it follows that things along the whole temporal dimension robustly change their intrinsic properties as time goes by. As we have already pointed out, Cameron's view is an example of what we have called an articulated moving spotlight view, one according to which the passage of time is captured by the qualitative change of entities across the temporal dimension. Cameron explicitly states that his view overcomes the frozen, or stuck, present problem:

> For the stuck spotlighter, ... [n]othing would be lost – you would not do a worse job of describing reality – if you ... simply gave a tenseless description of reality, saying what there is, and what things are like, including that one time is (tenselessly) present. By contrast, in saying that things were a certain way, my moving spotlighter is saying something about the very nature of things. It is of the essence of things that have such-and-such a temporal distributional property and so-and-so an age that they are a certain way now, but it is also of the essence of things that have those properties that they were and will be some other way.
> Cameron 2015: 209

The job that in the classic picture is done by primitive tensed facts about the position of the present, here is done by the constantly changing ages of things. While in the classic picture what is explanatorily more basic is the absolute, non-time relative position of the present, and the primitive facts about its changes (while the ages of things are derivative), in Cameron's picture the base level is given by the absolute non-time relative ages of things, *and primitive facts about their changes* (while the position of the present is derivative on them). How exactly is the charge of ad-hocness avoided by this swap of primitives? Here is how Cameron replies:

> [T]here is no costly ideological notion introduced to do a minimal amount of work. *Ages* are introduced, of course: they are postulated as constituents of some of the states of affairs whose existence is taken to be fundamental. But ages do *lots* of work: they play a role in making true every truth about how things were or used to be, not merely in making it the case that the spotlight used to be elsewhere.
> Cameron 2015: 210–11, italics in the original

The main reason why Cameron's position is not *ad hoc* is that age properties enter into the explanatory mechanism concerning truthmaking. What makes it true now that Cleopatra commanded the army to move forward is that it is of the essence of Cleopatra that she exemplifies a certain distributional property, and that she has *now* a certain age. But even if Cameron is correct here, and his position is indeed better (or less ad hoc at any rate) than the introduction of primitive tense operators (and even if ages do many further valuable jobs), our initial point still stands. Also, Cameron's moving spotlight view merely captures primitive passage, but does not have the means for providing an explanation of it. The reason why passage happens in Cameron's picture is that there are fundamental facts about the ages of things *constantly changing*. And as in all standard pictures, these are presently obtaining facts (although they concern things located in the past and the future too), since how presently things are is how things are *simpliciter*. No explanation in terms of how reality encompasses also other temporal perspectives besides the current one (the one that we happen to occupy) is forthcoming. Of course, Cameron can insist that we do not *need* a further explanatory step, that capturing passage is all we need – as we have seen in general standard realists can do.

Perhaps here we have hit the rock bottom of the dialectics, and the issue is so deep that no argument can reach. As we pointed out above, some philosophers are simply not persuaded by the claim that taking passage as primitive is enough to avoid the frozen present. Some, such as Akiko Frischhut (2013) and Natalja Deng (2010), are suspicious of the idea of realism about passage altogether. Others, such as Kit Fine (2005) and Brad Skow (2015), think that something more than one privileged perspective has to be introduced to explain why the present is not stuck. We are more moderate than either. We think that taking passage as primitive is enough to avoid the stuck present, but only in the sense of providing a theory that captures passage, not one that explains how come the present is not stuck.

To conclude, we would make a hypothesis about why one may be led to think that the articulated view (or at least Cameron's take on it) has an explanatory advantage over the classic one.

One can agree that Cameron's introduction of ages as intrinsic, explanatorily basic properties is not ad hoc because it follows from an independently motivated general picture, one in which primitive passage is captured by the intrinsic properties of the entities located across a changing temporal dimension. And they can agree that the classic moving spotlight theory, in which various tensed facts about the position of the present are taken as primitive is ad hoc in that introduces those facts merely to avoid the frozen present problem. Indeed, there is an explanatory advantage of Cameron's position here. However, it does not concern *passage*, but rather *presentness* and the other A-properties. The latter are explained in terms of the basic tools of distributional properties and ages:

> What makes it true that noon (GMT) on January 1st 1980 was present? That simply amounts to the question: what makes it the case that everything was the way it was at noon on 1/1/80? Well, we know what makes that the case: the ages and temporal distributional properties that things have now makes that the case. What makes it the case that *this* time is present? That question amounts to asking: what makes it the case that things have the properties they have now? Again: their having the fundamental properties that they have makes that the case.
>
> Cameron 2015: 189, italics in the original[13]

Now, one may be tempted to carry over this explanatory advantage to the issue of robust passage as well. But there is no reason to do so. The fact that ages change, that I have now a certain age property but that I had different ones and I will have still different ones is an explanatory basic fact in the picture.[14] Besides, although it is true that facts about 'pure' tensed properties (that is, the A-properties of times) are derivative in Cameron's view, it is not clear to us that *all* tensed facts are derivative. Cameron seems to think that *also* qualitative tensed facts are derivative:

> There are no fundamental tensed facts: nothing of the form 'such-and-such was/will be the case' is fundamental; all such facts are made true by things having a certain age and distributional property and their being located where they are.
>
> Cameron 2015: 210

But do facts about A-properties of times and qualitative facts exhaust the logical space of the tensed facts? Even if ordinary, 'mundane' qualitative tensed properties are derivative on the distributional properties and the age properties of things, it is hard to see how the facts that things *had* certain ages, *are now* a certain age, and *will have* certain ages can be reduced to anything else in this picture.[15]

Even if it is *also* of the essence of things that their age properties change, and not merely that they have (absolutely, non-time relative) the ages that they have, it still seems false to say that *nothing* of the form 'such-and-such was/will be the case' is fundamental in this picture. *All* facts of that form that are about mundane qualitative properties, or A-properties of times are indeed derivative, but facts of that form encompassing ages, if the stuck present problem is to be avoided, are not.

Finally, we do not wish to bestow the 'tense realist' label to Cameron's view at all costs. The difference between classical moving spotlight and his is radical and remarkable enough to justify a shift of label after all. What is important for us to stress here is that in Cameron's view there is a piece of the theory that captures primitive passage, the age properties. And even though age properties are not introduced ad hoc since they have a crucial role in explaining what A-properties, and what mundane tensed properties are, they do not bring us closer to an explanation of how the passage of time comes about.

1.1.4.3 Reductionism to the rescue?

As we have pointed out in the Introduction, we think that by considering all temporal perspectives – understood as fragments – metaphysically on a par, we have at our disposal the relevant theoretical tools to provide an explanatory discourse with respect to the passage. Standard tense realists may object that we do not need more than they can provide too, a view that captures primitive passage. But what about a specular view, one in which we give up the idea of capturing robust passage (through a primitive of the theory at least), and aim solely at explaining what passage is?

This use of the resources of the non-standard framework is what characterizes what we call tense realist *reductionism* about the passage. The reason of the label comes from its model: the reductionist account of qualitative change in terms of at-at change. Such a reductionist theory of change is grist of the mill of B-theorists. One can give an analysis of qualitative change in terms of *variation across temporal locations* of incompatible *qualitative* properties, possessed by the same (persisting) object. Traditionally, A-theorists have complained that in such an account *genuine* change is lost. But the complaint seems unfair. This is what, according to the theory, change *is*, after all![16] Besides, most agree that the at-at theory of change captures *something* of the intuitive idea; indeed, often the debate is framed in terms of whether ordinary change is merely at-at change or we need something *more* (tenses or some dynamic oomph).[17]

A non-standard A-theorist can engage in a similar project with respect to robust change, and identify the passage of time with it (see section 0.4).[18] According to a reductionist theory of robust passage, the passage of time is analysed in terms of *variation across temporal perspectives*, or *fragments*, of incompatible tensed properties, possessed by the same temporal locations. And if the standard A-theorist complains that by doing so one loses robust passage, they can be offered a reply similar to the one that we have just seen: the objection is unfair, according to the reductionist theory, this is what the passage of time *is*. Besides, as in the case of the at-at theory of change, it seems reasonable to maintain that the thesis that robust passage requires variation of tensed properties across temporal perspectives is a minimal requirement upon which realists (and possibly even anti-realist, given the appropriate understanding of 'perspectives' and 'tensed properties') agree.

Although there is something to the reductionist approach, we think that it fails to *capture* robust passage, and so dialectically is not a viable option for us. It is true that, unlike any standard account, it provides an explanatory story about what passage consists in. But if ordinary passage *is* robust passage, then the explanatory story is no good. Maybe there are good reasons to think that ordinary passage is neither robust passage nor anaemic passage, and reductionism will turn out to be the best realist account of ordinary passage that we can have.[19] But if we aim at explaining what robust passage is (and thus assume that ordinary passage is robust passage), it is clearly a non-starter.

Flow Fragmentalism is not a reductive theory in this sense, and it does not entail that the passage of time is *merely* variation of A-properties through fragments. Rather, we follow a strategy that is closer to that of the standard approach in this respect. As in the latter, the idea is to consider passage as primitive, and then choose something in one's theoretical toolbox to encode it. However, we do not stop there, as it were, but aim at explaining how passage comes about by looking at the temporal dimension from more than one temporal perspective.

1.1.4.4 *Priorian flow*

In this and the next subsection, we will spell out our explanation of the nature of passage in seven steps. For the first step, we rely on the original insight by Prior to take tense operators as the encoding tool, tense logic as the background theory, and capture the passage of time in terms of the satisfaction of Priorian Flow, which is repeated below.

Priorian Flow It was the case that p, and is not now the case that p

The problem with stopping at this first step is the one that we encountered in section 1.1.4.1: it is difficult to distinguish the picture that comes out of it from a picture in which the present time is 'frozen'. If all reality provides us is *one* temporal perspective, then how can the primitive notion of the passage that is encoded by the tense operators be put in action, so to say?

The second step is to enter the non-standard framework and consider the other temporal perspectives as equally legitimate to tell us what facts constitute reality. Now, one may suspect that if Neutrality holds and no time is privileged over the others, the situation is not very different. The only difference being merely the number of 'frozen presents' that we have. Each fragment is like a universe stuck in an everlasting present. But this would be a mistake. A way to resist the collapse of the view into a scenario of frozen fragments is to understand constitution not merely as absolute, but also as inherently *dynamic*. Tensed facts constitute a genuine flow of time by constituting reality in a way that warrants that when a future-tensed fact obtains within a fragment F, this is so *because* reality *will* contain the corresponding present-tensed version of it – that is, because a fragment that comes 'after' F contains it; and when a past-tensed fact obtains within a fragment F, this is so because reality *did* contain the corresponding present-tensed version of it – that is, because a fragment that comes 'before' F contains it.[20] Flow Fragmentalism supplements Prior's account by adding a story based on the 'harmonic' behaviour of the tensed facts in different fragments. The theory does not merely capture passage, by exploiting some bit of ideology that encodes it, but it provides an explanation of how it comes about. From a global perspective, the flow is an incoherent amalgamation of incompatible facts, all constituting reality in an absolute sense, but at the level of obtainment, from the perspective of each time so to speak, the flow is a coherent order across fragments.[21]

1.1.4.5 *Temporal pushes and pulls*

We have now cleared the difference between a standard account of robust passage and what we aim at achieving with Flow Fragmentalism. So far so good. But how does Flow Fragmentalism exactly exploit the pluralist approach just described to supplement the standard picture with an explanation of the temporal flow? The core idea we need to articulate is that facts that are future- or past-tensed obtain in a given fragment *in virtue of* the present-tensed facts that obtain within fragments that are, respectively, in its past and in its future. But how to make sense of talk of fragments that are 'in the past' and 'in the future' of other fragments? Unlike for the external relativist (as seen in section 0.4), for the fragmentalist reality is one, and the fragments can be seen as containing facts that are all about what happens at the various locations of a single temporal dimension. Imagine that two fragments F_1 and F_2 are such that within F_1 all facts that obtain at a certain instant t_1 obtain, and within F_2 all facts that obtain at a certain instant t_2 obtain. Informally, we can say that t_1 and t_2 are the 'present times' of F_1 and F_2, respectively. It is natural to think that fragments can be ordered in a sequence, which can play the role of a temporal succession of times ordered by an earlier/later relation. We will see the details of how to achieve such an order through the notion of fragments overlapping with one another in the next chapter. For now, let us assume that such a 'pseudo B-relation' $<_{ps}$ (as we will call it) is in the toolbox of the flow fragmentalist.[22] We can then stipulate that $F_1 <_{ps} F_2$ if and only if $t_1 < t_2$.

We are now in a position to make the third step towards an explanation of the passage of time. By ordering the fragments, we can put them to use as times in a standard semantics for tenses. More precisely, we treat our official idiom $\mathcal{L}^{+\odot}$ as an indexical language, and give fragment-relative truth-conditions to its simple and complex sentences.[23] Let be a model $\mathcal{M}$ a triple $\langle \mathcal{F}, <_{ps}, v \rangle$ such that (i) $\mathcal{F} = \{F_1, F_2, \ldots\}$ is a set of (points informally representing the) fragments, (ii) $<_{ps}$ is a linear order on $\mathcal{F}$, and (iii) v is a valuation function that, given a fragment in $\mathcal{F}$, assigns a truth-value in $\{T, F\}$ to each atom in $\mathcal{L}^{+\odot}$. The truth-conditions of sentences of $\mathcal{L}^{+\odot}$ are the following:

$[p]^{F_n}_{\mathcal{M}} = T$ iff $v_{F_n}(p) = T$, where p is atomic[24]

$[\neg \phi]^{F_n}_{\mathcal{M}} = T$ iff $[\phi]^{F_n}_{\mathcal{M}} \neq T$

$[\phi \wedge \psi]^{F_n}_{\mathcal{M}} = T$ iff $[\phi]^{F_n}_{\mathcal{M}} = [\psi]^{F_n}_{\mathcal{M}} = T$

$[\odot_{F_x} \phi]^{F_n}_{\mathcal{M}} = T$ iff $[\phi]^{F_x}_{\mathcal{M}} = T$[25]

$[WILL \phi]^{F_n}_{\mathcal{M}} = T$ iff there is a fragment F_m such that (i) $F_n <_{ps} F_m$, and (ii) $[\phi]^{F_m}_{\mathcal{M}} = T$

$[WAS \phi]^{F_n}_{\mathcal{M}} = T$ iff there is a fragment F_m such that (i) $F_m <_{ps} F_n$, and (ii) $[\phi]^{F_m}_{\mathcal{M}} = T$

Truth in a model $\mathcal{M}$ is defined in a non-recursive way as follows:

$\mathcal{M} \vDash \phi$ iff for some fragment F_n, $[\phi]^{F_n}_{\mathcal{M}} = T$

Logical truth and logical consequence are defined as usual:

$\vDash \phi$ iff, for any model $\mathcal{M}$, $\mathcal{M} \vDash \phi$

$\Sigma \vDash \phi$ iff, for any model $\mathcal{M}$, if $\mathcal{M} \vDash \Sigma$, then $\mathcal{M} \vDash \phi$

We take truth in a model to be the relevant notion for expressing metaphysical cogency (in the sense described in section 0.1). Although the sentences of $\mathcal{L}^{+\odot}$ are evaluated relative to fragments, there is – unlike in the standard framework – no privileged time. The simple sentences that are true in $\mathcal{M}$ express what facts constitute reality, whereas the complex sentences allow to articulate their obtainment. For instance, if $\phi \wedge \psi$ is true in $\mathcal{M}$, within at least one fragment the fact that ϕ and the fact that ψ obtain together, and if $\odot_{F_x}\phi$ is true in $\mathcal{M}$, the fact that ϕ obtains within the fragment F_x.

Now, providing truth-conditions for tensed claims of an indexical language in a fragmentalist framework in itself does not amount to providing an explanation of real passage. However, from the truth-conditions of past- and future-tensed claims, we can learn something about the behaviour of tensed facts along the temporal dimension. In particular – and this is the fourth step of the explanation – assuming that in general within each fragment, not only present tensed facts, but also past- and future-tensed facts obtain, we will have the correlation expressed by the Basic Principle of Flow Fragmentalism below.

Basic Principle$_{FF}$ For each fragment F_n,

(a) Within some fragments F_x such that $F_x <_{ps} F_n$, present-tensed versions of the past-tensed facts that obtain within F_n obtain.
(b) Within some fragments F_y such that $F_n <_{ps} F_y$, present-tensed versions of the future-tensed facts that obtain within F_n obtain.

Through Basic Principle$_{FF}$, Flow Fragmentalism articulates the idea of an inherent dynamism of the tensed facts along the temporal dimension. As anticipated at the end of the previous section, from the point of view of constitution, the flow is an incoherent coalescence of incompatible tensed facts, but at the level of obtainment, the flow is a coherent order of successively obtaining tensed facts. Notice that there is coherence not only at the level of individual fragments, but also in how past- and future-tensed facts and their present-tensed versions correlate within different fragments. However, stating a mere correlation is not providing an explanation either. We need to know more about how this correspondence is explanatory of a robust conception of the passage of time.

To see how, it may be useful to make explicit reference to how reality is characterized in Flow Fragmentalism, and compare it with the picture in the standard framework. In the latter, what happens *from the perspective of the present time* is what explains what will happen from the perspective of future times, and what happened from the perspective of past times. That is so, since how reality is (full stop) is how reality is from the perspective of the present time. We can express this idea by the following tenet (in the context of tense realism, in which the antecedent is true).

Presentist Flow If it will be the case [it was the case] that in reality a present-tensed fact obtains, it is so because in reality its future-tensed [past-tensed] version obtains at present.[26]

In this picture, reality 'pulls itself' as it were towards the future and 'pushes itself' away from the past. This is the Munchausen still movement of the present that we have briefly hinted at in the Introduction (p. 14). For reasons that should be obvious from the discussion so far, it seems to us explanatorily deficient to appeal to *the present only* to explain the flow of time, which is a notion that necessarily involves more than one temporal perspective (cf. Leininger 2015).

One may object that a standard tense realist (being her a presentist, a growing blocker, or a moving spotlighter) does *not* have to endorse Presentist Flow; and thus this criticism is irrelevant. More precisely, the standard tense realist could *reverse* the explanatory order. After all, tenses *are* part of their basic theoretical tools, so why not take as explanatorily more basic that it will be the case [it was the case] that in reality a certain present-tensed fact obtains? Our reply is that, as long as we stay in a standard framework, all but the privileged perspective (the one that is from the time that is present *simpliciter*) are *hypothetical* perspectives (cf. Fine 2005: 279). If so, past and future perspectives simply cannot be explanatory *prior* to the present one, which is the only non-hypothetical one. But that it will be the case [it was the case] that in reality a certain present-tensed fact obtains is a way to state what facts obtain from the perspective of a time that is *not* present, and hence it cannot be taken as explanatorily more fundamental. We are aware that in the literature, there are various attempts to appeal to a primitive tense language in a non-committal way to explain how the past was or the future will be.[27] Here we do not want to defend in full our methodological principle, but just to point out that if one accepts that it is in the business of metaphysical theories to provide a metaphysically cogent description of reality that allows us to formulate explanatory hypotheses, then between Presentist Flow and its reverse the standard theorist has only one option.

In the non-standard framework, we have more options than the resort to an 'all powerful' present that has all it takes to explain the passage of time. In particular, and this is the fifth step of the explanation, the flow fragmentalist can explain the present obtainment of future- and past-tensed facts in terms of the future and past obtainment of the correspondent present-tensed facts, since non-present perspectives have the same status than the present one for her. We can express this idea by the following tenet (in the context of tense realism, in which the antecedent is true).

Fragmentalist Flow* If in reality a future-tensed [past-tensed] fact obtains at present, it is so because it will be the case [it was the case] that in reality its present-tensed version obtains.

If we compare this thesis with Presentist Flow, the difference is clear. What bears the explanatory burden here is how reality was or will be like. It is the past that 'pushes' the present away from it, and the future that 'pulls' the present towards it. And that can be the case, because in the non-standard picture of fragmentalism every perspective is born equal and has equal right to the overall picture of reality.

Now, although the difference in the direction of explanation between Presentist Flow and Fragmentalist Flow* is, hopefully, clear, the flow fragmentalist cannot take Fragmentalist Flow* as it is at face value. There are two problems. The first is shallow, but the second is deeper and overcoming it will lead us to the core of our theory of passage. The first problem is that the difference between Presentist Flow and Fragmentalist Flow* is expressed by exploiting the 'in reality' idiom explicitly, and the difference between the two is essentially a difference in the scope of this expression and tense operators. However, in our official idiom, in order to express what is the case in reality, we have stipulated that we will use a sentence that is not prefixed by one of the 'within fragment F' operators. Thus, it looks like impossible to have a difference *in scope* here. It is like trying to spell out the difference in *de re* and *the dicto* readings through a language that has neither quantifiers nor modal operators.

One may think that then what we should do is simply to *introduce* an 'in reality' operator in the official idiom, so that it can interact with the usual tense operators and allows us to express the central idea of Fragmentalist Flow*. After all, in Fine's original formulation, the official idiom does contain such an operator. We have nothing against using an explicit 'in reality' operator, but for the formulation of the the explanation at issue, this manoeuvre will not save the day. The problem (and this is the second, deep problem) is how to make sense of (i) in the context of Flow Fragmentalism, assuming that it must mean something different from (ii).

(i) It will be the case that [It was the case that] in reality ϕ
(ii) In reality, it will be the case that [it was the case that] ϕ

To see the point, think of the following. If a tense operator takes wider scope on a reality operator, the perspective *from which the claim is made* 'takes over'. After all, what does it mean that it will be the case that reality is such and such, if it is not that it will be such and such from the perspective of the fragment in which I am speaking? But constitution cannot be relativized to times (or fragments) in Flow Fragmentalism, and thus the flow fragmentalist has no way to state how reality will be like (or was like) from the perspective of a given time, unless she does not simply mean to talk about what future- or past-tensed facts constitute reality, namely unless she conflates (i) and (ii). In other words, she is not in a position to say that reality will be (or has been) *updated* in some absolute sense, since that would require a privileged perspective on reality, which she has given up by interpreting Neutrality as the pluralist view according to which constitution is absolute and obtainment is relative. What we will do is to 'sneak in' our official idiom of tense operators and 'within fragment F' operators the idea of reality getting updated in an absolute sense, although not from the point of view of any fragment in particular.

In order to do that – and this is the sixth step – we number the fragments in a way that reflects their $<_{ps}$-order. We choose an arbitrary fragment zero,[28] and postulate that given any two fragments, the modulo of the difference in their numbers corresponds to the temporal distance between their 'presents' in a given scale. Then we unify the past and the future tense operators in one operator '$TENSE_n$,' which expresses the distance of n units (in the same scale) from the present. Thus, if n is negative, '$TENSE_n$' is synonymous with 'it was the case n units of time ago that' and if it is positive it is synonymous with 'it will be the case in n units of time that', while if $n = 0$, it expresses the present tense (and thus is redundant). We can now make the seventh and last step of our explanation and express Fragmentalist Flow* in a way that is compatible with Neutrality, by claiming that for any x and $n \neq 0$ and some ϕ:

Fragmentalist Flow $\odot_{F_x} TENSE_n \phi$ because $\odot_{F_{(n+x)}} \phi$

With this last seventh step, we have arrived at a rather elegant formulation of the idea that in a universe where there is robust passage, the flow of time is not given by a self-propelled present, but rather by the fact that from the perspective of each time there are a push from the past and a pull from the future that explain how reality is globally updated. Flow Fragmentalism captures the flow of time through the same tools of standard tense realism. However, thanks to its 'wider' toolbox, it supplements the standard view with an explanation of the flow, which does not reduce the flow to the variation of tensed properties across fragments (cf. p. 33), and is *more* than an idle multiplication of the Priorian idea within each fragment (cf. p. 34).

1.1.4.6 The analogy to the modal case

It is important to stress that, unless one takes passage as primitive, the resort to a full array of temporal perspectives is not itself enough to deliver a dynamic picture of time. It is only with the *combination* of the explanation in terms of temporal 'pushes' and 'pulls' and the assumption that there is robust passage that one can finally account for the idea that time is inherently dynamic. An analogy to the modal case might help see why this is so. Consider the modal analogue of fragmentalism.[29] As Fine (2005: 284) underlines, both in the temporal case and in the modal one 'we have ... a certain aspectual feature ... [– respectively, the tensed nature of facts and their being worldly (or contingent) –] and an associated form of relativity' – the relativity being, respectively, to a time and to a world. Within a realist framework, this 'aspectual feature' is taken to be irreducible: the worldly fact that *Socrates is a philosopher* cannot be reduced to the non-worldly fact that *Socrates is a philosopher in the world w*, just like the tensed fact that *Socrates is drinking the hemlock* cannot be reduced to the tenseless fact that *Socrates is drinking the hemlock at the time t*. By exploiting the analogy between times and worlds, we can reinterpret Realism, Absolutism and Neutrality as follows (p. 285; Coherence will be left untouched):[30]

Worldly Realism Reality is composed of worldly facts.
Worldly Absolutism The constitution of reality is an absolute matter, i.e. not relative to a world.
Worldly Neutrality No possible world is privileged, i.e. the facts that constitute reality are not oriented towards one possible world as opposed to another.

We can now give the modal analogue of the debate between standard and non-standard tense realists. As Fine has it:

> The standard realist will claim that there is a privileged world, namely the actual world, while the non-standard realist will treat all worlds on an ontological par (but still hold to the reality of worldly facts).
>
> Fine 2005: 285

Call *Modal Fragmentalism* the realist view that rejects Coherence, while maintaining both Worldly Absolutism and Worldly Neutrality. Under this view, the modal dimension will be fragmented into maximally coherent collections of worldly facts, playing the role of concrete possible worlds.[31] Arguably, there are different ways to pin down the idea that the modal dimension lacks metaphysical unity, depending on one's preferred interpretation of fragmentalism (see section 1.3 of this chapter). One can extend our approach to the modal case by taking the absolute constitution of worldly facts and their relative obtainment as two equally fundamental features of the modal dimension.[32] The Obtainment-Constitution principle can then be rephrased as follows (where 'modal fragment' refers to a maximally coherent collection of worldly facts).

Obtainment-Constitution' A worldly fact obtains in some modal fragment iff it constitutes reality.

Although, by Obtainment-Constitution', there cannot be facts that constitute the modal dimension without obtaining relative to at least one modal fragment, reality is not 'of a piece' in that not all facts that constitute the modal dimension obtain in each modal fragment. This means that if two facts constitute the modal dimension, there is no guarantee that they also obtain together within some modal fragment.

As we just saw in discussing the temporal case, the idea that each fragment is A-theoretically present serves an important role in overcoming Fine's frozen-present objection, an objection that is meant to uncover an explanatory lack at the root of standard tense realism. Unless Neutrality is adopted, the explanatory burden of accounting for the passage of time lies inevitably on the present, for how reality is *sic et simpliciter* is nothing but how reality is at the present moment. But once Neutrality is taken on board, what happens in our moment does not exhaust the totality of what is absolutely present. This allows the fragmentalist to reverse the explanatory direction of her theory of passage: the explanatory burden is put on how reality was or will be like, the past and the future respectively 'pushing' and 'pulling' the present along the temporal dimension.

Now, in analogy to the temporal case, the adoption of Worldly Neutrality allows for an explanatory reversal: it is not the case that what happens in our world explains what happens in the other ones; rather, it is what happens in the other worlds that explains what happens in ours. Suppose that, among the many concrete worlds, there is one that is absolutely actual.[33] In such a framework, the explanatory burden lies on the actual world, for how reality is *sic et simpliciter* is how reality is from the perspective of that world. If it is the case that there are talking donkeys, it is so because the fact that there might have been talking donkeys obtains in the actual world. But once Worldly Neutrality is adopted, what happens in our world does not exhaust the totality of what is absolutely actual. If it is the case in our world that there might have been talking donkeys, it is so because the fact that there are talking donkeys is actual, by being part of another world.

It should be obvious that in this case we observe no modal analogue of the passage of time. This is so because the availability of an explanatory reversal is not itself enough to make the modal dimension inherently dynamic. Unless the fragmentalist assumes the existence of some sort of modal 'flow' – and there is no reason why one should do that, for there is obviously no 'flow' in the modal case – she won't end up with a dynamic picture of modality. Analogously, the explanation of the flow of time offered by the flow fragmentalist does not exempt her from taking passage – just as in the standard framework – as primitive. In the absence of this primitive, the explanatory toolbox of the flow fragmentalist would fail to vindicate the inherent dynamism of time.

1.2 Some objections and replies

In this section, we discuss four objections that may naturally arise against Flow Fragmentalism. This will give us the chance to further develop certain aspects of the view, in particular the nature of times in their double role of location and perspectives, and its take on the incompatibility between presentism and perdurantism.

1.2.1 The update test

The previous section gives our explanation of the passage of time as formulated in the official idiom of Flow Fragmentalism. As we have just stressed, the theory aims at being more than a reductive account of passage. Yet one may protest that it is not clear that in our theory passage is something more than variation of tensed properties across temporal perspectives. The problem is not that there is never an update in how reality is *constituted*. Once we enter the non-standard framework, it is fair to concede that constitution is not a tensed matter.[34] The problem is that in Flow Fragmentalism nothing changes as time goes by with respect to what facts *obtain* within each fragment. What Fragmentalist Flow states is just how tensed facts vary *across fragments*, and it tells us how they relate to each other along the order of fragments. What exactly is the difference with the reductionist claim according to which ordinary passage is variation of tensed properties across temporal perspectives?

Let us formulate the worry in terms of the *update test*, which Flow Fragmentalism fails when formulated in its official idiom. The test is the following. Assume a theory $\mathfrak{T}$ and a language $\mathcal{L}$ in which the theory is expressed, and in which we aim at making metaphysically cogent claims. Write down on a sheet what is the case with respect to a certain object o according to $\mathfrak{T}$ using $\mathcal{L}$. Wait for o to change in some respect, and then write down how o is in the new situation. The couple $\langle \mathfrak{T}, \mathcal{L} \rangle$ passes the test if and only if one needs to bar something written before not to write on the sheet incompatible sentences. Standard tense realism with the language of tense logic passes the test. If o is P at the beginning of the test, one has to write something like 'o is presently P'. If then later on o is Q (a property incompatible with being P), one has to bar the former sentence and write down 'o is presently Q'. Test passed. Tense *anti*-realism with a tenseless language, on the other hand, fails the test. In the same situation just described, the anti-realist would write something like 'o is P at t_1', and 'o is Q at t_2', with no need to bar any sentence.

What about Flow Fragmentalism and its official idiom? One may be tempted to point out that $\mathcal{L}^{+\odot}$ is tensed, and its semantics is that of an indexical language. The context of utterance naturally selects a fragment (roughly, that in which the utterance is present), and thus as in the standard case, we should write 'o is presently P', and then later on bar it and write 'o is presently Q': the couple $\langle$Flow Fragmentalism, $\mathcal{L}^{+\odot}\rangle$ thus passes the test. But this, unfortunately, is not quite right. As we said above (p. 23) simple sentences of $\mathcal{L}^{+\odot}$ express what facts constitute reality, and given that constitution is captured by the notion of truth in a model, both 'o is P' and 'o is Q' can be legitimately written down at *any* time to state how things stand with respect to o (although for epistemic reasons one may not know which she is legitimate to write down). However, as we pointed out at the outset, it would be unfair to require that a non-standard realist adopts the idea that constitution varies as time goes by, since they abide with Neutrality. But if we test the behaviour of obtainment, we are not better off, since in Flow Fragmentalism the language for obtainment behaves like the tenseless language of the anti-realist. If we write down '$\odot_{F_1} o$ is P' and then '$\odot_{F_2} o$ is Q', no sentence needs to be barred to maintain coherence. To stress again the point, that does *not* mean that we are expressing two fragment-indexed facts that are compatible with one another. There are no indexed facts in Flow Fragmentalism. The operator '$\odot_{F_x}$' does not stand for a fact constituent, it just allows us to state something about the facts, namely in which fragment they obtain. Yet what we say about the facts involving o at different times does not require us any sentence barring to maintain coherence. The couple $\langle$Flow Fragmentalism, $\mathcal{L}^{+\odot}\rangle$ fails the update test.

The objection can be then formulated as follows: since Flow Fragmentalism in its official idiom fails the update test, it fails to capture robust passage. If ordinary passage is not robust passage, the theory may have its virtues. Indeed, the flow fragmentalist explanation of ordinary passage may turn out to be the best that we have. But *as an account of robust passage*, it cannot be better off than the reductionist one.

We do not think that the update test objection is fair, for the simple reason that the test itself is not fair. A theory that is *about* a constantly updating reality needs not *itself* to constantly update what it takes to be metaphysically cogent.[35] Think of the analogy with a theory of vagueness. It has to tell us something about the situations in which vagueness shows up, and what it says has to be explanatory with respect to those situations, but it does not have to be *itself* vague. The same goes for Flow Fragmentalism and robust passage. The theory captures robust passage by encoding it in one of the elements of its primitive ideology, namely the operator '$TENSE_x$'. As long as standard tense realism captures passage by encoding it in Priorian operators, Flow Fragmentalism does so as well. When we use $\mathcal{L}^{+\odot}$ to express a fact that constitutes reality, for instance by stating that something will be the case in x units of time (or was the case x units of time ago), we are making a claim that is no different from the analogous one that the standard tense realist would make. Our claim, as the one of the standard realist, if true, entails a robust change in reality. The difference is that Flow Fragmentalism allows us to say something *more*. Thanks to Fragmentalist Flow, we can provide an explanation of such a change, and state what it takes for it to happen. The fact that the explanation itself does not need to be updated as time goes by can hardly be taken as a defect of the view.

1.2.2 Labelling the fragments

Another objection to Flow Fragmentalism comes from the problem of the nature of times. Fine (2005: 308–10) argues that one of the reasons to prefer fragmentalism over external relativism is that according to fragmentalism we can simply identify times and fragments, whereas the external relativist does not seem to have any viable account of what times are. In light of our distinction between times as locations and times as perspectives, we can formulate Fine's worry as follows. The ontology of temporal locations is not particularly problematic for the non-standard tense realist. Roughly, in the Priorian tradition, temporal locations are collections of tensed facts.[36] The flow fragmentalist can make an analogous move and identify each fragment F_x with a temporal location. More precisely, all the present-tensed facts in each fragment F_x can be thought of as about a 'slice' of the universe at an instant, a concrete Newtonian time t_x. The fragment F_x enables t_x to play the role of location by providing the information about what entities inhabit it, and what properties they have there – as it were. What about the temporal perspective role? The fragmentalist can take fragments to enable times to play also that role. In each fragment F_x there are not only present-tensed facts about t_x, but also past- and future-tensed facts about other temporal locations. And, crucially, the facts in F_x 'treat' t_x as the *perspectival centre* of the fragment. To paraphrase Fine, the tensed facts that obtain within a fragment are all oriented towards their 'present'.[37] The external relativists, however, can identify the location role by appeal to a collection of tensed facts, but they cannot do the same with respect to the perspective role. They need to take temporal perspectives as the entities relative to which reality loses its unicity. Therefore, they cannot identify them with collections of tensed facts, which *are* the various realities of the relativist. To paraphrase what Fine says in a slightly different context: if the indexing to temporal perspectives is to have any real significance, we need an independent conception of temporal perspective, one that gives them an identity that is separate from the realities to which they give rise.[38] In other terms, external relativism cannot take temporal perspectives to be collections of tensed facts, since that would turn it into a position according to which there is *one* reality (constitution is at bottom absolute), and many incompatible perspectives (there is no global coherence), namely it would collapse it into fragmentalism. However, it is difficult to see what else these perspectives could be for the external relativist.[39]

Now, we suggested that a reason to prefer Flow Fragmentalism over external relativism is that the former but not the latter permits us to posit explanatory links between the different temporal perspectives on the same temporal dimension (cf. pp. 14, 35). In order to spell out those links, we make essential use of an irreducibly relativized notion, that of obtainment. One may think that we are then subject to a kind of 'revenge argument' here.[40] Consider our $\odot_{F_x}$ operator, which can be used in sentences to be read informally as stating that within fragment F_x such and such is the case. One may argue that for *this* relativization to be taken seriously, we cannot simply, on pain of circularity, take F_x to be a collection of tensed facts. But this is not quite right. It is true that in other versions of fragmentalism (see section 1.3) the objection does not take off the ground, since they do not resort to a language in which the fragments can be explicitly labelled. However, the problem for the flow fragmentalist is not one of circularity. What a sentence such as '$\odot_{F_x} \phi$' states is simply that the fact that ϕ is part of a certain collection of facts (which cohere with one another).[41] Clearly there is no worry of collapsing the view into fragmentalism, since Flow Fragmentalism *is* a form of fragmentalism!

The only real problem here is that of telling a story about how the labelling can be realized, and the story is all but trivial. In principle, in order to label the fragments, it suffices that we *can refer* to them, but how do we *actually* refer to them and introduce their labels? Let us begin with labelling times, a practice that requires quite basic referential capacities. We can baptize (no scare quotes needed) a certain time t_0 by uttering something like:

Baptism This (snap of fingers) is t_0

In baptizing t_0, we give a name to a temporal location (whatever it may turn out to be), at which entities (which possibly exist at other temporal locations) have properties and enter relations. And we can establish by convention that by doing so we are also labelling all the other times in the past and the future with the corresponding labels t_{-n} and t_{+n}, depending on how many units of time n they are, respectively, in the past and the future of t_0. That is an awful lot of baptizing, but conventions are (well, this convention is at any rate) cheap to get. Indeed, nothing prevents us to adopt a further convention, to the effect that by baptizing t_0 and all its comrades in the temporal series, we are also baptizing the maximally coherent collection of tensed facts that obtain at t_0, which we will call F_0. And the new convention expands also to all maximally coherent collections of tensed facts obtaining at the various t_{-n} and t_{+n}, which get the corresponding labels F_{-n} and F_{+n}. Let us call 'convention $\mathfrak{F}$' the whole labelling convention. Convention $\mathfrak{F}$, or something analogous to it, is the one that we have implicitly used all along for $\mathcal{L}^{+\odot}$ in presenting the official idiom of our theory.

1.2.3 Presentism

Another problem for Flow Fragmentalism is about its ontological commitments. As we have stressed many times already, the way in which robust passage is captured in Flow Fragmentalism is analogous to the way in which it is captured in the standard framework: by endorsing a primitive ideology of tenses. Now some may argue that it is possible to genuinely capture robust passage through tense operators only if we have a changing ontology, namely if we endorse presentism.[42] Some, perhaps many, would disagree.[43] However, it would be nice if Flow Fragmentalism would turn out to be compatible with this tenet, since it is crucial for the position that it can *capture* the flow in the same sense in which the standard position can. Indeed, in published works,[44] we have defended a version of Flow Fragmentalism that explicitly aims at vindicating certain aspects of presentism. In this book, we wish to leave open the issue of the correct ontology to adopt, but precisely for that reason we want to defend the *possibility* that Flow Fragmentalism has a presentist ontology. There is an obvious problem though. As with all forms of non-standard tense realism, Flow Fragmentalism rejects Presentness and endorses Neutrality (cf. section 1.1.1). All times are equal, in the sense that the facts that obtain at times that are past and future (from the standpoint that we happen to have) constitute reality as much as the facts that obtain at present. But among those facts there are plausibly also existential facts, such as the fact that *Socrates exists*, the fact that *Jenann Ismael exists*, and the fact that *the 144th president of the United States exists*. It seems then inevitable to conclude that Flow Fragmentalism, and indeed any non-standard form of tense realism, is compelled to have on board an *eternalist* ontology.

Let us clear this point, and see how we can rejoinder. The label 'presentism' has been used for very different positions.[45] Again following Fine, we will distinguish between Factive Presentism and Ontic Presentism. The former is nothing but the thesis that we have called Presentness, namely the claim that only tensed facts obtaining at present constitute reality (see p. 20). Factive Presentism is not a thesis about what exists, but a thesis about how reality is like, and together with Realism and Absolutism, constitutes the core of standard tense realism.[46] Ontic Presentism is a thesis about what exists, and in this context can be expressed as follows.

Ontic Presentism Only present entities exist.

While Factive Presentism is compatible with different ontologies – with presentism, but also with an eternalist ontology (i.e. a moving spotlight view), or an ontology encompassing the present and the past (i.e. a growing block view) – Ontic Presentism seems to require Factive Presentism. Apparently, even Fine thinks so:

> It is readily possible for a factive presentist not to be an ontic presentist. Indeed, he may endorse a full ontology of things past, present, and future. . . . Ontic presentism, by contrast, does not really make sense except in the context of factive presentism. There is no strict implication from one to the other but, *given that all the facts are tenseless*, it makes no sense to restrict the ontology to presently existing things.
>
> Fine 2005: 299; italics added

We have to be careful here. The negation of Factive Presentism, that is, the negation of Presentness, is not equivalent to tense *anti*-realism. A realist who accepts instead Neutrality, namely a non-standard tense realism, also denies Presentness.[47] Therefore, from the fact that tense anti-realism requires (not in a logical sense, but to make sense as a theory of time) an eternalist ontology, it follows that a non-eternalist ontology (such as the presentist one) requires the negation of tense anti-realism, but it does *not* follow that a presentist ontology requires Presentness. If the facts are *not* all tenseless, there can be variation in existential facts across fragments. We trust the reader can see that in principle, but how exactly does one make sense of Ontic Presentism in a context where Presentness does not hold, even granting that the relevant existential facts are tensed?

In order to couple Ontic Presentism and Flow Fragmentalism, we have to distinguish between two kinds of existential facts. The ones that involve existence *at a temporal location*, and the ones that involve *simple* existence.[48] Tensed talk about existence is ambiguous in this respect. We can say that Socrates exists to say that he is located in the present, but also to express the fact he is one of the entities that populate our world (abstracting, as it were, from any temporal reference), namely to say that he exists *simpliciter*. Both presentist and eternalist agree that it is not a fact that Socrates exists in the first sense, but disagree on whether the fact that *Socrates exists simpliciter* obtains or not. But while the standard presentist maintains that the fact that *Socrates exists simpliciter* fails both to obtain and to constitute reality, a flow fragmentalist that endorses a presentist ontology maintains that the fact that *Socrates exists simpliciter* constitutes reality absolutely speaking, but it obtains only within certain fragments (those where he is temporally located).[49]

We can now see why the initial objection does not reach its target. The idea that Neutrality entails eternalism follows from the idea that the ontology of a theory is dictated by which facts according to the theory constitute reality, rather than which facts obtain. If it were so, then Flow Fragmentalism (as any other non-standard theory) would by no means be able to vindicate the idea that *only* present entities exist, since facts about the simple existence of future and past entities do constitute reality in the flow fragmentalist's picture. However, if in Flow Fragmentalism the facts about simple existence that obtain within different fragments involve only the entities that are located at the 'present' of the fragment, it seems unfair to say that the position does not vindicate the presentist insight about existence in a non-standard framework. Clearly, if we look at (irreducibly relative) obtainment, the flow fragmentalist, within each fragment, can (and perhaps should) be presentist.[50] The issue of whether ontology is to be decided by constitution or by obtainment seems largely an arbitrary one. Perhaps we should say that it depends on the explanatory purpose at issue. But the issue here is whether the flow fragmentalist can capture the primitive flow as much as the presentist can. So it looks like begging the question to *deny* any relevance to an ontology relativized to fragments. Be that as it may, once we have facts about simple existence on board, we open up the possibility of having versions of fragmentalism in which what exists *simpliciter* (not merely what is located at the 'present' of the fragment) varies across fragments. Within each fragment, thus, the tensed facts are the same as those a standard presentist would accept. Therefore, it is plausible to think that the primitive flow is captured by the tenses in the same way in both theories.

The presentist version of Flow Fragmentalism opens up also another interesting possibility. We have argued that in Flow Fragmentalism both the location role and the perspective role that a time t_x plays are enabled by the corresponding fragment F_x. Now, we have so far informally talked of the *temporal dimension* and how each fragment has a perspectival centre on it. The temporal dimension is the succession of temporal locations, ordered by the earlier/later relation $<$. However, if the ontology within each fragment is presentist, in each fragment F_x, only the concrete t_x that corresponds to its 'present' exists. In which sense then are the facts obtaining within F_x facts from the perspective of t_x on the other times t_y, t_z, etc. given that the latter do not exist within F_x? Notice also that, even though within fragments different from F_x those other concrete entities exist (t_y exists within F_y, and t_z exists within F_z, say), there are no cross-fragment facts linking them, neither through $<$ nor by means of some other external relation (we will come back to this point in several occasions in what follows, starting from p. 53). What is, then, the temporal dimension in the presentist version of Flow Fragmentalism? Strictly speaking, there is no temporal dimension within each fragment. As in presentism, we can talk of a temporal dimension only to refer to the *metric* aspect of the tensed facts which are about what goes on *outside* of the perspectival centre. However, the flow fragmentalist (with a presentist ontology) can do something more. While for the presentist time is the change in what constitutes the present, the flow fragmentalist can individuate a succession of *fragments* based on the internal relation $<_{ps}$ between them, which follows from which metric tensed facts obtain (we will say a lot more about this in section 1.2.4 and Chapter 2).

1.2.3.1 Perdurantism

Before moving to the last problem, let us spend some words on a remarkable feature of the presentist version of Flow Fragmentalism: it offers a fresh take on the debate about the incompatibility between presentism and perdurantism.[51] The latter is the view that concrete particulars, such as tables, cats, and persons, persist by being mereological sums of instantaneous spatiotemporal parts – called stages – belonging to different times. According to many, a strong reason to prefer perdurantism over other theories of persistence is that it solves the problem of identity through change.[52] This solution, however, is incompatible with the idea that there is genuine change in the world, that is, that entities genuinely gain and lose properties.[53] Suppose that Socrates is now sitting and then standing. The perdurantist describes this case in terms of mere qualitative variations of Socrates' temporal parts: the mereological sum called 'Socrates' has a stage having the property of being seated; at a later point of the sequence of Socrates' stages, we find another stage having the property of being standing.

Brogaard (2000) explored a version of perdurantism that promises to save the idea that there is genuine change. This view – called presentist four-dimensionalism – maintains that concrete particulars have

> four dimensions in the sense that they have an unfolding temporal dimension in addition to the three spatial ones ... No stage is wholly present at more than one time; every stage is wholly present at exactly one time. There is a new stage for every moment at which a given thing exists.
>
> Brogaard 2000: 343

There is an obvious crucial objection against Brogaard's view. Perdurantism is *incompatible* with presentism: if there were no time except the present, then nothing could have more than one stage, the present one. But then nothing could be a sum of stages from different times.[54] In preventing this objection, Brogaard insists that

> [it] rests on the idea that objects must have their temporal parts in the same way that they have their spatial parts. That is, temporal parts, like spatial parts, must exist *in their entirety*. This does indeed hold of those smallest temporal parts which are our successive stages. But it does not hold of temporal parts in general. That this need not be a problem is seen in the fact that events are commonly understood as having temporally extended parts even though these never exist as a whole but only through their successive stages. Similarly, objects, such as you and me, may have extended temporal parts even though these are parts which

exist always only in the sense that they unfold themselves, incrementally, through their successive stages.

Brogaard 2000: 346, italics added

As a counter-reply to Brogaard, one might argue that despite the appearances, the perdurantist is *forced* to take all the stages as existing in their entirety. An argument in favour of this idea can be found in Tallant (2018). He claims that the perdurantist is bound to accept cross-temporal identity dependencies, which are incompatible with the presentist ontology. Following Lowe (2010), he characterizes the notion of identity dependence as follows.

Identity Dependence x depends for its identity upon $y =_{df}$ There is a function f such that it is part of the essence of x that x is $f(y)$.

As an example, Lowe considers a marriage x between two people y and z. Since 'the identity of a marriage depends on the identities of the two people being married' (2010: § 4), saying that x depends for its identity upon y will be tantamount to saying that there is a function f, that is, the *marriage with z* function, such that it is part of the essence of x that x is the f of y. Similar considerations can be extended to mereological sums. A sum x – Tallant argues – depends for its identity upon its parts y.[55] This means that there is a function f, which Tallant (2018: 2212) calls the 'having y as a part' function, such that it is part of the essence of x that x is the f of y (in other words, it is part of the essence of x that y is a part of x). Now suppose that x stands for a mereological sum of stages from different times. The trouble for the presentist is that, since she takes no more than one stage at a time to be real, she can at best say that x depends for its identity upon its *present* parts. But given that which stages are present changes as time goes by, the identity of the sum itself will change as time goes by (Tallant 2018: 2212). The unwelcome conclusion is that no object can persist.

Now, it is interesting to note that, within a presentist version of Flow Fragmentalism, there is no need to reject the idea that temporal parts, like spatial parts, must exist *in their entirety*. Let us take Socrates' stages as spread along a series of $<_{ps}$-ordered fragments: no stage is wholly present at more than one fragment, every stage is wholly present at exactly one fragment. For each stage S of Socrates, the fact that *S exists simpliciter* constitutes reality in an absolute sense, so doing justice to the idea that every stage of a given concrete particular is literally part of reality. At the same time, the view has the tools to capture the relentless succession of purely present stages described by Brogaard. Within each fragment, the only facts about existence *simpliciter* that obtain are those concerning the stage located in that fragment. No fact about the existence *simpliciter* of the stages located 'before' or 'after' in the pseudo-B series can obtain. At the level of obtainment, from the perspective of each fragment, there is a new stage for every moment at which Socrates exists.[56]

1.2.4 Cross-temporality

The last problem we consider comes from the issue of cross-temporality. It seems that there are potentially at least two kinds of facts, among those required by our picture, which do not seem to obtain in any fragment, and thus do not constitute reality, according to our Obtainment-Constitution principle (p. 22). Those are facts that involve links between facts that obtain in different fragments. First, we have the facts involving the pseudo succession relation $<_{ps}$, and secondly the explanatory facts such those expressed by Fragmentalist Flow above. We will discuss in more detail the first kind in the next chapter, and come back to this problem. Here we want just to notice that claims involving $<_{ps}$ are not claims linking facts, but rather fragments, which are collections of facts. These claims are not in the object language $\mathcal{L}^{+\odot}$, but rather in its metalanguage. As we will see, they do not express facts at all, but simply state that one fragment is partially contained in another, namely that there is an overlap between the facts contained in the first and those contained in the second. The relation between the fragments in question is *internal*, in the sense that it is completely resolved by what facts constitute the first collection and what facts constitute the second collection. It is analogous to the relation expressed by the claim that my niece is taller than me, which is 'given' as soon as my height and my niece's height are given. It is not an external relation, such as a spatial relation between *a* being on the left of *b*, something requiring a fact involving both entities to obtain, and thus to constitute reality.[57] This is why we call the relation *pseudo*-temporal, and not properly temporal, and we say that the order of fragment *mimics* rather than exemplifying the temporal order.

As for the explanatory claims such as Fragmentalist Flow, the situation is somewhat similar. Even if one interprets 'because' as a sentential operator in the object language $\mathcal{L}^{+\odot}$, in our picture there are no explanatory facts, as little there are conjunctive or negative facts. It is true that what 'because' does here is more than just modulating the way in which certain facts obtain. However, also in this case nothing forces us to take on board external relations between entities that exist in different fragments. The explanatory link in question is entirely resolved by the *qualitative profile* and *tense profile* of the facts in question. Consider the tensed fact that *the apple was 3 units of time ago red*. We can think of this fact as involving a qualitative profile (something like *redness*) and a tense profile (something like *3 units of time ago*). Now for there being an explanatory link between this fact and the fact that *the apple is presently red*, all that is required is that (i) they obtain within fragments that are linked by $<_{ps}$ in the appropriate way, (ii) they have the same qualitative profile, and (iii) they have the appropriate tense profile (roughly, one 'past' and the other 'present'). But none of the above requires external links between these two facts: (i) is an internal link between fragments, (ii) and (iii) just require that the first and the second fact have a certain qualitative and tense profile.

The case can be strengthened by a parallel with the modal case. Regardless of how one understands possible worlds, as representational entities, or as spatiotemporally unrelated concrete ones, *if* one takes a modal property such as *being such that I could die if I jump in the caldera of an active volcano* to be explained in terms of the obtainment of non-modal properties of appropriately related possible worlds, it is difficult to think that one should then accept the consequence that their explanations require external relations between possible worlds. If I say that I am *such that I could die if I jump in the caldera of an active volcano* because I (or a counterpart of me)[58] died by jumping in the caldera of an active volcano in some other possible worlds, I do not commit myself to having a relation with me in another possible world (or my relevant counterpart there) that is comparable to the one I have with Petunia the guinea pig, by being on her left, or by feeding her her favourite lettuce. Although the modal context is different from the fragmentalist one, we see no reason why *explanatory* links of this kind, namely links that do not involve external relations between entities existing in different worlds and at different times respectively, should be treated differently.

Finally, we note here that our understanding of the 'rule of coherence' (the specification of what facts obtain together) as positing a veto – as it were – on what substantive links between entities can obtain, and thus constitute reality, is another (and quite decisive in our eyes) element of distinction between non-standard tense realism and tense anti-realism. Remember that both non-standard tense realism and tense anti-realism reject Presentness and abide by Neutrality. In our interpretation of the non-standard framework, the non-standard and the anti-realist understanding of Neutrality do not only involve a different stance towards tensed facts. Also for us, of course, the non-standard tense realist takes tensed facts as explanatorily fundamental, while the tense anti-realist takes the tenseless facts as more basic. However, we also postulate a further difference in how, and whether, obtainment constrains the possibility of substantive links between facts. According to the tense anti-realist there is no constrain at all coming from whether two facts obtain together or not. After all, it would be strange if the derivative level of tensed facts imposed constraints on the more fundamental level of tenseless facts. Therefore, for the tense anti-realist is perfectly kosher that entities that are located at different temporal locations enter in substantive, external relations, and thus in tenseless facts. But for the non-standard tense realist of the flow fragmentalist sort, there cannot be substantive cross-fragment facts, namely facts involving external relations between entities located at different locations of the temporal dimension. This is as it should be, if a 'liberalized' cross-temporality is a characteristic mark of tense anti-realism.[59] This concludes our discussion of cross-temporality in the flow fragmentalist framework. We now turn to a discussion of the main close competitors of Flow Fragmentalism.

1.3 The rivals

In this section, we will compare and contrast our version of fragmentalism with other notable interpretations of the view. We begin by highlighting some differences between Flow Fragmentalism and the original proposal by Kit Fine (section 1.3.1). We then discuss the proposals by Martin Lipman (section 1.3.2) and Roberto Loss (section 1.3.3). Finally, we tackle the reductionist (in our terminology, see p. 33) approach by Brad Skow (section 1.3.4).

1.3.1 Fine's original insights

Although Flow Fragmentalism is inspired by Kit Fine (2005)'s original proposal, there are several aspects in which we depart from the letter, if not the spirit, of Finean fragmentalism. The main difference concerns the issue of constitution and obtainment. In discussing the McTaggartesque problem that arises from endorsing Realism, Absolutism, Coherence and Neutrality, and the two non-standard ways out of external relativism (which rejects Absolutism) and fragmentalism (which rejects Coherence), Fine (2005: 270–84) considers whether the notion of constitution should be taken to be tensed or tenseless, and absolute or relative. Although (at least some of the) facts that constitute reality for the realist are tensed, their constituting reality is not necessarily a tensed matter. A *tensed* and absolute notion of constitution is what characterizes standard tense realism and its core principle Presentness. The facts that obtain at the current temporal standpoint are the ones that absolutely constitute reality, and this is why what facts constitute reality changes as time goes by in the standard realist framework. However, once Presentness is dropped in favour of Neutrality, we have no reason to think of what we state (by using a tensed language) from the current temporal standpoint as metaphysically more cogent than what we could state from other (past and future) standpoints (pp. 278–9). This means that constitution in the non-standard framework is a tenseless notion (although, to stress again, the facts that constitute reality are irreducibly tensed): what facts constitute reality does not change with the passing of time. If we choose the external relativist option, constitution is tenseless and relative. Here is a passage in which Fine stresses the difference between the relativization that an anti-realist, and the standard realist, on the one hand, can accept, and the radical, irreducible one of the external relativist, on the other hand.

> For the anti-realist, reality at a time is what one might call a *facet* of reality; and what properly belongs to reality is not the facet itself but the fact that it is instantiated at the given time. For the standard realist, reality at a time (other than the present) is a *hypothetical* reality; what properly belongs to reality is not the hypothetical facts constituting this reality but the fact that they would be the facts were this reality to obtain. For the [external relativist], by contrast, reality at another time is an *alternative* reality. It is neither a facet of the one true reality nor a hypothetical determination of the one true reality, but another reality on an equal footing with the current reality; and the facts belonging to such a reality are full-fledged facts, sharing neither in the incomplete status of a facet nor in the insubstantial character of a hypothetical fact.
>
> Fine 2005: 279, italics in the original

If we choose fragmentalism, constitution is tenseless and absolute. In the official idiom of Finean fragmentalism, such a notion is expressed by the 'in reality' sentential operator (Fine 2005: 268). Given that the position is a form of tense realism, and that plausibly at different times tensed sentences that are incompatible with one another will be true, we need to renounce to the idea that reality is globally coherent. This means that it could be the case both that *in reality ϕ*, and *in reality ψ* (where ϕ and ψ state incompatible facts). However, the view is compatible with various 'rules of coherence' that allow us to keep local versions of coherence. The difference between the way constitution is captured in Finean fragmentalism, through the 'in reality' operator, and in Flow

Fragmentalism, through the idea of truth in a model for $\mathcal{L}^{+\circ}$, is interesting, but we will not spend much time on it here. What we are more interested in is the way in which this idea of local coherence is articulated in both views. Flow Fragmentalism does it through a time-indexed notion of obtainment (we will see in the next sections how other theories adopt different strategies): if we can state correctly that two facts obtain at the same index, the two facts cohere one another. Obtainment, thus, is relative (facts obtain only relative to fragments, and never *simpliciter*) and tenseless (what obtains relative to a fragment does not vary across time). A notion of obtainment that were both tenseless and absolute would be, of course, useless to articulate the position. Although Fine here gives the broad-brush picture, and does not articulate in any detail how to capture the idea in more formal terms, the difference between his take and ours is clear. Rather than organizing the various fragments in locally coherent pluralities of facts through a time indexed language, he suggests that the language of obtainment be taken as *tensed* and absolute. As sameness of indices is tantamount to co-obtainment for us (cf. p. 22), for Fine sameness of tense gives us a way to express co-obtainment. In a sense, while we resort to an *explicit* time indexing to express obtainment (as opposed to constitution), Fine resorts to an *implicit* one, via the tensed language.

By taking obtainment to be tensed and absolute (as opposed to constitution, tenseless and absolute), Finean fragmentalism reflects a duplicity of points of view on the temporal dimension. Constitution corresponds to an external, global point of view, one that encompasses the whole 'über-reality' of the totality of fragments. Obtainment corresponds to the internal point of view, the one that entities located along the temporal dimension occupy.[60] Here is how he puts it: 'in stating that a fact belongs to reality [that is, constitutes reality], we adopt a general perspective, but in stating that a fact obtains, we adopt the current perspective' (2005: 297). As the use of 'current' makes it clear, obtainment is confined to the present. However, since we are in a non-standard framework, 'the present' cannot be here understood as picking out *the* privileged perspective or fragment. Rather, it is the fragment in which we happen to formulate a thought or utter a sentence.

The reason why Fine chooses an implicit temporal indexing rather than an explicit one seems to be semantic rather than metaphysical. Indeed, the above quote is from a passage at the end of his discussion of the 'argument from truth' against tense realism. Briefly, the argument aims to show that the following four plausible principles entail a contradiction.

Truth-Value Stability If an utterance is true (false), then it is always true (false).
Content Stability If an utterance states that p, then it always states that p.
Link An utterance is true if and only if what it states is verified by the facts.
Relevance A tensed utterance is only verified with the help of tensed facts.

Consider an utterance U_1 of the tensed sentence 'Socrates is standing' done when Socrates is standing, and another utterance U_2 of the same sentence done when Socrates is sitting. Given that U_1 is true and states the proposition that Socrates is standing, by the left-to-right direction of Link, there are facts, $f_1, \ldots, f_n$, that verify that Socrates is standing, and given Relevance those facts are tensed. Since U_2 stated the proposition that Socrates is standing, by Content Stability, U_2 states that Socrates is standing. Given that $f_1, \ldots, f_n$ verify that Socrates is standing, by the right-to-left direction of Link, U_2 is true. But *ex hypothesi* U_2 was false and hence, by Truth-Value Stability, U_2 is false.

For the tense anti-realist the problem does not get off the ground, since clearly Relevance is a principle she will not accept. According to her, tensed claims, even granting that they express tensed propositions, are verified by tenseless facts. The standard solution for the tense realist (e.g. Priest 1987) consists in denying Truth-Value Stability. Fine (2005: 295) has arguments against a solution of this kind which we do not need to consider here. What we are interested in is the non-standard solution which he defends, and which consists in denying Link and endorsing Relative Link instead:

Relative Link An utterance is true if and only if what it states is verified by the facts that obtain at the time of utterance.

What the non-standard realist needs to solve the predicament is a way to single out the perspective or fragment that is involved in the verification[61] of (the proposition stated by) a given utterance. In order to have that, we need to give up, as Fine explicitly says, that 'any fact belonging to reality [that is, constituting reality] obtains' (p. 297). While a tensed language, through its implicit reference to the time of utterance, can be used to that effect, it does not necessarily reflect a deep metaphysical feature of the position. The important point, as we have stressed over and over, is that local coherence among facts is recovered, and in order to do that, we need a notion that is *not* the tenseless and absolute constitution through which the 'über-reality' of the totality of fragments is captured. In replying to the argument from truth, Fine resorts to a tensed and absolute notion of obtainment. However, it is not clear that a distinctively tensed language of obtainment is part of the official idiom of Finean fragmentalism. More importantly, it would be a mistake to regard the fact that Fine takes obtainment as tensed as having to do with the core idea of tense realism, namely that the *content* of the facts that constitute reality is tensed. The core idea, in Finean fragmentalism, is captured by the fact that there are true sentences of the form ⌜in reality, ϕ⌝, in which ϕ is a *tensed* statement.

In that respect, Finean and Flow Fragmentalism are not profoundly different. In Flow Fragmentalism, we express constitution through the basic sentences of the tensed language $\mathcal{L}^{+\odot}$, which captures the tensed nature of the content of the facts that constitute reality. Although the facts are tensed, constitution, as per the non-standard framework in general, is tenseless, and this is why constitution is given by what is true in the model and not in a particular fragment (cf. p. 36). Therefore, when it comes to state what is metaphysically cogent, the indexical feature of $\mathcal{L}^{+\odot}$ is treated like a gauge of the theory, as it were. Our way to capture a general point of view on the temporal dimension is thus analogous to Fine's use of the 'in reality' operator. Both articulate the idea of tenseless and absolute constitution as applied to tensed facts. The way in which, in Flow Fragmentalism, we capture an internal point of view is different. As we saw, we are not confined to the internal point of view, to the perspective of the speaker, but we can express what facts obtain also relative to perspectives that are not necessarily *ours*. We think that this is more in harmony with Neutrality and thus the general non-standard framework, in which the present or current perspective is not metaphysically privileged in any sense. Indeed, once we realize that a tensed obtainment per se does not cut much metaphysical ice, it should be clear that the only reason to single out our current position in time must be semantic.

Moreover, endorsing an explicit indexed language for obtainment yields explanatory resources that would be desirable for Finean fragmentalism as well. One of the motivations to abandon the standard framework that Fine gives is the frozen present problem (p. 12). Endorsing Neutrality, and thus abandoning the idea of a temporally privileged point of view on reality, is a *first step* in the direction of solving the problem. Here is Fine:

> The two forms of non-standard realism are not subject to these difficulties since they do not single out any one time as the present. . . . [I]n either case, presentness, in so far as it is a genuine feature of reality, applies equally to all times. Presentness is not frozen on a particular moment of time and the light it sheds is spread equitably throughout all time. Of course, this feature, by itself, does not account for the passage of time. Consider the analogous first-personal case. Here the non-standard, or neutral, realist will suppose that no person is privileged – me-

ness applies across the board to everyone. But that is hardly enough to secure a moving me! So clearly, something more than the equitable distribution of presentness is required to account for the passage of time. But at least, on the current view, there is no obvious impediment to accounting for the passage of time in terms of a successive now. We have assembled all the relevant NOWs, so to speak, even if there remains some question as to why the relationship between them should be taken to constitute a genuine form of succession.

Fine 2005: 287–8

Finean fragmentalism does not take us further than the first step. But Flow Fragmentalism can be seen as an attempt to spell out how the relationship between the various presents across the fragments constitutes a 'genuine form of succession'. By resorting to the time indexed language of obtainment, we can spell out the relevant explanatory connections between the different perspectives, and provide an account of how robust passage comes about.

1.3.2 Lipman's co-obtainment and his theory of passage

Lipman (2015) offers a different interpretation of fragmentalism by characterizing it through the elucidation of a primitive (tenseless and absolute) notion of *co-obtainment*, rather than by distinguishing relative obtainment from absolute constitution. When two facts co-obtain 'they form a unified qualitative manifestation of the relevant objects, one single bit of world within which the things are a certain way' (2015: 3127), while when two facts do not co-obtain, 'relative to the one fact, the other fact is not there at all', they cannot be 'the case together, … they do not make for a unified chunk of world' (2015: 3128).[62] In a sense, Lipman and we make a step in the same direction away from Fine's original insight that obtainment has to be treated as tensed, since we both take the relevant notion to be tenseless. However, Lipman also makes a step in the direction opposite of ours in that he thinks that absolute co-obtainment is explanatorily more basic than relative obtainment.

Lipman's informal paraphrases of co-obtainment can be pinned down in formal terms, by introducing a semantics of co-obtainment (Lipman 2015, 2016). Let us consider a model $\mathcal{M} = \langle \mathcal{F}, v \rangle$, where $\mathcal{F}$ and v are defined as above (section 1.1.4.5). The co-obtainment of two facts is formalized by exploiting a co-obtainment operator '∘'. Formulae of form ⌜$\phi \circ \psi$⌝ read 'ϕ insofar as ψ'. The following recursive clause extends the valuation v for atomic sentences relative to fragments to a valuation for co-obtainment sentences:

$[\phi \circ \psi]_{\mathcal{M}}^{F_n} = \mathrm{T}$ iff $[\phi]_{\mathcal{M}}^{F_n} = [\psi]_{\mathcal{M}}^{F_n} = \mathrm{T}$

These are the recursive clauses that define truth in a model:

$\mathcal{M} \vDash p$ iff for some fragment F_n, $v_{F_n}(p) = \mathrm{T}$, where p is atomic

$\mathcal{M} \vDash \neg\phi$ iff $\mathcal{M} \nvDash \phi$

$\mathcal{M} \vDash \phi \wedge \psi$ iff $\mathcal{M} \vDash \phi$ and $\mathcal{M} \vDash \psi$

$\mathcal{M} \vDash \phi \circ \psi$ iff for some fragment F_n, $v_{F_n}(\phi \circ \psi) = \mathrm{T}$

Logical truth and logical consequence are defined as in section 1.1.4.5. Lipman defines truth in a model in a way that reflects a global conception of negation: the fact that ¬ϕ constitutes reality only if *nowhere* in reality it is the case that ϕ. If ¬ϕ is the case within a fragment, but ϕ is the case within some other fragment, then the fact that ϕ will constitute reality, but *not* the fact that ¬ϕ. As Lipman rightly notes, his approach requires that we decide which sentences express instantiation of 'positive' properties.

As a consequence, *conjunctions* of sentences describing incompatible (positive) facts, such as 'Socrates is sitting' and 'Socrates is standing' can, and usually would, be true. It is *not* the case, however, that conjunctions of sentences describing contradictory facts, such as 'Socrates is sitting' and 'Socrates is not sitting', can be true. And this last consequence is prevented because of his differentiated treatment with respect to (positive) atomic sentences and their negations. If an atomic sentence is sometime true, then the positive fact that the sentence expresses constitutes (absolutely speaking) reality, but that is not the case for its negation, since the corresponding fact constitutes reality only if the negation is *always* true. Another interesting feature of Lipman's approach can be highlighted by contrasting the inferential behaviour of our conjunction with his co-obtainment operator. While both of them fail to satisfy the rule of adjunction, the converse rule of simplification holds only for our conjunction: $\phi \wedge \psi \vDash \phi, \psi$.[63]

Although we grant that Lipman's theory is an interesting route to explore, we think that it fares worse as a theory of time than Flow Fragmentalism. Firstly, accepting that it can be true that Socrates is both sitting and standing does not strike us as much better than accepting both that Socrates is sitting and that Socrates is not sitting. After all, if we accept that something that is completely green can be also completely red in the sense that it will be completely red, then we should also accept that it can be non-green, since when it will be completely red, it will not be green. It is true that in Lipman's theory conjunction is not co-obtainment. Still, it strikes us as strange that negation is treated in this asymmetric way, and that as a consequence the theory allows for conjunctions of incompatible claims.

Secondly, Lipman's differentiated treatment of atoms and their negations forces him to admit that there is a fact of the matter with respect to which one of many pairs of incompatible expressions ('is alive' and 'is dead', 'good weather' and 'bad weather', . . .) expresses a positive property, and which one is just a way to express a negation. Of course, in certain cases he can probably just accept both pairs as primitive, but in other cases, like in the case of weather, it seems that one is just the negation of the other (rather than a distinct, but contradictory positive condition), although it is not clear which of the two should be taken as the positive one. The objection has been originally raised by Simon, who observes:

> There are some challenges faced by [fragmentalists, like Lipman,] who distinguish between facts that obtain and those that merely co-obtain. For example, shape properties like 'round' and 'square' or 'straight' and 'bent' may seem like basic, positive properties, but on closer inspection there are reasons to suspect otherwise. Arguably, part of what it is to be round is to *not* have any right angles in one's boundary, and part of what it is to be square is for there to *not* be any central point such that all of one's boundary points are equidistant from it, on any relevant metric. But then [they] cannot allow that something that changes from being round to being square is both round *simpliciter* and also square *simpliciter*. Which is it? Similar problems arise with mereological predicates like 'overlap' and locative ones like 'exact location'.
>
> Simon 2018: 129–30, italics in the original

In contrast to Lipman's approach, we do not take a stance on whether there is a substantive class of 'positive' properties, and it seems to us a good result that from a metaphysics of *temporal* reality, no substantive commitments on the nature of properties follows.[64]

As for the flow of time, Lipman takes passage to be captured by a primitive and inherently dynamic *relation* between facts belonging to different fragments. His official idiom includes a passage-operator '$\hookrightarrow$'. A formula like '$\phi \hookrightarrow \psi$' reads '$\phi$ passes into ψ' (Lipman 2018: 112). The model $\mathcal{M}$ will now be a triple $\langle \mathcal{F}, \prec, v \rangle$. $\mathcal{F}$ is defined as before. $\prec$ is an irreflexive, antisymmetric, transitive and connected binary relation on $\mathcal{F}$. The valuation function v is extended along two different lines. First, the following clause is added:

$[\phi \hookrightarrow \psi]_{\mathcal{M}}^{F_n} = F$

The clause states that a passage formula is always false if evaluated relative to a single fragment. The reason is obvious: ϕ cannot pass into ψ within one and the same fragment.[65] Second, v is extended to a valuation for all formulae relative to each member of the relation $\prec$; here we give only the valuation for '$\hookrightarrow$':

$$[\phi \hookrightarrow \psi]\langle {}^{F_n,F_m}_{\mathcal{M}} \rangle = T \text{ iff } [\phi]{}^{F_n}_{\mathcal{M}} = [\psi]{}^{F_m}_{\mathcal{M}} = T \text{ and } (\phi = \psi \text{ or } \phi = \neg\psi \text{ or } \neg\phi = \psi)$$

According to this last clause, a passage formula $\phi \hookrightarrow \psi$ is true if and only if v is relativized to a pair of fragments $\langle F_n, F_m \rangle$ such that ϕ is true in F_n, ψ is true in F_m, and ϕ and ψ are either the same or one the negation of the other. Intuitively, the clause expresses the idea that there are three possible cases of passage: (i) the case in which a fact obtains repeatedly, (ii) the case in which the fact ceases to obtain, and (iii) the case in which the fact comes to obtain (Lipman 2018: 113).

Lipman adopts this strategy for reasons that have to do with Fine's frozen present problem. Lipman argues that the present-tensed facts that obtain at the current perspective cannot capture the passage from one moment to another. In the standard picture, what we can do is only to 'add' past- and future-tensed facts. This does not help, after all, for we are just considering more *presently obtaining* facts, and no 'conflicting facts' enter the picture. For that we need to adopt an atemporal point of view, that embodied by the passage operator '$\hookrightarrow$'. Lipman's point can be read as the claim that tenses do not even suffice to *capture* passage. In order to capture it we need a *relational* tool such as the operator '$\hookrightarrow$'. This is a stronger claim than the one that we accepted above (cf. p. 26), that a standard framework do not have the tools to *explain* passage. Now, if Lipman's criticism is correct, our position may be liable to an analogous one, given that Flow Fragmentalism purports to capture the passage of time in terms of tensed facts (as standard tense realism does), and then explain it in terms of the relations between tensed facts obtaining in different fragments. However, we think Lipman here is combining two legitimate criticisms in a way that leads him to an undue generalization.

He is right in claiming that if tenses are understood merely as indexical and perspectival tools of representation, they cannot capture genuine passage. In order to capture it, we need to understand them as expressing a primitive dynamic notion.[66] And he is also right in pointing out that explaining passage requires taking into account more than one moment of time: adding more present content to the present alone won't be enough. However, those two tenets does not force us to endorse a view – such as Lipman's – in which a primitive dynamic ingredient is bestowed *on the relation* between facts, considered in an a-temporal way.

According to Flow Fragmentalism, *tenses* are inherently dynamic. As in the standard, Priorean picture, they are not mere indexical instruments,[67] they reflect the idea that if now reality is such that p will be (was) the case, then reality will be (was) such that p. Yet, as distinctive of non-standard forms of tense realism, according to Flow Fragmentalism, the robust form of change expressed by tenses requires that no single time is privileged. So, the difference between Lipman's account of passage and ours is where to locate the primitive notion of passage: whether within each fragment, or in some fundamental relation between them. And even if Lipman's alternative is viable, it strikes us somewhat against the spirit of fragmentalism. Unlike external relativism, fragmentalism does admit an absolute way to speak of reality, yet the obtainment of a relation between distinct fragments seems to require some sort of 'bridging' fragment, or at any rate some way to consider what happens in distinct fragments at once.[68] The reason why we take this to be problematic is that it seems to require an unduly duplication of the rules of coherence. While it may be correct that there are different rules of coherence (for instance, by passing from a Newtonian framework to a relativistic one, we need to change the way facts obtain together to make sense of the new scenario; see Chapter 4), it seems ad hoc to admit both a rule of coherence that involves the facts that obtain together, and another one that involves facts that have contradictory contents. However, we do not want to insist on this point, since it is of course possible that Lipman takes the operators '∘' and '↪' to obey different rules of coherence simply as a brute fact.

A related final point concerns the semantics of the passage operator '↪'. As we just saw, in Lipman's model theory there is a total order relation between (points informally representing) fragments, and the semantic for '↪' is given in relation to ordered couples $\langle F_n, F_m \rangle$ thereof. Even if his 'set-theoretic machinery is merely a heuristic tool' (2018: 106), we find suspicious that sentences *in the object language* can be evaluated with respect to distinct fragments *at once*. Lipman seems to be happy to admit matters of fact connecting or bridging the fragments. However, as we just pointed out, this may be problematic. Be that as it may, we want to stress a difference here between Flow Fragmentalism and Lipman's view. As we saw above (p. 53), explanatory links between fragments can hold without there being facts grounding them. They are resolved by the qualitative and tensed profile of the facts alone. The situation is radically different in Lipman's picture of reality. Consider again the comparison with the cross-world situation. If we say that a certain fact, f_1, that obtains in a world w_1 passes into another, f_2, that obtains in w_2, then it is either the case that $w_1 = w_2$, or if w_1 is distinct from w_2 then they are somehow in contact; maybe they are somehow spatiotemporally linked.[69] Of course Lipman does not want to say that there are cross-world passage facts, but the point stands. Lipman's reality is not so fragmented after all, since facts with contradictory contents are 'linked together' although not in the sense that they co-obtain. As in the framework of tense anti-realism, co-obtainment of tensed facts does not set a line between the facts that can be linked together. Although we do not wish to press the issue further here, it seems to us that, by admitting such substantial links between facts that do not co-obtain, Lipman blurs the distinction between non-standard tense realism and tense anti-realism.

1.3.3 Loss' subvaluationism

The idea at the root of Loss (2017)'s interpretation of fragmentalism is to treat the latter as a form of subvaluationism:[70] a sentence ϕ is true if and only if there is some fragment where ϕ is true. Just like in our formal approach, the valuation for the atomic sentences is extended to a valuation for only negations and conjunctions, via the following clauses:

$[\neg \phi]^{F_n}_{\mathcal{M}} = T$ iff $[\phi]^{F_n}_{\mathcal{M}} \neq T$

$[\phi \wedge \psi]^{F_n}_{\mathcal{M}} = T$ iff $[\phi]^{F_n}_{\mathcal{M}} = [\psi]^{F_n}_{\mathcal{M}} = T$

The definition of truth in a model is the same as ours:

$\mathcal{M} \vDash \phi$ iff for some fragment F_n, $[\phi]^{F_n}_{\mathcal{M}} = T$

Logical truth and logical consequence are defined as above. This approach allows one to evaluate both the sentence 'Socrates is sitting' and the sentence 'Socrates is not sitting' as true. However, it does *not* allow one to evaluate the conjunction of the two claims as true as well, for in light of the valuations provided, the following principle, which is a version of the law of non-contradiction, turns out valid: $\vDash \neg(\phi \wedge \neg\phi)$. Conjunction does not obey the rule of adjunction: $\phi, \psi \nvDash \phi \wedge \psi$ (but it obeys the rule of simplification: $\phi \wedge \psi \vDash \phi, \psi$). This is crucial in vindicating the idea that reality is a fragmented place. Even if the fact that ϕ and the fact that ψ constitute reality absolutely speaking, there is no guarantee that the fact that $\phi \wedge \psi$ constitutes reality as well. But the two facts can obtain together only if the fact that $\phi \wedge \psi$ constitutes reality. It follows that, even if the fact that ϕ and the fact that ψ constitute reality absolutely speaking, there is no guarantee that the fact that ϕ and the fact that ψ obtain together. From a formal point of view, our proposal is obviously closer in spirit to Loss' view than Lipman's. In fact, both Loss' approach and ours fall into the category of subvaluationist interpretation of fragmentalism.

Our framework, however, is more expressive than Loss'. As underlined above, the adoption of a family of 'within' operators '$\odot_{F_1}$', '$\odot_{F_2}$', ... allows us to preserve adjunction in its uniformly prefixed version, which we recall here for readers' convenience:

$$\odot_{F_x} \phi, \odot_{F_x} \psi \vDash \odot_{F_x} (\phi \wedge \psi)$$

Let us stress, once again, that these operators are introduced to express the irreducibly relative nature of obtainment, in the metaphysically robust sense discussed above. In Loss' view, on the contrary, no relativization of obtainment is required. Metaphysically speaking, then, the difference is quite deep. Although in both frameworks, the idea that reality is a fragmented place in expressed in terms of adjunction failure, in our view, which is a pluralist one, obtainment and constitution are treated as two ways, irreducible to one another, in which facts relate to reality. The same cannot be said of Loss' approach, where nothing prevents a principle like Obtainment-Constitution from being read as a *definition* of obtainment in terms of absolute constitution.

1.3.4 Skow's supertime and MST-Time

Another author that has explored a theory of time that pertains to the non-standard landscape is Brad Skow. Although his theory is not a form of fragmentalism, it is interesting to consider it here, since it comes close to a form of – in our terminology (cf. p. 33) – reductionism of robust passage in a non-standard framework. Let us begin with a first attempt of formulating a theory that explains, and not merely captures robust passage (in two articles, 2009 and 2012). His first attempt is not an account of passage as variation across temporal perspectives, namely a reductionist account, but it is rather an explanation through an appeal to what he calls *supertime*, in a framework that is standard. The context is that of articulating the moving spotlight theory (i.e. an eternalist A-theory). We can explain the idea that the present (or the NOW, in his terminology) moves from one instant to the next one in the temporal series, by resorting to a further dimension – viz. supertime – in which this movement takes place. Points in supertime are ordered by a relation that 'mimics' the linear topology and metric of the B-series of instants. Thus, from the perspective of a point of supertime T_n, a time t_n is present, and all those coming before it (all t_x such that $t_x < t_n$) are past, and all those coming after it (all t_x such that $t_n < t_x$) are future. This allows us to provide an account of the flow of time as the movement of the NOW through the temporal series.[71]

> So with supertime we can make sense of the NOW's motion: for the NOW to move is to be located at different times relative to different points of supertime.
>
> Skow 2012: 224

Although here the framework is standard, it should be clear how this account could be expanded into a non-standard version. Points of supertime closely resemble fragments (or perspectives). As with fragmentalism, facts obtain within fragments (and as with external relativism, reality is constituted by tensed facts relatively to perspectives), in the supertime story *from the perspective of* different points of supertime, different times are past/present/future, and hence (we can assume) certain tensed facts rather than others obtain. However, in the two articles cited above Skow's supertime is a *metaphor*,[72] a heuristic tool that helps us understand how standard forms of eternalist tense realism work. More precisely, supertime is a metaphor of irreducible tensed facts, expressed by primitive tense operators.

> Talk of the NOW's motion is to be understood using primitive tense operators . . . . 'The NOW is moving into the future' means (roughly) 'The NOW is located at *t*, and *it will be the case that* the NOW is located at a time later than *t*'.
>
> Skow 2012: 224

That is what makes this theory a standard picture, in which one time is present *simpliciter*, and not relative to perspectives or fragments. The movement of the NOW along the supertime series is thus a metaphor for the changes in which facts are absolutely present.

As we read the proposal in the 2009 and 2012 articles, the notion of supertime has no metaphysical import. However, Pooley (2013), in discussing Skow's view, points out that there are *two times* in his picture: there is the A-theoretic supertime, understood in primitively tensed terms, and there is the B-theoretic time of the temporal series on which the spotlight shines and moves.[73] We will not discuss here Pooley's criticism. We just notice that in Skow's 2015 book, where he considers (and dismisses) the Moving Spotlight Theory-Supertime (MST-Supertime), a theory in which supertime is explicitly taken non-metaphorically, the situation seems different. In MST-Supertime, the second time-like dimension yields the points relative to which the temporal dimension is in different ways. Unlike in his previous accounts, then, the supertime dimension is similar to a B-theoretic order. While the tensed nature of the facts involving the 'ordinary' temporal dimension makes it closer to an A-theoretic order. The idea is to trade off this 'crazy' (in his own words)[74] commitment to supertime with a more reasonable commitment to *perspectives* as further irreducible and fundamental *roles* of times (beside that of location) in the theory that he calls MST-Time.[75]

Given that no perspective is privileged, Skow's proposal in the 2015 book is a non-standard form of tense realism that aims at explaining robust passage, as ours is.[76] However, unlike Flow Fragmentalism, it is a form of reductionism of the passage, in which the temporal flow is real, but it is identified with variation across times as perspectives. As we have seen before, there is an analogy between this idea and the way B-theorist, typically, reduces ordinary change to variations across times as locations. Indeed, Skow agrees that what we have in MST-Time is *not* robust passage; however, he insists, perhaps correctly, that it is not either the same as the anaemic passage that we have in the B-theoretic scenario. The dialectic here is murky as it is always when a reductionist theory of X is accused to be a theory that 'does not respect X', and we do not want to enter it (but see our remarks in section 1.1.4.3). We just notice, again, that even if the idea of variation across perspectives (or, better, across fragments as they are ordered by the pseudo-temporal relation $<_{ps}$) is part of our account of passage, it is not the whole of it. Quite the contrary, our account is based on the explanatory link between the different fragments, and the fact that there is variation through the order of fragment is a consequence of this.

2

Open Future

In this chapter, we will drop the assumption that the temporal dimension is linear, namely a total order of times. We will thus develop a *branching-time* version of Flow Fragmentalism. The chapter is divided in two parts. Section 2.1 discusses two distinct kinds of openness of the future, ontological and topological openness, focusing on their connections with robust passage. In section 2.2, we will show how to vindicate the openness of the future within the flow fragmentalist framework. We will argue that our view constitutes a middle ground between ontological and topological openness, which is able to retain the benefits of both of them, while avoiding their drawbacks. At the end of the chapter, the reader will find an appendix (2.3) devoted to the logical details of our branching framework.

2.1 The varieties of openness

The idea that there is an elective affinity between a robust conception of passage and a robust openness of the future has seduced many scholars.[1] The image of a relentlessly changing reality, with no determined script, and yet not necessarily chaotic is indeed suggestive. But how can we make this picture more precise? As we have seen in the previous chapters, the idea of robust passage, while elusive, can be clarified at least in part through the notion of real tense (cf. p. 25). There are at least two prima facie different ways to capture the idea of an open future in more regimented terms. Both present themselves as quite natural if we think of robust openness in terms of metaphysical indeterminacy, that is, indeterminacy that is neither purely epistemic, nor purely semantic (more broadly, representational). Both follow from the idea that in reality there is no such thing as *the* future. For the *ontological* conception of metaphysical openness, the future is not there, because there are no future entities at all, no future individuals, no future states of affairs, no future nothing. For the *topological* conception, the future is not there, because there are many futures, and none of them is more or less real than any other. One can think of the distinction between the two conceptions by analogy with the semantic behaviour of definite descriptions, such as 'the commander in chief'. If there is one commander in chief (in the relevant context) then it is determined to what the description refers. But if there is no commander, then it is not determined what the expression refers to, and the same goes if there is more than one person fulfilling the role.[2] The analogy is not perfect, because in the case of 'the commander in chief' we are dealing with a semantic case of indeterminacy, but it is enough for a first approximation.

The ontological conception of the open future requires a non-eternalist ontology. Presentists and growing blockers alike can treat the future as open in this sense.[3] However, notice that such a picture of reality does not entail per se two further aspects that are sometimes also associated with robust openness, namely *bivalence failure* for future contingent claims, and *indeterminism* with respect to the laws of nature. If bivalence holds for future contingents, future-tensed claims about contingent matters of facts, such as (1) below are either true or false. If it fails, (1) has no determinate truth-value – that is, it is neither true nor false.

(1) It will rain tomorrow

While the lack of existence of the future may be a reason to think that (1) has no determinate truth-value, it is neither necessary nor sufficient for it. Maybe the future exists, and yet (1), when uttered today, has no determinate truth-value, because the semantic rules leave it undetermined whether what is uttered is true or false. Maybe the future does not exist, but something else makes (1) determinately true (or false). The laws of nature, the will of a god, or brute facts about the future, for instance. If nomological indeterminism is true, the present state of the world, together with the laws of nature, does not entail a unique future history of the universe. If determinism is true, it does. While the lack of existence of a single future may be congenial to an indeterministic universe, it is neither sufficient nor necessary for it. Maybe there is no future as in the presentist universe, but in principle one could still derive from the laws of nature and the present state of the universe *the* way in which things will go. Or maybe the laws are not enough to fix one single future, but as a matter of fact one single future exists (more on this in section 2.1.1).

More generally, bivalence failure is a *semantic* kind of openness, and indeterminism is a *nomological* kind of openness; and even though a given metaphysical picture may invite certain semantic and nomological interpretations rather than others, bivalence failure and indeterminism are logically orthogonal to ontological openness.

The topological conception of openness requires an eternalist ontology. If there is more than one future, a fortiori there are future entities, beside the present and past ones.[4] But we will set aside this exotic ontology for the purpose of this book. Moreover, it requires that certain topological relations obtain between times. Roughly, the future is topologically open if the temporal dimension is *branching*. That is, while if we go from the present towards the past we find a linear succession of times (the trunk), if we go from the present towards the future we find distinct paths (the branches). The present (the upper bound of the trunk) is connected to one past, and to several futures. The linear past together with each of the future branches forms what are usually called *histories* ($h_1, h_2, \ldots$).

Topological openness is a form of metaphysical openness, and it is thus likewise orthogonal to bivalence failure for future contingents, and nomological indeterminism. As for bivalence, even if according to different histories h_1, h_2 different futures will happen, there may still be one actual history, the one that dictates the determinate truth-value of future contingents like (1). And even if there is only one story, that is, the future is linear as the past, it may still be indeterminate whether (1) is today true or false. As for indeterminism, the histories may reflect the alternative paths that the laws of nature allow for, but there may be a branching future also in a deterministic world, if the histories reflect some other kind of alternative future (what would happen if the laws of nature were different, or if the present were different, for instance). Conversely, there may be one history of the world, what will actually happen, even if what happens is not (entirely) determined by the laws.

It is important to understand that in both versions of metaphysical openness – the ontological and the topological – the idea that the future is open because there is not one future is not the idea that we are on the verge of the end of time. Although this is in a sense obvious, it is not obvious how to spell out the difference at issue. One way to do it connects nicely future indeterminacy and passage. The idea is that *as of now*, the future does not exist – either in the sense that there is no single future, or in the sense that in front of us there is nothing at all. Yet, unless it is the end of time, which is the option that we are ruling out, there *will be* one future. In other terms, that there is not one future means that nothing (or nothing determinate) exists *as future*. Rather, future things will exist – we just have to wait for them to come into existence (or to become determinate).

Although this picture does not entail robust passage, it seems to us clear that the latter completes it harmoniously. We are authorized to take seriously the lack of existence, or of determination, of the future because reality robustly changes, and how it is as of now can be radically different from how it is as of a future time: it can contain entities that it did not contain, or it can be determinate with respect to what was indeterminate.

Another important point is that although the ontological and the topological conceptions of openness seem to require quite different metaphysical pictures, they are less distant from one another than one may suspect. First, the topological conception can also capture the idea that when we *talk* about the future, for instance, by making a future-tensed claim such as (1) above, what we express involves an open future because *something* in the future does not yet exist. A universe with a branching future may not contain a determinate future, even if it contains a plethora of future things. Indeed, it may fail to contain a determinate future, because there are conflicting states of affairs on the different histories. For instance, there may not be a determinate tomorrow with respect to rain in Milan, because there are branches in which tomorrow it rains, and branches in which it is sunny.[5]

Second, even if the presentist cannot have a branching temporal dimension, they can still *represent* the future in a branching way. Indeed, in order to better articulate the points concerning the relation between ontological openness and semantic and nomological openness, a presentist (or a growing blocker) may need to exploit a representation of alternative histories, or some ersatz entities that play their role.

To recap. The fundamental varieties of openness of the future are *metaphysical* openness, *semantic* openness, and *nomological* openness. Metaphysical openness comes into two guises, the *ontological* and the *topological* conceptions. In both forms, metaphysical openness can be seen as supporting, or 'naturally going with', robust passage, while there is no reason to think that semantic and nomological openness do the same.

As we will argue, the core of Flow Fragmentalism as formulated in the previous chapter can be completed in a way that accommodates elements from both ontological and topological openness. Although we are aware that not everybody agrees that the openness of the future should be accounted in metaphysical terms, and that others may want to capture openness with more radical means than those allowed by Flow Fragmentalism, we think the latter comes with certain advantages, which will be discussed in the next sections.

2.1.1 Ontological openness

In section 1.2.3, we pointed out that positions with a presentist ontology may have an advantage over eternalist positions when it comes to capture passage. And that is why it is dialectically important to us that the fragmentalist *can* adopt a presentist ontology, in the sense that within each fragment, the only existential facts that obtain are those about the entities that are located at the 'present' of the fragment. If a tense realist thinks that a presentist ontology is crucial for passage, and agrees that robust openness and robust passage support each other, it is a natural option for them to capture openness in ontological terms.

Let us have a closer look at the relationship between ontological openness and semantic openness. If we capture openness in presentist terms, it is quite natural to interpret future contingents, such as (1) above, as lacking grounds. After all, we should expect that what grounds the truth-value of (1), namely what makes it true or false, is something in the future. But if, as of now, the future does not exist in the presentist universe, then why should we expect (1) to have a determinate truth-value? The rationale can be repeated for any future contingent, and the conclusion is that ontological openness leads naturally to the denial of an unrestricted principle of bivalence.[6] However, as we pointed out in the previous section, ontological openness and semantic openness are orthogonal theses. Now, one may wish to preserve bivalence when possible; after all, bivalence is a very elegant and well-behaved logical property. Therefore, if our aim is to capture metaphysical openness in ontological terms, and if that can be done *without* rejecting bivalence, why not do it? A natural thought is that the grounds of future contingents do not need to be in the future, they can be in the present. There are least two candidates for present grounds here.

The first option is to endorse nomological determinism. If present truths, together with the laws of nature, necessitate future-tensed truths, there is no reason to deny a determined truth-value to future contingent claims even if they lack future grounds.[7] But the issue of nomological determinism vs. nomological indeterminism is an empirical one, and it would be nice if the presentist could save bivalence even if the universe we happen to live in turns out to have indeterministic laws. Therefore, in what follows, we will not rule out that indeterminism holds.

The second option is to introduce in the present reality 'brute facts' that settle which history among all the nomologically possible alternatives will be the actual one. If we represent, as is customary, nomologically possible histories through a tree-like structure, such brute facts single out among all future branches the branch that will turn out to be the actual future history of the world. In the literature, this option has been thought of as the introduction of a *thin red line*.[8] The branch is *red*, because it is singled out among the others, but it is also *thin*, because the difference between the actual branch and the others is not a substantive metaphysical difference, as if the red line is concrete, while the others are merely abstract, or the red line has a metaphysically distinctive property of some sort. The red line is singled out simply because 'one among the alternatives... will "in fact" happen' (Belnap et al. 2001: 133). Many have criticized the idea for not being at bottom compatible with a robust openness of the future. We will not review those criticisms here.[9] Rather, we want to investigate whether, for the presentist, the red line can be 'thin' in the sense just outlined. One obvious reason to think that that is not the case is that the brute facts about the red line are *further* facts, which cannot be 'reduced' in any sense to facts about the present. What future *contingents* are about, after all, is states of affairs that might or might not happen regardless of how the present is. This means that while the branches that do *not* represent the actual future are mere representations, they represent what might happen but will *not*, the red line is constituted by the presently obtaining future-tensed facts about the actual future. Maybe if you have already set your mind to having topological openness and an actual future, you are willing to pay the cost of a thick red line. However, we think that, all in all, if an option for having a thin red line is available, it should be preferred.

Let us dwell on this a bit more, and see if the presentist has a way out. Firstly, we need to make a distinction between future facts in the weak and strong sense.[10] Consider the tensed fact that *Socrates is sitting* – as opposed to the tenseless fact that *Socrates is sitting at t*. If Socrates is presently sitting, reality is constituted by the fact that *Socrates is sitting*. Assume that in a few minutes Socrates will be standing: can the presentist accept the future fact that corresponds to such a (stipulated) future-tensed truth? It depends on how we read 'future fact'. A future fact in a *weak* sense is a future-tensed fact that obtains at present. If Socrates will be standing in a few minutes, the fact that *Socrates will be standing* obtains at present (and hence it constitutes reality now). A future fact in a *strong* sense is a present-tensed fact that will obtain in the future. If Socrates will be standing in a few minutes (and he is now sitting), the fact that *Socrates is standing* will obtain in a few minutes (and hence it will constitute reality, which it does not now).

Presentists can accept future facts in the weak sense, at least insofar as they resort to slightly 'exotic' but presentist-friendly ideology or ontology – for instance, by resorting to 'Lucretian' properties. The Lucretian presentist takes properties such as *being such that Socrates will be standing* to be an irreducible element of reality, and identify the future fact, in the weak sense, that *Socrates will be standing* with the fact that *the mereological sum of all the presently existing things is such that Socrates will be standing*.[11] However, presentism is *not* compatible with accepting future facts in the strong sense. Indeed, for the presentist future facts in the strong sense are not facts at all, i.e. the extension of the very concept is empty. The facts that obtain at present are the facts that obtain *simpliciter*, and that constitute reality, namely the only facts there are.

We can then formulate our previous worry as follows. The presentist needs weak future facts to ground the red line, and to signal it out from the other alternatives. Therefore, the actual future is grounded in weak future facts, but alternative futures that lie outside the red line are not so grounded. This difference makes the presentist's red line thick. Now, a presentist may have the following rejoinder. It is true that *as of now*, only future facts in the weak sense obtain. However, future facts in the strong sense will obtain also for the presentist (remember, we are not at the end of time). That is to say that *as of future times* future facts in the strong sense obtain. But then, why can't the presentist simply appeal to how reality *will* be like, to ground a thin red line? If future contingents have a determinate truth-value in virtue of the strong future facts that will obtain, then the actual future history is red, in that it is the only one that is actual, but it is thin, in that there are not further weak future facts that ground it.[12]

There are two problems with this strategy. One is specific to the issue of futurity, and the other is a version of a more general methodological point that we have already encountered. The specific issue is that, if how reality will be the case grounds a thin red line in the presentist picture, then the thin red line is the *only* option available to the presentist. Presentism with bivalence failure for future contingents would not be an option. To see why, consider again the point about the distinction between a doomsday scenario, according to which there is no future because we are at the temporal edge of reality, and presentism. As we say, in order to distinguish the presentist claim from the doomsday claim, the presentist has to say that while as of now, there is no future, there will be a future. But if the red line is grounded by the fact that there will be a future, then the presentist cannot opt out bivalence, as it were.[13] If the fact that there will be a future holds independently of bivalence (since it holds because we are not at the end of time), then what makes it the case that bivalence holds cannot be that very fact. If there is a red line, thus, there are irreducible weak future facts obtaining as of now that ground it. Therefore, the line is thick.

The second reason is analogous to what we encountered when discussing Presentist Flow (p. 38). The presentist is right in pointing out that according to them too, as of the future, certain strong future facts obtain. However, they cannot take those facts as explanatorily prior to what happens in the present. What happens as of the future is what happens merely in a *hypothetical* fashion. The actual fact that a future contingent has a determined truth-value now cannot be explained in terms of the hypothetical fact that in the future a certain state of affairs obtains.[14]

To conclude, ontological openness has the advantage that it allows us to capture passage in a way that according to some non-eternalist is more cogent. However, if at the same time we want to have a red line among the future alternatives to maintain bivalence, we have to pay the price of irreducible weak future facts and thus a thick red line. As we will see, the flow fragmentalist can have the first advantage without paying the second price. Let us now move on to topological openness.

2.1.2 Topological openness

Eternalists cannot spell out metaphysical openness as ontological, but they can still argue that there is a connection between robust openness and robust change. Openness can be interpreted as a topological notion. More precisely, it is the topological asymmetry in the temporal order relation <. Towards the past the relation is linear, and thus the past is entirely determined, but towards the future it is branching, it allows for many alternative futures, which make indeterminate which future facts obtain. The flow of time is the passage from the undetermined to the determined, from the branching future, passing through the fleeting present, into the linear past. As in standard tense realism with linear time, there is global change in the temporal dimension, but here the change involves the topological relations: the 'trunk' of past determined facts grows, and the present is constantly changing its connections not only with new past events, but also with different future alternatives, since the branches that have failed to be realized die out of existence altogether.[15]

Although nomological indeterminism and topological openness are logically independent theses, the idea that the different branches or histories are embodiments of the alternatives that the laws of nature leave alive at different times is particularly attractive. Of course, that does not mean that nomological indeterminism per se supports robust passage or robust openness. However, it may be that nomological indeterminism invites a metaphysical picture of the openness of the future, namely topological openness, which in turn can be cashed out in terms of a relation of mutual support with robust passage.[16] Given that our focus here is on metaphysical openness, we will not discuss further indeterminism. However, the aspects of topological openness that we are going to incorporate in Flow Fragmentalism rule out neither that nomological indeterminism is true, nor that the branching structure of time reflects this feature of the fundamental laws of nature. And this is a point of strength of the position.

A defect of topological openness is that, like presentism, it seems to require a thick red line if we want to save bivalence in its framework. The reason is obvious. *Any* form of standard tense realism cannot rely on facts *as of future times* to explain how the present is like. Hence, the facts that explain why a certain future contingent claim has a certain determinate truth-value must be explanatorily prior to the facts that will obtain if the claim is true. Such facts won't require Lucretian properties, since they can involve future entities, which in this picture exist *simpliciter* just like the present ones, but are still weak future facts obtaining at present, since only the facts that obtain at present obtain at all (and constitute reality) according to the standard tense realist. However, unlike ontological openness, topological openness is also compatible with tense *anti*-realism about tense and anaemic passage. This should not be surprising since topological openness comes with an ontology, eternalism, that is compatible with tense anti-realism, whereas ontological openness requires tense realism (although it does not require Presentness; more on this in section 2.2). We will discuss the anti-realist version because the kind of metaphysical openness that we will incorporate in Flow Fragmentalism shares an advantage with this view, without sharing an obvious drawback of it (as we will see), and of course without sharing the anti-realist stance towards tense.

First, let us note that the B-theoretic eternalist can accept future facts in both the weak and the strong sense – at least in so far as they are derivative and not fundamental. Tensed facts are the only kind of facts for which it makes sense to distinguish between facts that obtain in the present, in the past, and in the future. Tenseless facts, such as the fact that *Socrates is sitting at t_1* and the fact that *Socrates is standing at t_2*, are such that either it does not make sense to talk about them as obtaining in the present rather than in the past or the future, or they obtain indifferently in the past, in the present, and in the future. Now, as we have put it, the distinction between weak and strong facts is defined only for tensed facts, and hence, *at the fundamental level*, it makes no sense for the B-theorist. However, if she accepts tensed facts at a non-fundamental level, as obtaining (and constituting reality) only relative to times, she will have future facts both in the weak and in the strong sense.

Furthermore, if < branches towards the future, we need to introduce a further relativization to *histories*. We thus need to introduce a few modifications. First, we need < to hold between *moments*, that is, entities that play the role of *alternative* times. Each moment can be thought of a spatially maximal instantaneous event, something like a slice of the universe at a time. Accordingly, *histories* are defined as maximal sequences of moments. Two histories h_x and h_y can overlap in their initial segment up to a certain moment, the *node* at which they diverge. Second, we need all histories to be 'synchronized' not only in their overlapping parts but also in the parts in which they diverge. For that we need *instants*, that can be thought of as collections of moments that are all at the same temporal distance from any moment in their past (see the appendix, 2.3, for the details). In general, if we couple tense anti-realism and topological openness, tenseless facts (specified as what happens at an instant) will obtain only relative to histories h_x,[17] and tens*ed* facts will obtain relative to (or 'at') ordered couples of instants and histories $\langle i_x, h_x \rangle$. Imagine that the fact that *Socrates is sitting at* i_0 and the fact that *Socrates is standing at* i_1 obtain relative to a branch h_1, and that i_1 is future with respect to i_0. With respect to the non-fundamental level of tensed facts, the future fact (in the weak sense) that *Socrates will be standing* obtains at $\langle i_0, h_1 \rangle$, and the future fact (in the strong sense) that *Socrates is standing* obtains at $\langle i_1, h_1 \rangle$. We can then say that both facts obtain 'on the history h_1'.[18]

Since the tense anti-realist can have (derivative) future facts in the strong sense, they *can* have a red line without postulating extra weak future-tensed facts, namely they can have a *thin* red line rather than a thick one. Whether *there is* a thin red line, and bivalence holds depends only on how we interpret the whole temporal dimension in this picture. Specifically, it depends on whether the anti-realist is talking about time in a *universe* or in a *multiverse*. To see the point, note that from a 'god's eye' view, namely if we do not consider any specific time, the whole temporal dimension is more like a *bush* than a tree. If we assume, for simplicity, an event with which time begins (like the Big Bang, if we give a physical reading of the model), the general representation of the topological relations looks as follows (Fig. 1).

How do we interpret the bush? Is this picture representing a universe, where there are many alternative histories to the actual *one*, or a multiverse, where *all* alternative histories are actual in the same sense? Given that we are in an eternalist framework, in which all branches exist *simpliciter*, it is natural to interpret it as a multiverse. If so, every possible future alternative is part of an

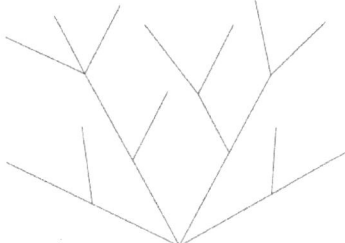

Figure 1 The temporal dimension as seen from a 'god's eye' view.

alternative universe, and there is no reason to think that there is a red line at all. In a multiverse, there is no single future, and to ask what will be the case is an ill-posed question, since things do not happen *simpliciter*, but only relative to worlds or universes, which are here represented by the various histories. Unrestricted bivalence will then not hold, since contingent future-tensed claims will not have a definite truth-value. But if we are in a universe, then one of the histories will stand for how things actually are. To see this, first consider that even if the picture is that of a bush, the temporal relation < is still branching *only* towards the future, but it is linear towards the past. This means that if you pick up a node in the graph, if you 'go down' you will follow a line, whereas if you 'go up' there will be many paths that keep on bifurcating. Hence for each moment there is a tree-like structure determined by its topological relations, and we can say that if we *consider as present* a given moment, the 'trunk' downwards represents its past, while the 'head' above its future(s).

In a multiverse scenario there will be many partially overlapping trees relative not only to different instants, but also to different histories. But if we make the hypothesis that we are in a *universe*, rather than a multiverse, then there is an absolute matter of fact with respect to which history (that is, world) is the actual one, although there will not be an absolute matter of fact with respect to which instant on it is present (since we are in a anti-realist framework). In other words, from a 'god's eye' view, only one history is the actual one, and thus relative to an instant (and *not* an instant and a history) there is a *single* succession of future facts in the strong sense: the ones that will actually obtain relative to that instant. Therefore, the B-theoretic eternalist does not need to postulate weak future facts to single out a thin red line. The ground of the thin red line is in the future facts in the strong sense, or the tenseless facts that ground them, which are part of the picture anyway. Crucially, the reason why, in a universe scenario, the tense anti-realist red line is *thin* rather than thick is that there is *not a single privileged present*, and *not* that there are no irreducible tensed facts. That is, the failure of Presentness, rather than anti-realism per se, is explanatorily crucial here. Of course, the anti-realist can appeal to the non-reality of tenses to motivate their rejection of Presentness. But, as we have seen (p. 20), tense realists too can reject Presentness.

Now, the combination of tenseless open future with a universe is not very 'natural', as we already suggested by pointing out that the multiverse option is suggested by the adoption of the eternalist itself, in a branching scenario. There are, indeed, many objections to the universe view. To begin with, why should one accept the existence of non-actual branches? Given that the actual one is not such in virtue of some distinguishing property,[19] since otherwise it would be a thick red line, in which sense the other alternatives are not also legitimate futures? Of course, if they were legitimate futures, we would be in a multiverse scenario. Luckily, we do not need to answer those questions here. Our point is just that the red line of the tense anti-realist who assumes that we are in a universe is thin, and that is so because there is no privileged present, and thus what will happen in the future can be what makes it determinately true (or false) now a certain future contingent claim. *This* aspect is one that will be inherited by Flow Fragmentalism, but without the drawbacks that we have just pointed out. Let us see then how Flow Fragmentalism can combine elements of ontological and topological openness to account for the open future in a framework where the passage of time is taken to be robust.

2.2 Fragmentalist openness

As we have seen in the previous chapter, Flow Fragmentalism is the thesis that the temporal dimension is constituted by internally coherent pluralities of tensed facts (fragments) that are mutually incompatible. This means that although absolutely speaking reality is constituted by future facts in the strong sense (since each fragment constitutes reality on a par with all the others), within each fragment only future facts in the weak sense obtain. From the point of view of obtainment, thus, the future is unreal and can be open in an ontological sense, while from the point of view of constitution, the future is on a par with the present and the past, and can be open by not being singular, as in the topological version of openness. Let us see in detail how we can develop this position, and what its benefits and costs are.

2.2.1 Branching fragments

As we underlined in section 0.5, one of the defining features of fragmentalism is the idea that reality lacks genuine cross-fragment relations. In the attempt to recover a temporal order between fragments, then, in the previous chapter we introduced a 'pseudo B-relation' $<_{ps}$. Take two times, t_1 and t_2, as usually understood in a standard framework. Since fragments are taken to play the same role as them, there will be two fragments – say, F_1 and F_2 – such that within F_1 all facts that obtain at t_1 obtain, and within F_2 all facts that obtain at t_2 obtain. This licenses the hypothesis that $F_1 <_{ps} F_2$ if and only if $t_1 < t_2$. Interestingly, the same holds in the case the relation $<$ branches towards the future. Remember that in the branching scenario we need to introduce histories as maximal chains of moments, that diverge at nodes, and that are synchronized, so that we can ask what happens at a certain instant i_x on a given history h_y. Roughly (for details, see the appendix, 2.3) the idea is that each fragment F_n is individuated by an instant i_x and a history h_y, and thus it can be named by the corresponding ordered couple $\langle i_x, h_y \rangle$. Thus, each history h_y individuates a corresponding *pseudo-history*, namely the linear sequence of fragments that 'lie on' h_y, that is, a sequence like $\langle i_n, h_y \rangle$, $\langle i_m, h_y \rangle$, ... (where the indices of i establish the order). Notice that although within each fragment F_n only future-tensed facts about *one* history h_n obtain, $<_{ps}$ is a partial branching order between fragments, as $<$ is between moments.

Also in a branching scenario the 'pseudo B-relation' $<_{ps}$ can be exploited to provide truth-conditions for tensed claims that piggyback the more familiar ones for indexical languages. For readers' convenience, we briefly recall the truth-conditions for the tense operators 'WILL' and 'WAS' presented in section 1.1.4.5:

$[WILL\phi]_M^{F_n} = T$ iff there is a fragment F_m such that (i) $F_n <_{ps} F_m$, and (ii) $[\phi]_M^{F_m} = T$

$[WAS\phi]_M^{F_n} = T$ iff there is a fragment F_m such that (i) $F_m <_{ps} F_n$, and (ii) $[\phi]_M^{F_m} = T$

However, it is well known that in a situation in which time is branching towards the future the clause for WILL is problematic.[20] Suppose we ask whether it will be the case that p within a fragment F_0:

$[WILLp]_M^{F_0} = ?$

Assuming that p is contingent, there will be two (simplifying things) future histories h_1 and h_2 such that according to h_1 it will be the case that p, and according to h_2 it will be the case that $\neg p$. Accordingly, there are two pseudo-histories on which two fragments F_1 and F_2, respectively, are both 'in the future' of F_0 and are such that within F_1 it is the case that p and within F_2 it is the case that $\neg p$.

$[p]_M^{F_1} = T$

$[\neg p]_M^{F_2} = T$

We will say that a pseudo-history[21] h_y 'passes through' a fragment F_x when F_x is one of the fragments in the sequence h_y (see Fig. 2).

Clearly both pseudo-histories h_1 and h_2 pass through fragment F_0. Of course, within F_0 only the facts about one of the corresponding histories obtain. However, unless we stipulate that the history of F_0 determines the pseudo-history relative to which a future-tensed claim is to be evaluated, evaluating future contingents merely relative to fragments is like evaluating them relative to instants: they lack a determinate truth-value. While if we also specify a pseudo-history, then depending on which pseudo-history we consider, we will have opposite truth-values.

$[WILLp]_M^{i_0} = \text{Ind}$

$[WILLp]_M^{i_0, h_1} = T$

$[WILLp]_M^{i_0, h_2} = F$

Now, the plurality of pseudo-histories in this picture can be exploited in providing a theory of metaphysical openness in terms of future alternatives at each *node* in the temporal dimension. The idea is that if we consider one instant i_n, there will be overlaps of *present* tensed facts among the fragments that share the same instant index $\langle i_n, h_1 \rangle, \langle i_n, h_2 \rangle, \ldots$ This 'horizontal' (partial) overlap[22] leads to equivalence classes of fragments that map one to one to the *nodes* of the tree

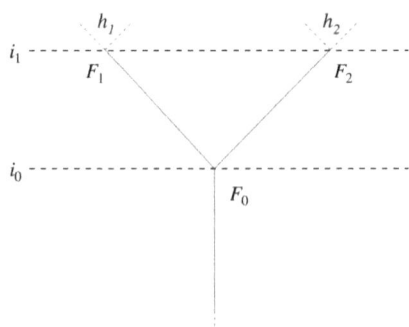

Figure 2 h_1 'passes through' $F_1 = \langle i_1, h_1 \rangle$, while h_2 'passes through' $F_2 = \langle i_1, h_2 \rangle$.

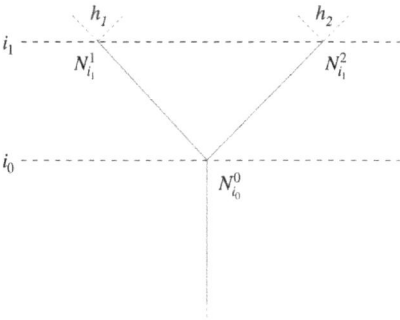

Figure 3 Three nodes.

where branching happens (see, in Fig. 3, the two nodes that intersect the i_1 dotted line). Each node is such that in every fragment in it, the same present-tensed facts obtain, but possibly different, alternative future-tensed facts obtain. How the nodes are labelled is straightforward: we index the symbol N (that stands for 'node') with a subscript to identify the instant, and a superscript to differentiate the various equivalence classes of fragments that share the same present-tensed facts: $N^x_{i_y}$.

The *rule of coherence* that dictates the behaviour of obtainment within each fragment can be complemented by a rule of coherence for nodes, which captures metaphysical openness in Flow Fragmentalism. In general, the tensed fact $TENSE_x p$ obtains relative both to a node $N^n_{i_m}$ and a history h_y, if and only if there is a fragment $\langle i_m, h_y \rangle$ in $N^n_{i_m}$, in which $TENSE_x p$ obtains.[23] While relative to instants, tensed facts of any sort (past-, present- and future-tensed facts) will obtain relative to histories, relative to nodes only the obtainment of future-tensed facts is 'sensitive' to histories. In other words, the relativization to histories is idle for present- and past-tensed facts, but it does make a difference for future-tensed facts. If we go back to our previous example, we can say that there is no determinate answer to the question whether it will be the case that p with respect to a node $N^0_{i_0}$, because within the fragment $\langle i_0, h_1 \rangle$ the fact that *it will be the case that p* obtains, while in the fragment $\langle i_0, h_2 \rangle$ the fact that *it will be the case that ¬p* obtains, and both fragments belong to $N^0_{i_0}$.

This 'branching fragments' openness is clearly similar to the topological openness that we discussed above. However, it can also be integrated with a form of ontological openness. As we saw, Flow Fragmentalism *can* adopt a non-eternalist ontology, as much as this is doable in a non-standard framework. To remind the reader, given that within each fragment F_n only tensed facts that obtain at the 'present' time t_n of F_n obtain within it, and that facts about *simple existence* may vary across fragments, the non-standard tense realist is not forced to have an eternalist ontology within each fragment (see section 1.2.3). This is obviously true also in the branching scenario. And, if you think that robust passage requires not merely irreducible tenses, but also a future which is open in an ontological sense, then you have (at least) two options. You can take that the only facts about simple existence that obtain within F_n are those concerning entities located at t_n (presentist scenario), or are those concerning entities located either at t_n or at the times $t_x < t_n$, that is, the ones that come before it (growing block scenario).

In the rest of the chapter, we will take care of two refinements of this picture. First, we are going to explain what makes it the case that two fragments are $<_{ps}$-connected. Our theory of temporal order respects the idea that there should not be robust cross-temporality in a tense realist context, even a non-standard one (cf. section 0.5). Second, we are going to show how in Flow Fragmentalism it is possible to salvage bivalence, through a red line that is thin, but it does not come with the disadvantage of the anti-realist option.

2.2.2 Overlap and branching ordering

In introducing informally the pseudo B-relation $<_{ps}$, we have appealed at the temporal order of times that in the standard framework can be expressed by the earlier/later relation $<$. One may wonder whether this informal gloss can be taken literally. If we admit facts about the relation $<$ between times $t_1, t_2, \ldots$ and facts about whether any given time t_x is present within each fragment, we can think that the order of fragments is given as follows. If a fragment F_n contains the fact that t_n is present, and a fragment F_m contains the fact that t_m is present, and both contain the fact that $t_n < t_m$, then F_n 'pseudo precedes' F_m, namely $F_n <_{ps} F_m$. Although we have used it as a useful heuristics to informally introduce the idea, we do not think that this strategy is in line with the spirit of our proposal. First of all, the fact that $t_n < t_m$ is a tenseless fact, and even if it is not incoherent to admit in Flow Fragmentalism primitive tenseless facts, we would rather having tenseless facts in our framework to be reduced to tensed facts. There is a strategy that dates back to Prior (1967) and can be clearly adapted to the flow fragmentalist case. Very roughly, we can associate to each time t_x a proposition that is true only at that time; let us call it p_{tx}. We can then interpret claims involving $<$ as follows:

(2) $t_x < t_y =_{df}$ Always, if p_{ty}, then $WASp_{tx}$

Setting aside now the complications that 'always' raises here, claims about $<$ are equivalent to disjunctions of tensed claims. Flow Fragmentalism admits sentential operators in its metaphysically cogent language, but no *disjunctive* (*conjunctive, negative*, etc) facts. That is why the truth of claims about the conjunction or disjunction of facts requires only that certain facts obtain in the relevant fragments. For instance, the truth of $\odot_{F_n} \phi \wedge \odot_{F_m} \psi$ requires only that ϕ and ψ obtain in fragments F_n and F_m, respectively. Analogously, if claims such as $t_x < t_y$ are translated into disjunctions, we should have a story *about what is going on within the fragments involved*. Of course, we do have a story: in each fragment in which p_{t_y} is the case, $WASp_{t_x}$ is also the case. However, notice that we have just *stipulated* that for any x, the sentence p_{t_x} is true only at t_x, and thus individuates the fragment (we can call it F_x) whose 'present' is t_x. Nothing genuinely explanatory is going on here, we are just assuming that the fragments reflect the order of times, which is what we have been doing all along in the previous chapters.

At any rate, there is a second problem, which is both strictly connected to the first one and more serious. As also Fine (2005: 308–10) points out, the tense realist is better off if they reduce times to collections of facts, or at any rate they do not take them as individuals. We would then rather have an *independent* way to order the fragments, and then derive the temporal order from it, rather than starting with facts about how times $t_1, t_2, \ldots$ are connected by $<$. This is why we take $<_{ps}$ to be pseudo-temporal. We call it 'pseudo' *not* because it is not a relation, but because it is not temporal. It mimics, or reflects, what we informally and pre-theoretically take to be the temporal order. But if Flow Fragmentalism is true, the temporal dimension is at bottom an order of fragments, rather than of times – things like events or 'containers' thereof. That is why our metaphysically cogent description of reality is given by using $<_{ps}$ and not $<$.

One may still object that, even if the relation is not temporal, it is still a relation *between fragments*. Therefore, if the problem is not to have cross-fragment facts, we have not really solved it. Our answer, as we have already anticipated in section 1.2.4, is that $<_{ps}$ is an *internal* relation between fragments. We do not need extra facts to accept it (more precisely, to explain the truth of claims of the form $F_x <_{ps} F_y$), we just need the facts that we find within each fragment involved. To be more precise, the order is given by the *partial overlap* in the tensed facts that obtain within the fragment related by $<_{ps}$.

We will make a comparison exploiting a mundane example. Imagine you have to prepare a game for kids with red and blue balls inside sacks. The setting of the game is the following (we do not need to care about the rules of the game here). Each sack has twenty balls in it, and each has a different distribution of red and blue balls. In one there is one red ball and nineteen blue balls, in another there are two red balls and eighteen blue balls, and so on and so forth. It is clear that given the setting, there is a way to order the sacks depending on how many red balls (or blue balls) contain. A bit contrivedly, we can reason as follows. All the sacks that have at least nineteen red balls in them are 'after' those that have at least eighteen red balls in them. All sacks that have at least eighteen red balls in them are 'after' those that have at least nineteen red balls in them. And so on. Analogously, if tensed fragments share certain tensed facts, we may have a way to order them in virtue of the facts that they contain, and without appealing to facts about the temporal order of times. The analogy is of course not perfect. First of all, there is 'type' (of balls) overlap in the game example, but not actual sharing of parts. In the case of fragments, as long as we take the facts that obtain within a fragment to be parts of it, there is actual overlap of parts. Secondly, in the example there is someone who puts the balls in the sack, and this is why there is type overlap. But in the case of fragments, the overlap is given by there being one reality, and the facts involved in the various fragments being facts about the very same entities and properties that constitute the one reality.

Let us get into the details of the construction of the order. The key idea comes from Fine himself, when he spells out the account of the flow of time in the fragmentalist picture: 'Any fact is plausibly taken to belong to a 'fragment' or maximally coherent collection of facts; and so reality will divide up into a number of different but *possibly overlapping* fragments' (2005: 281, italics ours). Roughly speaking, two fragments are said to be partially overlapping if they share some tensed facts, such as the fact that *there were dinosaurs*. Intuitively, the fragmentalist can hold that, since a tensed fact of this kind is 'temporal', the relation of overlap between these two fragments is sufficient to order them in a (pseudo) temporal succession.

In criticizing the idea that there can be genuine overlap between fragments, Tallant (2013) argues that

> the trouble with such a proposal ... is that these facts are insufficiently refined to act as suitable ground for true propositions about the past (and future) and when they are replaced with facts that *are* suitable, we find that the distinct fragments of reality will no longer overlap.
>
> Tallant 2013: 293, italics in the original

As an example, Tallant proposes to consider the proposition expressed by 'Jonathan was hungry five minutes ago'. Its truth – he underlines – cannot be adequately grounded by the tensed fact *Jonathan was hungry*, but rather by the more precise tensed fact that *Jonathan was hungry five minutes ago*. But it is easy to see that this more specific tensed fact *cannot* overlap with the fragment that represents how things will be in another minute, 'for, in another minute, the tensed fact that we will require is not *Jonathan's having been hungry five minutes ago*, but *Jonathan's having been hungry six minutes ago*' (p. 294). Nothing prevents us – Tallant concludes – from thinking of the fragments as constituted only by tensed facts of this kind. But then it is hard to make sense of the claim that different fragments can overlap. Hence, the fragmentalist cannot explain how to order the fragments in a temporal sequence in terms of overlap.

We think there is a way to overcome Tallant's reply. We are willing to admit that there are many propositions whose truth supervenes on more specific tensed facts, such as the fact that *Jonathan was hungry five minutes ago*. Consequently, we admit that we are required to think of fragments as constituted by such metric tensed facts. However, we disagree about whether this is sufficient for claiming that fragments cannot overlap. To be clear, consider a fragment F_0 containing the tensed fact that *dinosaurs became extinct at least 65 million years ago*. Given that tensed fact, in F_0 the proposition expressed by 'Dinosaurs became extinct at least 65 million years ago' is true. Note that if in F_0 this proposition is true, then in F_0 the proposition expressed by 'Dinosaurs became extinct at least 64 million years ago' is also true, since the former entails the latter.[24] It follows that F_0 must also contain the tensed fact that *dinosaurs became extinct at least 64 million years ago*. Now, nothing prevents the fact that *dinosaurs became extinct at least 64 million years ago* from obtaining in another fragment – call it F_n. But then F_0 and F_n share at least one tensed fact, namely the fact that *dinosaurs became extinct at least 64 million years ago*. In other terms, F_0 and F_n are partially overlapping. We have no reason to exclude tensed facts like *dinosaurs became extinct at least 65 million years ago* from the inventory of what we are calling 'more precise' tensed facts.[25] On the contrary, note that the former can be thought of as partially *supervening* on the latter. More precisely, they supervene on a combination of 'at least' facts and 'at most' facts (indeed, they can be defined precisely in those terms, as we will show in the appendix, 2.3).

The pseudo B-series of fragments can be reconstructed out of the overlap of 'at least' facts among fragments. No 'bridging facts' are needed, such as facts concerning the order of times. The relation $<_{ps}$ is thus internal, and very different from $<$, which is a prototypical example of an external relation. Even more interestingly for our purposes, an order can also be reconstructed in the case where the tensed facts are about a branching temporal succession and the relation $<_{ps}$ is branching towards one of its sides. Consider a fragment, F_0, containing the tensed fact that *dinosaurs became extinct at least 65 million years ago*, and thus also the tensed facts that *dinosaurs became extinct at least 64 million*

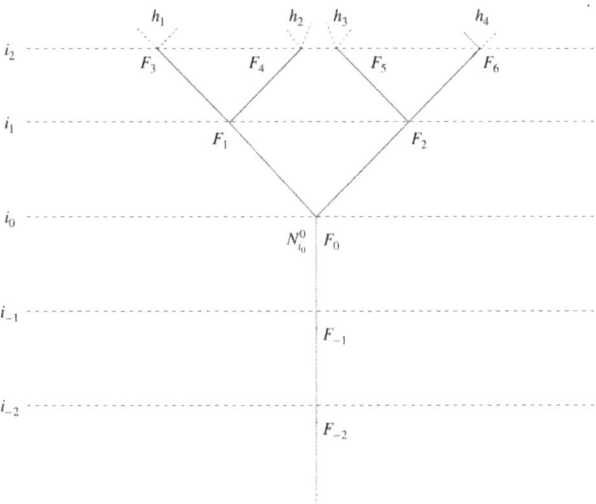

Figure 4 A branching succession of fragments with respect to F_0.

years ago, that *dinosaurs became extinct at least 63 million years ago*, and so on and so forth. Suppose also that F_0 does not contain the tensed fact that *dinosaurs became extinct at least 66 million years ago*. Now, we can order the fragments to be placed in the trunk whose upper bound is F_0 (see Fig. 4) by analysing how they overlap with F_0.

More precisely, a fragment F_x will be part of the trunk if and only if it does not contain the tensed fact that *dinosaurs became extinct at least 65 million years ago*. Conversely, it will be located in one of the branches if and only if it contains the tensed fact that *dinosaurs became extinct at least 65 million years ago*. Analysing the overlap relation also allows us to determine *the order* in which the fragments are disposed along the trunk. Take for example two fragments F_{-1} and F_{-2}. Suppose that F_{-2} contains the tensed fact that *dinosaurs became extinct at least 63 million years ago*, while F_{-1} also contains the tensed fact that *dinosaurs became extinct at least 64 million years ago*. In other words, there is at least one tensed fact obtaining in F_0 that also obtains in F_{-1}, but not in F_{-2}. In this case, F_{-1} will be closer to the upper bound than F_{-2} (in more formal terms, it holds that $F_{-2} <_{ps} F_{-1}$). To synthesize in a motto: the larger the overlap, the smaller the distance to the upper bound.[26] This would suffice to order completely the fragment in the case of linear time (i.e. if, within each fragment, time is linear). But if the future-tensed facts within each fragment are about a branching structure, as we are assuming, we need some further refinement.

In order to calculate the distance (from the upper bound of the trunk) of the fragments that are disposed along the branches we can adopt the previous strategy, but calculating their distance to the upper bound of the trunk may no longer be sufficient for pinpointing their location. Reconsider Fig. 4 above and remember that in this framework, future-tensed facts obtain relative to nodes $N^x_{i_y}$ and pseudo-histories h_x (cf. p. 82).[27] Assume that F_0 is a fragment in node $N^0_{i_0}$. If at $N^0_{i_0}$, relative to both history h_1 and h_3, it will be the case that dinosaurs become extinct at least 66 million years ago and it will not be the case that dinosaurs become extinct at least 67 million years ago, then there will be two fragments – say, F_1 and F_2 – that contain the tensed fact that *dinosaurs became extinct at least 66 million years ago* (that is, *within F_1 and F_2*, dinosaurs became extinct at least 66 million years ago), while they do not contain the tensed fact that *dinosaurs became extinct at least 67 million years ago* (that is, *within F_1 and F_2*, it is not the case that dinosaurs became extinct at least 67 million years ago). It follows that they are at the same distance to the fragments in $N^0_{i_0}$, and hence to F_0. This is sufficient for determining their position (in this case, the motto will be: the smaller the overlap, the larger the distance to the upper bound), but only because they are directly connected to the upper bound F_0. But what about the higher branches? Consider for instance F_3 and F_5. Even though we are told that they are disposed to the same distance to F_0 (assume both that they contain the tensed fact that *dinosaurs became extinct at least 67 million years ago* and that they do not contain the tensed fact that *dinosaurs became extinct at least 68 million years ago*), we cannot determine either whether F_3 is connected to F_1 or to F_2 or whether F_5 is connected to F_1 or to F_2. To do this we need to take into account more 'at least' facts. Assume that at node $N^0_{i_0}$, relative to h_1 humans will become extinct in one million years, whereas relative to h_3 they won't. Then, it is true in F_1 and false in F_2 that humans are extinct. It follows that in every fragment connected to F_1 it will be true that humans became extinct at least one million years ago, while in every fragment connected to F_2 it will be false. Hence, F_3 will be connected to F_1 if and only if it contains the tensed fact that *human beings became extinct at least 1 million years ago*, while F_5 will be connected to F_1 if and only if it does not contain this fact. This gives us the ordering of the fragments in a branching structure.

2.2.3 The invisible thin red line

As we have just stressed, $<_{ps}$ is a partial order, such that it is linear towards one of its sides, but non-linear towards the other. If so, the tree-like ordering of fragments is useless for providing *bivalent* truth-conditions for future contingents. At each node, time branches, and no future-tensed facts obtaining at any of the fragment in the node are privileged in any metaphysical sense. We could, of course, *insert* a red line at each node, just as the presentist can insert brute facts about which one of the possible future histories will be the actual one. For instance, at each node there may be matters of facts about which history is the actual one. But such a manoeuvre would give us a thick red line, rather than a thin one. This is not the only route that the flow fragmentalist can take if they want bivalence and a red line. As in the anti-realist case, if the model is intended to describe a *universe*, rather than a multiverse, there is a definite answer to the question which fragments contain facts that constitute reality, *simply* because there is no privileged present, and thus future temporal perspectives, in which the future is no longer open, are part of the picture anyway.

However, one may object that if what happens according to the rule of coherence that we have given for nodes reflects how the future is (in a metaphysically cogent way) in Flow Fragmentalism, then *relative to a node there is no fact of the matter about which future branch is the actual one*. As Pooley also notices when discussing a non-standard tense realist scenario, the only information we can recover is that a single course of events will be the actual future, but not which one.

> While a given branching structure (absent a thin red line) does not encode a single sequence of the kind we have been considering, it does encode that the future tensed facts that hold at later and later times correspond to some such sequence.
>
> Pooley 2013: 342

Pooley seems to think that the non-standard tense realist is compelled to have something like supervaluationist truth-conditions for future contingents, which would save the law of excluded middle, but jettison bivalence.[28] The reason is that there is neither a 'global' point of view, nor an 'end of time' perspective ('the end of time is never reached', Pooley 2013: 343) from which we can reconstruct the information about the whole of reality. In his words:

> Just as the tensed facts that hold as of some time are not reducible to tenseless facts, there is no need for them to be deducible from the tensed facts that hold as of other times. As of t, it is neither true nor false that there will be a sea battle at t'. As of t', it is true that a sea battle is raging.... it might seem that this open-future version of non-standard [tense realism] better captures the passage of time than a version in which the tensed facts as of one time can be read off from

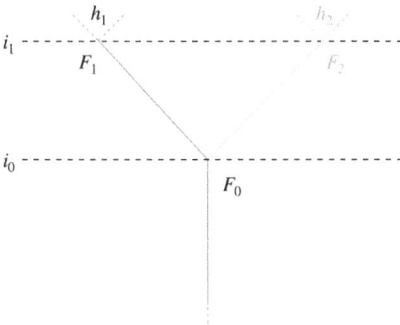

Figure 5 Reality is constituted only by facts in h_1.

those that hold at another. In the latter case, it is hard to see what the insistence that such facts are not reducible comes to, for there *is* a unique representation of reality – the block universe – from which the perspectival facts can be derived. This is no longer true of the open-future model. The primordial branching structure captures only how things might turn out, not how they will turn out.

Pooley 2013: 343, italics in the original

Also, according to Flow Fragmentalism, information about 'future' fragments cannot be recovered from 'earlier' ones. This is the gist of the rule of coherence for nodes. All the *weak* future facts are in the same boat. And yet there is something puzzling in the idea that the fragmentalist picture 'captures only how things might turn out, not how they will turn out'. Although we are barred from recovering information about the future when we look only at what present facts obtain, in the fragmentalist picture, if we are in a universe rather that in a multiverse, reality is *not* constituted by all the *strong* future facts on all the pseudo-histories. Therefore, the very hypothesis that reality is fragmented elicits the idea that one of the branches *must* be singled out as the thin red line, i.e. the one corresponding to the actual course of future events (cf. Fig. 5).

Once we assume we are in a universe and not in a multiverse, the flow fragmentalist picture entails the presence of a red line. And the red line is thin, since it is not given by any future-tensed fact obtaining in some 'privileged' fragment. It would be misleading to think of those future-tensed facts that both obtain at a node *and* are in correspondence with the present-tensed facts obtaining along the fragments constituting the red line as more substantive than the ones that correspond to non-actual future alternatives. At each node, the future-tensed facts are all on a par. There are no facts of the matter establishing a correspondence between some of the weak future facts and the strong future facts. It is only relative to nodes that contain fragments that are pseudo-after the one we are considering that we have matters of facts about the red line. As in the case of the anti-realist, it is the failure of Presentness what does the trick. Of course, the red line is thin also in the sense that it does not come with an epistemic marker. As Belnap et al. suggest (in an anti-realist framework), the thin red line is not visible from the present:

> You may think of the hue as infrared, to capture the idea that the Thin Red Line does not imply that mortals are capable of seeing the future.
>
> Belnap et al. 2001: 135

In the flow fragmentalist scenario, such 'invisibility' is not to be understood in merely epistemic terms. There is literally no fact of the matter as to which of the pseudo-histories at a node corresponds to the actual future.

That is why, as distinct from presentism, having a thin red line is no extra cost for the flow fragmentalist. In the standard picture, having a thin red line entails accepting *presently obtaining* facts about what the actual future will be within the perspective of the present time, which is the only real perspective. But in the flow fragmentalist version of the story, we are not required to accept facts about the actual future at each node. If fragmentalism is true, we know that an invisible thin red line (ITRL) can't fail to be out there, since only the fragments that form a certain sequence are part of reality; all others are not part of reality at all. At one point, Pooley seems to be sympathetic to such an idea:

> The model of the non-standard variant of the view *does* involve a particular sequence [a sequence of perspectives that stands for the actual future course of events]. Each element of it represents the irreducibly tensed facts that hold as of some time. This might seem to give us a more explicit representation of once open possibilities being settled by the passage of time: what is indeterminate as of *t* is settled in such-and-such a way as of *t'*. But care is needed: the sequence of trees does not represent how reality is absolutely, as conceived from no particular temporal point of view.
>
> Pooley 2013: 342, italics in the original

As we have seen, 'care' pushes Pooley to reject the idea that the fact that 'the view *does* involve a particular sequence' justifies the endorsement of a thin red line. That may be because Pooley uses a different version of non-standard tense realism from us – external relativism on his part, and fragmentalism on ours.

Remember that while both external relativism and fragmentalism accept Neutrality, external relativism rejects Absolutism while fragmentalism rejects Coherence, as we repeat below.

Absolutism The constitution of reality is an absolute matter, i.e. not relative to a time or other form of temporal standpoint.
Coherence Reality is not contradictory; it is not constituted by facts with incompatible content.

Therefore, the fragmentalist does not accept that the constitution of *reality* is irreducibly relative to fragments (or perspectives, or points in supertime, or what have you), although she does relativize what facts obtain to fragments: we are never allowed to claim that facts that we find in a different fragment from the one in which certain facts obtain also obtain. The fragmentalist reality is not 'of a whole' because as a whole it would be incoherent, but it is nonetheless constituted by all tensed facts in an *absolute* sense. On the other hand, in the external relativist picture, tensed facts do not constitute one reality, since they only constitute reality *relative* to perspectives. This makes a difference when it comes to ordering the fragment with $<_{ps}$. In an external relativist framework, it is not only that we don't find a global perspective or a perspective as of the end of time, we do not find a reality constituted by all the facts that we find along the thin red line. Hence, in an external relativist framework the postulation of a thin red line would entail that there is a further reality constituted by incompatible facts. This may be a price that someone endorsing such a version of non-standard tense realism – as Pooley in the paper we just quoted – may not be willing to accept. But in the fragmentalist version, since Coherence but not Absolutism is dropped, the postulation of such a reality is no additional cost at all; indeed, an incoherent but fragmented whole of incompatible tensed facts is the *only* reality that the model posits.

2.3 Appendix: The model theory

In this appendix, we provide more details on the logic exploited in this chapter. Let us start by offering the following syntactic rules of a language $\mathcal{L}$:

Syntactic rules

(a) $p, q, \ldots$ are well formed formulae (hereinafter, wffs. $p, q, \ldots$ are the atoms of $\mathcal{L}$)
(b) If ϕ and ψ are wffs, then $\neg \phi$ and $\phi \wedge \psi$ are wffs
(c) If ϕ is a wff, and x and y are numbers, then $ATLEAST_x\, \phi$, $ATMOST_x\, \phi$, and $\odot_{F_{ix},\, h_y} \phi$ are wffs

The model $\mathcal{M}$

A model $\mathcal{M}$ is a tuple $\langle \mathcal{F}, <_{ps}, d, ITRL, V \rangle$ such that:

(d) $\mathcal{F} = \{F_1, F_2, \ldots\}$ is a set of points, informally representing the fragments;
(e) $<_{ps}$ is a partial order on $\mathcal{F}$ that is linear towards the left and branching towards the right, and it is such that any two points have a common $\leq_{ps}$-ancestor, thus forming a tree structure. *Pseudo-histories* $h_1, h_2, \ldots$ can be defined as sets of maximal chains of $\leq_{ps}$-connected points.
(f) d is a *distance* function that, for each pair of $\leq_{ps}$-connected points in $\mathcal{F}$, gives a positive number x expressing their distance in time units.[29] Two points F_x, F_y are said to be *d-aligned* iff they lie at the same temporal distance from a point F_z that (improperly) precedes both of them. *Instants* $i_0, i_1, \ldots$ are defined as equivalence classes of d-aligned moments. For any instant i_x, we write i_{x-n} to indicate the instant that is n time units in the past of i_x, and we write i_{x+n} to indicate the instant that is n time units in the future of i_x.
(g) We require that the tree be *synchronized*,[30] so that any instant i_x intersects each pseudo-history h_y on precisely one point.[31] We write (i_x, h_y) to indicate the unique point lying in the intersection of i_x and h_y.
(h) *ITRL* is a selected pseudo-history, which informally represents the *invisible thin red line*, the sequence of fragments that constitutes the actual history of the universe.
(i) V is a valuation function that associates each atom in $\mathcal{L}$ with a function from points in $\mathcal{F}$ to truth-values in $\{T, F\}$.

The semantics

The truth-conditions are defined as follows:

(j) $[p]_{\mathcal{M}}^{(i_x,\, h_y)} = T$ iff $V(p)\,(i_x, h_y) = T$, where p is atomic
(k) $[\neg \phi]_{\mathcal{M}}^{(i_x,\, h_y)} = T$ iff $[\phi]_{\mathcal{M}}^{(i_x,\, h_y)} \neq T$

(l) $[\phi \wedge \psi]_{\mathcal{M}}^{(i_x, h_y)} = T$ iff $[\phi]_{\mathcal{M}}^{(i_x, h_y)} = [\psi]_{\mathcal{M}}^{(i_x, h_y)} = T$
(m) $[ATLEAST_n \phi]_{\mathcal{M}}^{(i_x, h_y)} = T$ iff for some k such that $k \leq (x - n)$, $[\phi]_{\mathcal{M}}^{(i_k, h_y)} = T$
(n) $[ATMOST_n \phi]_{\mathcal{M}}^{(i_x, h_y)} = T$ iff there is a k such that $(x - n) \leq k$, $[\phi]_{\mathcal{M}}^{(i_k, h_y)} = T$
(o) $[\odot_{F_{i_w}, h_z} \phi]_{\mathcal{M}}^{(i_x, h_y)} = T$ iff $[\phi]_{\mathcal{M}}^{(i_w, h_z)} = T$

We now define the following operators:

(p.1) $TENSE_n \phi =_{df} ATLEAST_n \phi \wedge ATMOST_n \phi$
(p.2) $WAS_n \phi =_{df} TENSE_n \phi$, when n is positive
(p.3) $WILL_n \phi =_{df} TENSE_n \phi$, when n is negative
(p.4) $WAS\phi =_{df}$ for some n, $WAS_n \phi$
(p.5) $WILL\phi =_{df}$ for some n, $WILL_n \phi$

Truth at an instant is defined as follows:

(q) $[\phi]_{\mathcal{M}}^{i_x} = T$ iff $[\phi]_{\mathcal{M}}^{(i_x, ITRL)} = T$

Truth in $\mathcal{M}$, logical consequence, and validity

Truth in a model $\mathcal{M}$ is defined in a non-recursive way as follows.

(r) $\mathcal{M} \models \phi$ iff for some i_x, $[\phi]_{\mathcal{M}}^{i_x} = T$

Finally, these are the definitions of logical consequence and validity:

(s) $\Sigma \models \phi$ iff for any model $\mathcal{M}$, if $\mathcal{M} \models \Sigma$, then $\mathcal{M} \models \phi$
(t) $\models \phi$ iff for any model $\mathcal{M}$, $\mathcal{M} \models \phi$

3

Causation

As we have pointed out in section 0.5, Flow Fragmentalism is committed to avoiding irreducible cross-temporal facts. Causation is, prototypically, an external relation that is cross-temporally instantiated, and thus it prima facie involves irreducible cross-temporal facts. In this chapter, we will discuss how Flow Fragmentalism can get around this predicament. We begin in section 3.1 by discussing which relations, if cross-temporally instantiated, seem to require irreducible cross-temporal facts, and thus are problematic for the flow fragmentalist, and we argue that causality poses a serious threat. We then discuss in section 3.2 the reductionist interpretation of Humean causation as an option for the flow fragmentalist. This will prepare the floor for our proposal, presented in section 3.3. Finally, in section 3.4, we make some reflections on the relationship between causal and temporal successions.

3.1 Cross-temporal facts

In section 1.2.4 (see also section 2.2.2), we argued that if we admit relations that are instantiated by entities that exist in different fragments, we risk of collapsing Flow Fragmentalism into tense anti-realism. We then showed how neither the truth of claims about the order of fragments (such as '$F_1 <_{ps} F_2$'), nor the truth of explanatory claims involving distinct fragments (such as '$\odot_{F_1}$ it will rain because $\odot_{F_2}$ it rains') require the cross-temporal instantiation of relations, namely irreducible cross-temporal facts. Roughly, in both cases the truth of the cross-temporal claims requires only that an *internal* relation between (entities in) distinct fragments obtains. But internal relations are *reducible*, precisely in the sense that we can make sense of true claims about them entirely in terms of the properties of the relata. Let us dwell a bit more on this, and see how it is possible to expand such a strategy, by starting with the case of relations of (*comparative*) *intrinsic similarity*.

Suppose that my niece, who has been shorter than me for a long time, has lately become taller than me. In order for this to happen, it seems not only necessary, but also sufficient, that her height now exceeds mine. Such a necessary and sufficient condition can be read as a *reductive analysis* of the comparative intrinsic similarity in question. If so, the fact that my niece is now taller than me is reducible to the following three facts:

(i) My niece is now n meters tall
(ii) I am now m meters tall
(iii) $m < n$

(i) and (ii) are *intrinsic* facts involving, respectively, only my niece and me,[1] and (iii), which is genuinely relational, does not involve my niece and me, but it is a general truth about heights (or perhaps numbers or quantities). Given that *relations of intrinsic similarities* are generally amenable to this kind of analysis, they are often understood as *internal* relations, that is, relations that are entirely reducible to the intrinsic properties of the *relata*, together with general facts like (iii).

However, note that the reducibility of a relation such as *taller than* is due to the fact that it is a relation of similarity, rather than to the fact that the similarity involved is intrinsic. Indeed, relations of *extrinsic* similarity are analogously reducible to the properties of the relata – although not reducible to their intrinsic properties alone. Consider the fact that Joanna lives on the same continent as Josephine, namely Asia. It is reducible to the following facts:

(iv) Joanna lives in Hong Kong
(v) Josephine lives in Tokyo
(vi) Hong Kong and Tokyo are both in Asia

According to such analysis, the extrinsic similarity between Joanna and Josephine is reducible to a collection of facts that do not involve any external relation *between them*: (iv) expresses an external relation between Joanna and Hong Kong (or an extrinsic property of Joanna that involves the city where she lives), (v) expresses an external relation between Josephine and Tokyo (or an extrinsic property of Josephine that involves the city where she lives), and (vi) expresses an external relation between Hong Kong and Tokyo. Lewis (1986) famously suggested a categorization of relations in internal, external, and neither internal nor external. An example of the latter would be *being married to* which holds between two persons in virtue of other facts, such as the presence in a given context of institutions and conventions. We take relations of extrinsic similarity to be of the third kind. They are not internal, since they are *not* reducible to intrinsic properties of the relata, together with general facts, and they are not external, since they *are* reducible to properties of the relata, together with general facts.² We will make the working hypothesis that if a relation is *non-external*, then it is amenable to a reductive analysis along the lines of (i)–(iii) or (iv)–(vi) above.

What interests us here is that non-external relations, under the working hypothesis, unlike external ones, do not commit us to irreducible cross-temporal facts, even if we accept true cross-temporal claims about them. Consider a different example, involving a relation of extrinsic similarity that is cross-temporally instantiated. Angela Merkel is born on the same planet Cleopatra was born: Earth. If we apply the analysis above, we have that this cross-temporal fact reduces to the following three facts:

(iv') Cleopatra was born in Egypt
(v') Angela Merkel is born in Germany
(vi') Egypt and Germany are on the same planet

Any view that allows for there being at present truths about the past[3] has no problem in accepting (iv')–(vi'), and thus the truth of the cross-temporal claim that Angela Merkel is born on the same planet as Cleopatra was. Since the truth of a claim involving a non-external relation between an entity *a* and an entity *b* requires only facts about *a* and *b* that do not involve external relations between *a* and *b*, the truth of a cross-temporal claim involving a non-external relation between *a* and *b* does not require that *a* and *b* cross-temporally instantiate the relation in question. Therefore, as long as it does not require other external relations to be cross-temporally instantiated, it does not require *irreducible cross-temporal facts*. However, not all cross-temporal claims involve relations that are non-external. External relations are metaphysically heavier than internal ones, because they require substantive links between their relata. More precisely, the truth of a claim involving an external relation between relata *a* and *b* requires an irreducible relational fact between *a* and *b*. And the truth of a *cross-temporal* claim about an external relation requires an irreducible cross-temporal fact. And if there are true cross-temporal claims that express external relations, they cannot be accounted for in terms of a conjunction (or some other 'operation') of facts about what happens to the relata at different times (namely, within different fragments). Thus the flow fragmentalist, if we are right in claiming that they should avoid cross-temporal facts to avert collapse into the anti-realist position, has a problem.[4]

Causation is clearly a troublemaker here. Typically, causes happen *before* their effects. This is true both for cases of *general* causation, as when we say that excessive watering causes succulent plants to rotten and die, and for cases of *individual* causation, as when we say that by accidentally bumping the knee against the table leg I have caused the vase to fall and break. If so, causation is at least sometimes cross-temporally instantiated. Besides, causation has all the marks of being an *external relation*, rather than an internal one, or one that is neither internal nor external. Consider a typical external relation, and how it differs from a relation of similarity. If I am on the right of my niece, it is difficult to see to which intrinsic properties of my niece and me this fact can be reduced. It looks like there *has to be* some matter of fact involving my niece and me 'together', so to speak. The relational element cannot be 'quarantined' into a fact about other entities (such as quantities or cities).[5] This is why spatial and temporal relations are usually understood as prototypically external: they are *not* reducible to the properties (intrinsic or not) of their relata.

Causation is on the side of spatial and temporal relations, rather than on the side of similarity relations. First, it is not obvious how it could be reduced to the intrinsic properties of the cause and of the effect respectively, along the lines of the reductive analysis that we have suggested above for relations of intrinsic similarity, such as *being taller than*. Second, it is not obvious how it could be reduced to extrinsic properties of the cause and the effect either. Whether it obtains or not puts demands on the position in space and time of the relata, but the fact that it occurs is not exhausted by properties of the spatial and temporal positions of the cause and the effect, as the relation of *being born on the same planet* is. Plausibly, it is not *merely* in virtue of the fact that the cause and the effect are at a certain spatial and temporal distance from one another that they are so related.

If causation is an external relation, true cross-temporal claims about causal links express irreducible cross-temporal facts, and the flow fragmentalist has a problem. There is an analogy between the problem that causality here raises for the flow fragmentalist and a problem that it raises for the presentist. Consider the fact expressed by the claim (vii) below.

(vii) Yesterday's heavy rain causes today's flood.

If (vii) is true, there is a connection between something that is happening today, and something that happened yesterday. The obvious idea is to identify such a connection with a relation between the past event of the rain and the present event of the flooding. However, as long as such a relation is *existence entailing* –

that is, as long as its relata have to exist for the relation to obtain – this analysis is not viable to the presentist. But external relations are existence entailing, and if causation is an external relation, the presentist cannot understand causal relations as cross-temporal links between a cause and an effect. This is not a knock-down argument for presentism, we agree; but it *is* a problem. And indeed in the literature on presentism it is discussed, along with the problem of past and future truths, and the problem of singular propositions about non-present entities.[6]

What the trouble for presentism and the trouble for Flow Fragmentalism have in common is that what creates the problem is that causality is prima facie both external and cross-temporal. Where they diverge is that the problem for the presentist is that external relations are *existence entailing*, while the problem for the flow fragmentalist is that they are not reducible to facts obtaining at different times. According to Flow Fragmentalism, there is no temporal perspective encompassing more than one fragment, and each fragment is centred on its *unique* 'present' time. Therefore, no fact linking a cause and an effect, as long as they are not simultaneous, can obtain.[7] In the rest of the chapter, we will see how to solve such a predicament. We will begin by considering a deflationist option: deflationist Humeanism.

3.2 Deflationist Humeanism

By discussing cases of individual causation above, such as (vii), while arguing that they entail irreducible cross-temporal facts we have implicitly treated them as cases of *singular* causation, that is, causal relations between individual events that hold *in*dependently of facts about the laws of nature. This is an option that some philosophers find appealing. Whoever endorses an ontology of primitive powers, for instance, is likely to think that the basic 'blocks' of causality, as it were, are robust causal links between individual entities.[8] That assumption leads us to think of causation as an external relation. But maybe there is *no* singular causation, and individual causal relations *are* dependent on facts about the laws of nature, along with facts about the properties of the causes and the effects. Think of a case involving two specific events: the hitting of the table leg by my knee (the cause c), and the falling of the vase (the effect e). Could the causal link between them consist entirely in the fact that the laws of nature entail that after c there will be a chain of events through space and time (the transmission of the vibrations from the leg, to the top, to the vase itself) which leads to e?

Let us make the point as clear as possible. We distinguish between *individual*, *singular*, and *nomic* (or *general*) causation. By 'individual causation' we mean causal links between individual events, such as the hitting and the falling in the example above. By 'nomic causation' we mean, roughly, the relations involving general features or properties that are expressed by the laws of nature. For instance, the relation stated by the claim that water freezes at zero degrees Celsius. Individual causation is *not* incompatible with nomic causation. It may be that individual causal relations are just instances of general causal relations. This individual event of cooling down the room caused this individual event of this parcel of water to freeze, because it is an instance of the general fact that water freezes at zero degrees. Or it may be that both claims about individual causes and nomic claims are just ways to describe patterns of properties across space and time. They are just different ways to talk about the regularities that we find in nature (more on this below). To the contrary, by 'singular causation' we mean individual causation that is *independent* of the laws of nature. Singular causation is thus incompatible with nomic causation, *unless* the latter is derivative on or reducible to the former. For instance, it may be that the laws of nature are mere generalizations of singular causal relations.[9]

As we will see, singular causation is problematic both for the presentist and for the flow fragmentalist, since singular causal relations seem to be particularly resilient to reductive analysis. However, not all philosophers think that we should take singular causation seriously, metaphysically speaking. Hume, famously, was highly sceptical towards the existence of robust causal links between particulars. The so-called *regularity theory* of causation, which is inspired by Hume's reflection on the topic, is sometimes interpreted as a deflationist view. In the deflationist interpretation, there are no singular links between events, and both individual and general causal relations are essentially psychological in nature.[10] When we say that a certain event c caused a certain effect e, what we are saying is that certain features with respect to which c and e are similar to the events in classes C and E, respectively, allow us to make certain generalizations.

In its crudest formulation, the generalization is that events of type E follow events of type C that are at the right distance in space and time. Thus, even if c preceded e, there is no need to look for an external relation that they cross-temporally instantiate. In order for the claim that c causes e to be true, it is sufficient that c is an event of type C and e is an event of type E, and that *the two abstract types* are related in a way that is reflected by *our* tendency to make certain generalizations. Even if the cause and the effect inhabit different fragments, and thus there is no fact that can involve both of them and make it the case that they are causally linked, we can truly say of them that one is the cause of the other because of the features they have (in their respective fragments) and because such features justify certain expectations. So if I encounter c I can reasonably expect that, if I am at the right position, I will observe e in a 'subsequent' fragment.

More sophisticated versions of the theory may involve other psychological attitudes than expectation, but the point stands. The deflationist reading dissolves the problem of causality for Flow Fragmentalism, because it reduces individual causation to general causation, and treats general causation as involving only psychological attitudes.

3.3 The ways of fragmented causation

Although the flow fragmentalist may welcome the 'neo-positivist' treatment of causation envisaged above, it would be nice if such a view of causation were not forced upon someone merely *by endorsing* Flow Fragmentalism. After all, given that it is not in the business of Flow Fragmentalism to explain certain aspects of temporality in terms of causality, or the other way around (for instance, to explain the directionality of time in terms of the directionality of causality, or vice versa, cf. section 3.4), methodologically it seems sound to leave to causality as much berth as possible. Luckily, the flow fragmentalist can accommodate a variety of views on the topic. In moving from a deflationist approach to causality to a *robust* one, the flow fragmentalist encounters two main problems. Both problems are there also for the presentist, but while the presentist can, arguably, solve the first one, the flow fragmentalist can solve both at once – for a reasonable fee.

The first problem is that in the robust reading of the Humean approach, individual relations of causality are derivative on the distribution of properties throughout space-time, rather than on psychological attitudes. It is thus the fact that *patterns of instantiation* in space-time, rather than psychological attitudes, play a crucial explanatory role what makes the position a form of robust realism. But those patterns are likely to require cross-temporal links that are not reducible to properties of the relata. Typically, temporal relations, and spatial relations among individual events located at different times. If so, both the flow fragmentalist and the presentist have a problem here, although for different reasons. The flow fragmentalist has to face a new sort of cross-temporal facts, while the presentist has to face a new sort of existence entailing relations that are cross-temporally instantiated.[11] The second problem is that of singular causation. If we do not want to rule out a priori the possibility that individual causal links are singular, and thus independent of nomic causation, accommodating cross-temporal facts about the locations of events in space and time is not enough. Rather, we need a way to reduce cross-temporal individual *causal* relations without appeal to general causal relations.

3.3.1 Presentist causation

Let us begin with the first problem, and see whether we can find inspiration from the various strategies that presentists have developed to account for cross-temporality, and individual causation more specifically.[12] One strategy whose spirit is particularly congenial to the approach we will develop is the following. Although *strictly speaking* no external relation between events that exist at different times can obtain in a presentist universe, there may be facts that are *in the ballpark* of such relations, so that claims about them can be 'quasi-true' although not properly true. Ted Sider, a critic of presentism, has explored this strategy, defining a notion of quasi-truth for presentism along these lines:

Quasi-truth$_p$ ϕ is quasi-true iff there is a sentence ϕ^* such that (i) ϕ^* is true, and (ii) if eternalism were true, ϕ^* would entail ϕ

Relatedly, we can call presentist *quasi-supervenience base* for a quasi-truth ϕ a collection of facts that makes ϕ quasi-true. As Sider points out, it is not unreasonable to assume a global quasi-supervenience base for all cross-temporal external relations:

> A presentist, therefore, will need to find a quasi-supervenience basis for all cross-time external relations .... But it is a reasonable hypothesis that, as the non-presentist would put it, all relations supervene (globally) on the totality of facts about i) where and when intrinsic properties are instantiated, and ii) nomological matters, including causal relations and laws of nature.
>
> Sider 1999: 335

Note that causality seems to play a double role here, as one of the cross-temporal relations that get a quasi-truth status thanks to the quasi-supervenience base, and as one of the constituents of the quasi-supervenience base. This may seem a problem. If causal relations are external cross-temporal relations that can be expressed only by quasi-truths, then how can the quasi-supervenience base contain facts about causation? But the problem can be overcome if we do a bit of divide and conquer. First, nomological facts. Consider *Humean Supervenience*, the thesis according to which the totality of facts about where and when intrinsic properties are instantiated settles all nomological facts. If Humean Supervenience is false, nomological facts require facts about necessary connections between universals (or they are primitive). As long as the presentist can accept those 'ethereal' denizens,[13] she will have all the nomological facts as well. Problem solved. If Humean Supervenience is true, the problem is overcome if the presentist's world encompasses 'enough' presently obtaining past-, present- and future-tensed facts to have all general causal relations, and thus nomological facts. Does it? It depends on whether the facts about the patterns of spatiotemporal instantiation of properties can be treated in a presentist-friendly manner. In order to do so, we need to consider the temporal and spatial aspects separately. The temporal relations between events can be expressed by the *metric* aspect of the tensed properties. If the ignition that caused a presently occurring explosion occurred 3 milliseconds before the explosion, then when the explosion is occurring, it is the case that 3 milliseconds before the ignition occurr*ed*. In the case of two simultaneous events e_1 and e_2, we need that e_1 occurs when e_2 occurs. And so on. The spatial relations can be expressed by external relations between events, or locations. The only problematic case is a cross-temporal case of spatial relation (e.g. e_1 happens 3 cm on the left of where e_2 happen*ed*), since spatial relations are external, and thus existence entailing. But as long as we can re-identify a location across time, the presentist can treat cross-temporal cases of spatial relations as relations of external similarity, and thus provide a reductive analysis of them. For instance, if the ignition that caused the explosion occurred 3 cm in a given direction from the place of the explosion, in the 'pattern facts' we will have that the location of the ignition and the location of the explosion stand in the corresponding spatial relation. Therefore, it seems that the presentist's world contains all the pattern facts and thus all the nomological facts.

Second, individual causal relations expressed by quasi-true cross-temporal claims. If individual causation is not singular, but reducible to nomic causation, the presentist is home and dry. A moment's reflection reveals that she has all it takes to implement a robust version of the regularity view of causation. In an eternalist universe where there is no singular causation, all individual causal relations supervene on the distribution of patterns of instantiation across space-time locations, and nomological facts. Analogously, in its presentist counterpart, all individual causal relations quasi-supervene on the nomological facts, and on presently obtaining tensed facts about the intrinsic properties of entities and relations between their spatial locations. We can now spell out the reductive analysis that the presentist can give of individual causal relations, by asking what is beyond the quasi-truths in question. The answer (assuming the effect is presently occurring) is: the facts expressed by (viii)–(x) below.

(viii) Metric past-tensed facts about the intrinsic properties of the cause c and its spatial location
(ix) Present-tensed facts about the intrinsic properties of the effect e and its spatial location
(x) Facts about the laws of nature that involve the properties of c and e

If individual causal relations are reducible to facts (viii)–(x), then even if causation is existence entailing, cross-temporal causal claims are quasi-true, and we have an explanation of their prima facie truth. Notice also that this scenario corroborates our working hypothesis that non-external relations are amenable to a reductive analysis along the lines of the relation of (extrinsic and intrinsic) similarity. If we are right, individual causal relations are reduced to general causal relations (that is, (x)) and non-causal facts (that is, (viii) and (ix)). Given that external relations are not amenable to reductive analysis of this sort, causal relations are not external relations. (They are not internal, because at least some of the properties of the cause and the effect involved in (viii)–(x) are extrinsic to them.)[14]

The case of singular causation is more problematic, because singular causation is not amenable to the same 'de-externalizing' treatment, and thus it is left out of the picture. If causal relations are independent of the laws, they have to be taken as substantive links between events.[15] But then we are back to the problem we started with: the events in question are one after the other, and thus cannot both occur in the present (or having occurred, or going to occur in the present). And the link in question is external, and thus existence entailing, which is problematic for the presentist, and substantive, which is problematic for the flow fragmentalist. In order to overcome this predicament, the presentist can express individual causal relations by using a *sentential connective*.[16] Given the role that reference to causal links and causal histories plays in explaining things (at both the ordinary and the scientific level), a natural option is to use a connective that expresses a causal explanatory link. Let us label it '$because_c$'. The connection expressed is explanatory, but, as the subscript reminds us, the explanation in question is of a causal nature.

In general, the presentist will express the causal link between the cause and the effect as the link between a present-tensed fact and a past-tensed fact, both presently obtaining and involving respectively the cause and the effect. The core thesis of presentist causation can thus be understood as the claim that the propositional scheme Presentist Causation below is sometimes instantiated in a way that the claim expressed is true. And if an instantiation of Presentist Causation obtained by substituting c and e for the two metalinguistic variables C and E respectively is true, then the corresponding relational claim Causation is quasi-true for the presentist.

Presentist Causation The effect E happens *because*$_c$ it was the case that the cause C happens
Causation c causes e

However, there are several problems that riddle this treatment of singular causation in a presentist context. Let us briefly review them before moving on to the official flow fragmentalist account. The first problem is, to our judgement, the less serious. In order to express singular causation, we need to *refer* to the event cause and the event effect somewhat directly, and not merely through some qualitative description of them. This is so because the causal link between them cannot be reduced to what the laws of nature state about individuals with such and such properties (and at the appropriate spatial and temporal distances one another). And direct reference to entities that no longer exist is problematic for the presentist. Perhaps this worry presupposes a theory of reference that puts too much ontological burden onto the reference relation, and by rejecting the underlying theory the presentist can claim that direct reference to past individuals is not problematic for them.[17]

However, even if presentists can directly refer to no longer existing past entities, they still have a second, more serious problem with claims of the form Causation involving no longer existing individuals. In this context, it seems natural to take such claims as expressing *singular propositions*. But how can singular propositions concerning past things exist *now*? Even if we can achieve reference to the past, a singular proposition about an individual c that no longer exists is a complex entity that has among its constituents an entity that does not exist. And this seems just contradictory. Think, by analogy, to the following claim: this vase is constituted by a very large lump of clay. However, only a tiny bit of the lump exists. Wait… what?

Finally, even if we bracket the problem of singular propositions too, there is a third problem that concerns the semantic status of the claims in question. If past entities do not exist (although we can refer to them, and somehow 'include' them in singular propositions), how comes that existence entailing cross-temporal claims about them are true? Of course, that is the problem we started with by considering why relations that are both existence entailing and cross-temporal, such as causation, are problematic for the presentist. And the quasi-truth strategy is precisely a way to go around that question. But remember that in this context, the causal relation is an explanatory link between facts that obtain at the same time, and at least one, the fact about the cause, is past-tensed, and thus cannot involve *individuals* that no longer exist, it can only involve *general features* (although perhaps in *stating* the facts we can unproblematically refer to no longer existing individuals). How, then, can the presentist make sense of a link between two events that is independent of (and possibly more fundamental than) the nomic relations between general features? Maybe resorting to Meinongian non-existing objects, or treating causation as a relation between present entities and *surrogates* for past entities, the presentist can get around those predicaments.[18] Be that as it may, as we will see in a moment the flow fragmentalist is not bothered by them.

3.3.2 Fragmentalist causation

Let us now see how to adjust the sentential operator account of causation to Flow Fragmentalism. There is a reading of Presentist Causation that is more natural in the context of a non-standard approach than the one we just saw. The presentist takes it as expressing a link between two facts that co-obtain in the present (the fact that e happens and the fact that c happened).[19] The flow fragmentalist has also the option of reading Presentist Causation as expressing a link between facts that obtain *in different fragments*. The link expressed by '$because_C$' is not taken to be a relation that enters as a constituent in a *further* fact. According to Flow Fragmentalism, Presentist Causation is not to be understood as expressing a cross-fragment fact. Remember that complex sentences in general do not express facts (see p. 24), and this holds also for sentences whose main operator is '$because_C$'. There is no 'relational causal fact' that Presentist Causation expresses, it just states something about the cause and the effect. And what it states, unlike in the presentist reading, does not require that facts about the cause co-obtain with facts about the effect. In the flow fragmentalist reading, Presentist Causation is about facts that do not share the same fragment. In order to make explicit the latter requirement, we can use a phrasing that puts the 'pastness' of the cause into the link itself, as in Presentist Causation' below.[20]

Presentist Causation' The effect E happens $because_C$-in-the-past the cause C happens

Presentist Causation' is a way to make explicit the reading of Presentist Causation that is available to the non-standard tense realist, but it is not yet what we are arguing the flow fragmentalist should adopt. The reason is that Presentist Causation' exploits an absolute notion of pastness, and this indirectly forces us to adopt the perspective from which it is uttered. Presentist Causation' is thus suitable for positions that take obtainment as an irreducible tensed notion (such as Fine's version of fragmentalism, see section 1.3.1), but not for the flow fragmentalist framework, in which the pastness in question is both *relative* to the temporal position of the effect, and metaphysically substantive. Remember that in the framework of Flow Fragmentalism, tense realism is in place (see section 1.1.1), hence the relative pastness of the cause can*not* be read merely in indexical terms, as resolved in the perspectival nature of the linguistic representation. But also Absolutism is in place (cf. p. 20), hence the substantivity of pastness attributions to a temporal location cannot be understood in terms of its absolute position in the temporal dimension either. What we can and should do is to adapt the strategy that we have used for the explanation of passage in section 1.1.4 by relying on the operator '$\odot_{F_x}$'. The first approximation of the principle of fragmentalist causation we want to defend is Fragmentalist Causation* below.

Fragmentalist Causation* $\odot_{F_m} \phi$ because$_C$ $\odot_{F_n} \psi$ (with $n < m$)

Now, the parenthetical on the right of Fragmentalist Causation* encodes the idea of the relative pastness of the effect, which is at the core of the principle (and it is the key feature that distinguishes it from Presentist Causation and Presentist Causation'). By adapting a strategy used before (see p. 40), we will 'sneak in' such information into the language more directly. We informally introduce a family of connectives of form ⌜because$_{Cx}^m$⌝ with an index m for the fragment where the effect takes place, and a metric parameter x for the temporal distance in the past of the cause. We assume that both m and x are positive numbers strictly greater than zero (we will come back to this assumption in section 3.4).

Because$_C$ ϕ because$_{Cx}^m \psi =_{df} \odot_{F_m} \phi$ because$_C \odot_{F_{(m-x)}} \psi$

With the connective so defined the core tenet of fragmentalist causation can be understood as the claim that the propositional scheme Fragmentalist Causation below is sometimes instantiated in a way that the claim expressed is true.

Fragmentalist Causation ϕ because$_{Cx}^m \psi$

This flow fragmentalist treatment of individual causation is flexible between a Humean reading and a singularist one, while avoiding the problems that riddle the presentist in the case of singular causation. A robust interpretation of regularist causation can be easily recovered. Remember that the problem with the robust take on Humeanism for the flow fragmentalist is that nomological facts require facts about the *patterns* of instantiation. As the presentist can appeal to the tensed facts that presently obtain to recover the 'behaviour' of instantiation at different times and places, in a way that does not commit them to external relations that are cross-temporally instantiated, the flow fragmentalist can appeal to the order of fragments to recover the pattern facts. Also, in this case, the spatial and the temporal aspects are treated separately. Spatial relations are treated as bona fide external relations within each fragment. There are thus spatial facts. Temporal relations are treated as internal relations between fragments. There are thus no facts about temporal relations in the same sense that there are spatial relational facts. As we saw in section 1.2.4, temporal relations in the flow fragmentalist framework are internal relations between fragments. Any temporal relation between events can be reduced to the fact that the cause happens in a certain fragment F_C, the fact that the effect happens in another fragment F_E, and the internal relation $F_C <_{ps} F_E$.

As before, the only problematic case is that of cross-temporal relations between spatial locations. Suppose that the individual causal relation between an ignition e_C and an explosion e_E is reducible to nomological facts, to the facts that e_C and e_E have certain intrinsic properties, and that they are temporally separated by n units of time, and spatially related by the relation R. In order to avoid cross-temporal facts, the flow fragmentalist has to treat the spatial and the temporal aspects of this link separately. But there is no reason to think that this is problematic. We just need that (i) within F_C, the location of e_C is s_C, (ii) within F_E, the location of e_E is s_E, (iii) $R(s_C, s_E)$, and (iv) $F_C <_{ps} F_E$. As in the presentist case, as long as we can re-identify locations through fragments, pattern facts can be treated in analogy with relations of extrinsic similarity.[21]

A singularist account of causation can also be recovered within the flow fragmentalist framework. According to the singularist, true instances of Fragmentalist Causation are not made true by facts about the laws (whether they are in turn reducible to pattern facts or not) together with facts about the cause and the effect. What does make them true? The explanatory burden of singular causation is shifted from the laws of nature to facts about the intrinsic nature of the cause and the effect, together with facts about their position in space and time. For the reductive analysis to go through then, it is not sufficient that cross-temporal spatial relations are reduced to relations of extrinsic similarity, but it is necessary that something in the intrinsic nature of the cause, and something in the intrinsic nature of the effect (along with their spatial and temporal locations) *explain* the causal link between the two.

This is where the small fee that we have to pay to the flow fragmentalist to get the job done shows up. In order for the reductive analysis to work, we have to endorse an account of singular causation that construes the causal link entirely in terms of the intrinsic properties of the cause and the effect. Maybe it is the fact that the cause had certain powers in it (together with its being at a certain spatial and temporal location) that made it the case that it produced an effect with such and such characteristics (and at a certain spatial and temporal location). Or maybe some other story involving the 'productive' nature of the cause and the intrinsic quality of the effect, together with their location in space and time is the correct account. In any case, all we need is that the cause and effect have the 'right' kind of intrinsic properties (and the right spatial and temporal locations).

3.3.2.1 *Events*

Let us now see why the flow fragmentalist is not bedridden by the problems that the presentist has with singularist causation. As a starting point, we need to regiment Fragmentalist Causation a little bit more. Even if we have been liberal with what can be substituted for ϕ and ψ in Fragmentalist Causation, implicitly allowing for having complex expressions involving connectives and embedded tense operators to express causes and effects, it may be wiser to require that any true instance of the scheme in some sense bottoms out in a claim about what presently occurs (respectively, relative to the 'cause' fragment and relative to the 'effect' fragment) that involves only present-tensed properties. Moreover, in order to accommodate singular causation, we need to allow for having not only definite descriptions of causes and effects in them, but also names or labels for events.

Although we want to stay as neutral as possible on the nature of events, and how they relate to other categories such as individuals and facts, we will put down here certain stipulations, to which we will adhere also in the following chapters. First, we will talk of an event as happening at certain time and in a certain place, and as *involving* individuals that have properties and enter relations at that time and place. For each event e, we can thus individuate the individuals x, y, etc. that are involved in it, and the properties that they instantiate at the temporal and spatial locations that they 'share' with e. (We do not make the further assumption that this correspondence is a reductive analysis of the event.) Second, unless otherwise specified, we take event to be temporally minimal, namely instantaneous. There is thus no risk that when talking of an event happening we entail that a cross-temporal external relation (between the individuals involved in it) is instantiated. Instantaneous events can be spatially minimal (i.e. with no spatial extension), and in that case we will talk of *point-like events*. But they can also be spatially maximal. The notion of spatial maximality is more elusive, but to a first approximation we can think of a spatially maximal event as the sum of all the events simultaneous to a given event; roughly, what we have called a Newtonian time t_x (cf. pp. 19, 45).

With these stipulations in place, we will expand on the labelling procedure introduced in section 1.2.2. Convention $\mathfrak{F}$ is apt only to name times and fragments. We can think of a broader strategy, which leaves the outcome of convention $\mathfrak{F}$ intact, while coming with *further* baptisms, which concern instantaneous and spatially minimal *events*. Convention $\mathfrak{F}^e$ expands convention $\mathfrak{F}$ precisely in that way. The idea is to name the events through a system of coordinates $\langle t_x, s_x \rangle$, the first one being a temporal coordinate, and the second one a (three-dimensional) spatial coordinate. Convention $\mathfrak{F}^e$ can be specified as follows: by uttering Baptism' below, one names (i) the occurring snapping of the fingers $e_{t0,\, s0}$, (ii) the time at which it happens t_0 and the spatial location in which it happens s_0, (iii) all times before (t_{-n}) and after (t_{+n}) the time t_0, and all other spatial locations s_x at various distances from s_0 in various direction, (iv) all various events located at those times and locations $e_{tn,\, sx}$, and (v) the various fragments F_n encompassing the all tensed facts that happen at the various times t_n.[22]

Baptism' This (snap of fingers) is $e_{t0,\, s0}$

Unlike convention $\mathfrak{F}$, which allowed us to introduce only names for times and fragments, convention $\mathfrak{F}^e$ allows us to introduce in the official idiom only names for individual events. We can thus restrict our attention to the sentences to be substituted in the metavariables ϕ and ψ in Fragmentalist Causation, that is, sentences of the form 'event $e_{tx,\, sy}$ is happening', which can be formalized as in the scheme Event below.

Event $H(e_{tx,\, sy})$

This is useful to introduce a *pseudo* causal relation that holds between any couple of events that are in the 'right' spatial and temporal position with each other. How to proceed is quite straightforward. We assume, as it seems reasonable, that for each fragment F_x, all events in the class $\{e : e_{tx,\, sx}\}$ are such that $\odot_{F_x} H(e)$ – namely, that the fact that an event e is happening obtains *only* in the fragment whose present time is the time at which e is located. And we assume, trivially, that no label for events introduced with convention $\mathfrak{F}^e$ lacks a referent. The necessary and sufficient condition for the pseudo-relation *causes*$_{ps}$ can be written as Causes$_{ps}$ below.

Causes$_{ps}$ e_C *causes*$_{ps}$ e_E iff there are locations s_C and s_E, and numbers k and x such that $e_C = e_{tk-x, \, sC}$ and $e_E = e_{tk, \, sE}$, and $H(e_E)$ *because*$^k_{Cx}$ $H(e_C)$

Sentences of the form ⌜e_C *causes*$_{ps}$ e_E⌝ do not bring in any of the problems that we saw for the presentist. Direct reference to past entities is not a problem for the flow fragmentalist, since she can talk about what constitutes reality, and constitution is tenseless in Flow Fragmentalism (cf. pp. 44, 56). As for singular propositions, claims of the form ⌜e_C *causes*$_{ps}$ e_E⌝ do not express a relational facts involving e_C and e_E. Rather, they state (by resorting to two singular non-relational propositions) that there is an explanatory relation between what goes on in two different fragments. And as long as the explanatory work is done by nomological facts or facts about the intrinsic nature of the entities involved, their truth does not force the flow fragmentalist to accept irreducible cross-temporal facts. Finally, the relation expressed in Causes$_{ps}$ clearly bears similarity with the relation $<_{ps}$ that we have exploited to order the fragments in Chapter 2. In both cases, the relation does not entail that an external relation is cross-temporally instantiated – that is, that there are cross-temporal facts. For $<_{ps}$ we exploited the overlap between fragments that follows from the theory, whereas for *causes*$_{ps}$ we exploited the explanatory links between facts obtaining in different fragments. Let us then have a closer look to their similarities and differences.

3.4 Temporal successions and causal successions

In section 2.2.2, we have shown as fragments can be ordered in virtue of their partial overlap in the tensed facts that obtain within them. The order that comes out of the construction, $<_{ps}$, is such that the truth-conditions that we have given for the past and future tense operators are vindicated. For instance, given that a sentence such as '$WILL_n \, \phi$' expresses the future-tensed fact that it will be the case that ϕ in n units of time, the truth-condition for the claim that within a fragment F_x, it is the case that $WILL_n \, \phi$, is that within the fragment F_{x+n}, it is the case that ϕ; and *mutatis mutandis* for the past operator 'WAS_n'. And given how we have informally characterized the behaviour of the 'because' connective, it follows also that the direction of the explanation is the same of that of the pseudo-temporal order. Remember that the idea is that the explanatory links are sensitive *only* to (i) the sameness in qualitative profile of the facts, and (ii) the 'harmony' between their tense profiles as encoded in the truth-conditions. Therefore, if within a fragment F_x a future-tensed fact is the case because in a fragment F_y the present-tensed version of the fact is the case, it follows that $F_x <_{ps} F_y$, and *mutatis mutandis* for past-tensed facts.

The order between fragments $<_{ps}$ is global, in the sense that the facts that obtain within a fragment 'fill up' the spatial dimension relatively to that fragment. Remember that fragments are informally thought of as collections of facts that encode what goes on at a 'Newtonian' time, which is a spatially maximal aggregate of simultaneous events (the concrete entities that we labelled $t_1, t_2, \ldots$). But the explanatory chains given by 'because' are inherently local, in the sense that they usually involve facts that are not about the whole spatial dimension. However, even if the explanatory order of the flow is local, it is necessarily constrained by the global order of fragments given by $<_{ps}$. The situation is different for the causal order given by *causes*$_{ps}$ (and thus by *because*$_C$). It is not just that the order derived by it is inherently local, but also that is not constrained by the global order of $<_{ps}$. When introducing '*because*$_{Cx}^m$', we have imposed that m and x are positive numbers strictly greater than zero. This was a simplification, and we did it because it was important to highlight how cross-temporality in the case of causation does not lead to irreducible cross-temporal facts. Simultaneous causation was thus a distraction, which we ruled out by not allowing x to be zero. And so was backward causation, which led us to the assumption that causal connections always point towards the future, namely, that x is never negative. However, in the flow fragmentalist framework per se the global pseudo-temporal order $<_{ps}$ and the local causal order *causes*$_{ps}$ do not have to align. The reason lies in how the explanations of the flow and the causal explanations are differently sensitive to the tense and qualitative profiles of the facts involved. The explanations of the flow are only sensitive to the sameness of the qualitative profiles of the explanans and the explanandum; apart from that (crucial) constraint, the whole explanatory work is done by the right correspondence in their tense profile and their position in the pseudo-temporal order. Causal explanations are thoroughly sensitive to the qualitative profiles of the cause (the explanans) and the effect (the explanandum), in the sense that whether the relation obtains or not crucially depends on their qualitative profiles. It does not fully depend on them though, since there are constraints on the relative spatial and temporal positions of the entities involved, but such constraints are set by the nature of causality, and not by the temporal order in itself.

In the case of the flow explanation, the fact that the explanans of a future-tensed fact lies in the 'future' of the explanandum (and vice versa for past-tensed facts) follows from the very way in which the order of fragments is constructed. In the case of causality, maybe a good theory *of causality* will eventually require that the cause is never simultaneous with the effect, or that it always precedes it, but the way the pseudo-temporal order is constructed per se has not bearings on the positions on it of the cause and the effect. We thus have no reason to think that we should not allow values of *x* that are negative, or the value zero.

Finally, although in its official formulation Flow Fragmentalism takes the causal and temporal order to be metaphysically independent, the framework is flexible enough to articulate other options too. In particular, one can exploit the causal explanatory link to give a causal theory of the temporal order,[23] according something like the following definition:

Causal Theory of Time For some n and m, $H(e_{t_x, s_n})$ $causes_{ps}$ $H(e_{t_y, s_m}) =_{df} F_x <_{ps} F_y$

Of course, causal chains of events are local, and thus there is no guarantee that $<_{ps}$ so defined will have any of the usual properties of the temporal order, such as being irreflexive. If we understand the fragments as informally characterized here, in terms of facts that obtain at a time in a Newtonian context, this will be the case. But of course as soon as we consider relativistic scenarios (see Chapter 4), or frameworks in which backwards causation is possible (see Chapter 5), this will no longer be the case.

Of course, one may actually welcome this situation, and drive the opposite conclusion. Rather than imposing a global order on causality, why don't we 'localize' temporality? Indeed, causal histories can be exploited to define a form of *local passage*. Formally, this is easily done by moving from actual causal connections, as expressed by $causes_{ps}$-claims, to *causal connectivity*. The latter can be expressed by the ancestral of the causal relation, which is defined in the usual way, and for which we will use the symbol '$<_{psc}$'. But rather than developing this option in a classical, Newtonian framework, we do it, in the next chapter, in the more natural context provided by the special theory of relativity.

4

Relativity

Metaphysics is empirically informed, in a minimal sense, when its results do not clash with well-established empirical results. It is well known that tense realism and the idea of an objective present time that comes with it are in contrast with Einstein's theory of special relativity, and the idea that simultaneity is relative to inertial frames of reference. Metaphysicians are aware of the tension, although they do not always choose to face it.[1] It is surely possible to interpret special relativity in a 'deflated' way that does not entail that there is no absolute simultaneity.[2] However, we think that the alternative strategy of adapting one's metaphysics of time to relative simultaneity is methodologically more sound.[3] In this chapter, we present the modifications that Flow Fragmentalism must undergo to make room for frame-dependent simultaneity. We take it as an advantage of our position that these modifications leave the core ideas of non-standard tense realism intact. In section 4.1, we explain in some details what the problem is for the non-standard tense realist. In section 4.2, we discuss Fine's version of relativistic fragmentalism, and point out its 'conventional' aspect, which we argue to be problematic. In section 4.3, we present our version, based on our account of causality (Chapter 3) and the related notion of relativistic pseudo-history; we argue that besides going around the problem of conventionality that Fine's version faces, it has certain independent advantages.

4.1 Time, space and space-time

In line with tense realism in general, both in its standard and non-standard forms, Flow Fragmentalism treats space and time differently. Each fragment can be seen as containing information about the whole temporal dimension and the spatial dimension, namely about what properties are instantiated when and where. But how this information is contained differs in the temporal and spatial cases. The information about the temporal dimension is encoded in metric tensed properties, and the internal relation $<_{ps}$ based on them (cf. section 2.2.2), while information about the spatial dimension is encoded in spatial relations. Now, we have to distinguish between how one can *represent* this information, and what we are saying about the nature of the temporal and spatial dimensions by stating that this information is encoded in the fragments. By introducing a system of coordinates $\langle t_x, s_y \rangle$ to name events e_{t_x, s_y}, (and using sentences of the form ⌜H(e_{t_x, s_y})⌝ to state that e_{t_x, s_y} happens) in Chapter 3 (p. 112), we have elaborated a way to represent the temporal and spatial relations (also in their metric aspect). This way of representing space and time is uniform, in the sense that the temporal and the spatial dimensions are presented as a *space-time*, a manifold whose locations can be identified with point-like events labelled by couples of coordinates. But even if the representation is uniform in this sense, temporal locations do not have the same status as temporal locations in this picture. The issue is not the vexed question whether space and time are a substance that contains the entities located at them, or a system of relations. Rather, the issue is that while the spatial dimension encompasses *bona fide* spatial relations, and thus irreducible spatial facts, there are no irreducible temporal facts in Flow Fragmentalism. The temporal relations between events or temporal locations are reduced to internal relations between the fragments containing them.

For instance, the fact that event e_{t_m, s_x} is k units of time earlier than event e_{t_n, s_y} is analysed in the following terms: (i) $\odot_{F_a}$ H(e_{t_m, s_x}), (ii) $\odot_{F_b}$ H(e_{t_n, s_y}), (iii) $F_a <_{ps} F_b$, and (iv) $|a - b| = k$. Notice that this reduction holds not only for the earlier/later relation, but also for simultaneity. In this picture, whether two events are simultaneous or not is reduced to whether the facts about their happening obtain within the same fragment or not.[4]

This differentiated treatment of space and time may look like a problem once we leave a Newtonian environment and enter a relativistic one. The manifold assumed in the representation of space and time implicit in the naming convention $\mathfrak{F}^e$ has a Newtonian structure in the following sense. We can arbitrarily define different *inertial frames of reference* ($I_1, I_2, \ldots$) on it (this means, roughly, putting the centre of the spatiotemporal coordinate system on any non-accelerating object, and consider it at rest), but temporal distances, and thus which events are simultaneous, will be invariant across frames (while spatial distances will generally vary: it may be that two temporally separated events happen in the same place in one frame of reference, but not in a different frame). In virtue of this feature, a Newtonian space-time manifold has a unique temporal *foliation* of the events in it, namely there is only one way to divide it into hyperplanes of simultaneity, each corresponding to a Newtonian time.

As it is well known, in special relativity space and time get somehow meshed up together.[5] In his seminal article, Fine (2005: 298–307) argues that non-standard forms of tense realism can be more easily expanded into their relativistic counterparts than standard forms can (to put it mildly). Although this is another advantage that non-standard positions share with tense anti-realism, it is not due to Neutrality (cf. p. 20) per se. It is clearly *not* enough to abandon the idea of a unique privileged present to make a theory compatible with special relativity. Consider the handbook version of standard tense anti-realism. According to this view, temporal relations between *times*, conceived as hyperplanes of simultaneity, are fundamental. Although the terminology is not always consistent, let us label it 'the B-theory'. The B-theory is Newtonian, and as incompatible with relativity as standard tense realism, since it is based on the assumption that there are hyperplanes of *absolute* simultaneity. However, one can easily move from the B-theory to what is sometimes called 'the Block view', namely a form of anti-realism according to which temporal relations between *events*, rather than times, are fundamental. The Block view allows for a Newtonian formulation, one in which the temporal relations (earlier/later and simultaneity) are absolute (namely, they are not frame-relative), but it can be easily adapted to a relativistic formulation, in which earlier/later and simultaneity are (non-vacuously)[6] relative to frames of reference. The reason why it can be adapted to a relativistic setting is not merely that it lacks a privileged present time, but also that in its framework, (i) the temporal relations are local, that is, they hold between point-like events rather than hyperplanes (namely, times), and (ii) their metric aspect varies across frames of reference (as spatial distances do).

Analogously, in order to have a relativistic version of Flow Fragmentalism, we need fragments or perspectives that encode information about space and time in a way that is local, and compatible with spatial and temporal relations being (non-vacuously) relative to frames of reference. There are various ways to do that. In what follows, we will first dwell on Fine's original insight, and then articulate the flow fragmentalist version and present some points in its favour.

4.2 Relativistic fragments: solipsism and frame-theoretic conception

As we have just pointed out, by exploiting convention $\mathfrak{F}^e$ to introduce coordinates to name events e_{t_x, s_y}, we have elaborated a way to represent the spatial and temporal information that is encoded in the fragments. Implicit in how we have characterized convention $\mathfrak{F}^{\mathfrak{e}}$ there is the assumption that the names are given on the background of a Newtonian manifold of events. For instance, the fact that a certain event is named e_{t_n, s_m} tells us its location in time (t_n) and space (s_m) in the Newtonian manifold that is encoded in the fragments. Let us now introduce a convention $\mathfrak{F}^{\mathfrak{R}}$ that is based on the assumption that the name of the events are given on the background of a Minkowskian manifold. In a spatiotemporal manifold with a Minkowskian, rather than a Newtonian, structure, there is an absolute spatiotemporal interval d between events or space-time points, but how the interval is 'divided' into spatial and temporal distances depends on the frame of reference that we consider. This means that not only spatial relations, but also temporal relations, and simultaneity in particular, are frame-relative. A Minkowskian manifold, differently from a Newtonian one, can be foliated in more than one way. In particular, for each inertial frame of reference I_x, there is a foliation in hyperplanes of simultaneity relative to which the manifold has a Newtonian structure.

Formulating convention $\mathfrak{F}^{\mathfrak{R}}$ requires certain preliminary technicalities. For our purposes, it is important to know that we can assign to each space-time point a quadruplet of Minkowskian coordinates $\langle x_{n_1}, y_{n_2}, z_{n_3}, k_{n_4} \rangle$, such that from them we can calculate the spatiotemporal interval between any two events e_x, e_y in the manifold and thus their spatial and temporal distances relative to any frame of reference I_n. By moving from $\mathfrak{F}^{\mathfrak{e}}$ to $\mathfrak{F}^{\mathfrak{R}}$ thus, we relativize to frames of reference both spatial and temporal metric information. For instance, if according to $\mathfrak{F}^{\mathfrak{e}}$ event e_{t_1, s_1} and event e_{t_2, s_2} are separated by a temporal distance of $t_1 - t_2$ and by the spatial distance $s_1 - s_2$, this will be the case according to convention $\mathfrak{F}^{\mathfrak{R}}$ only relative to the frame of reference in which $\mathfrak{F}^{\mathfrak{e}}$ was given, but generally different relative to other frames of reference.

Convention $\mathfrak{F}^{\mathfrak{R}}$ can be introduced as follows. By uttering Baptism" below, we label (i) the event of the finger snap (e_{x_0, y_0, z_0, k_0}) and (ii) all other events at the various space-time locations in the Minkowskian coordinate system ($e_{x_{n_1}, y_{n_2}, z_{n_3}, k_{n_4}}$).

Baptism" This (snap of fingers) is e_{x_0, y_0, z_0, k_0}

For simplicity, in what follows, we will use labels of the form ⌜e_x⌝ rather than spelling out the four coordinates, and set $e_0 = e_{x_0, y_0, z_0, k_0}$.[7]

Now, there is nothing particularly interesting in the convention that we have just introduced. Indeed, the technicalities on which it is based are the bread and butter of handbook treatment of special relativity.[8] The philosophically interesting issue is how the information about a Minkowskian manifold represented by it can be encoded in a collection of fragments. In other words, the philosophically interesting question is: what facts constitute the relativistic fragments? And can we still preserve the core insight of non-standard *tense* realism in a relativistic environment? When we introduced convention $\mathfrak{F}^e$ by individuating the event of the finger snap, we thereby also individuated its present time, that is, the hyperplane of absolute simultaneity in which it happens. This was in line with the idea that convention $\mathfrak{F}^e$ is simply 'expanding' convention $\mathfrak{F}$, which we used to label times and name the corresponding fragments, by adding names for events happening in the various fragments. But convention $\mathfrak{F}^\Re$ is not an expansion of the previous two, because – crucially – given that the naming of the events is done on the background of a Minkowskian manifold, there is no *unique* hyperplane of simultaneity of e_0 (or any other named event).

The problem is even worse if we think of how the temporal information is encoded in the fragments in the non-relativistic case: through the metric aspect of the *tensed* facts involved. The problem is that the very idea of tensed fact requires a *perspectival centre* to make sense (cf. section 1.2.2). We said that a collection of tensed facts encodes, along with the temporal (and spatial) information discussed above, a perspectival centre relative to which the temporal distances are given. In the standard framework, this perspectival centre is unique and absolute; in the non-standard framework, each collection of tensed facts has its own perspectival centre. But in both cases the perspectival centre is a Newtonian time. Therefore, our current formulation of Flow Fragmentalism is based on a notion of tense that is not compatible with special relativity. However, while in the standard framework creating a leeway to relax the notion of tense so to make space for frame-relative simultaneity is very difficult (see Fine 2005: 298–307), in the non-standard framework we can think of at least three alternatives for articulating a notion of relativistic fragment.

The first one is to take fragments to be collections of tensed facts that encode a *space-time point* as perspectival centre. We can use the names of the events in convention $\mathfrak{F}^\Re$ to build names for fragments: 'F_{e_1}', 'F_{e_2}', … According to this proposal, roughly, the only facts that obtain within a given fragment F_{e_n} are the facts that follow from the assumption that within F_{e_n}, e_n is happening here and now. We will briefly come back to this version to dismiss it; for now, we put it on the side.

The second one is the *frame-theoretic* conception that Fine favours. According to it, fragments are collections of tensed facts that encode information about the spatial and temporal positions of the events in the Minkowskian manifold given the selection of a frame of reference I_x and a hyperplane of simultaneity in it as its perspectival centre (its 'present'). We have already pointed out that a

Minkowskian space-time can be foliated in ways that correspond to (inertial) frames of reference, and relative to each frame the manifold has a Newtonian structure and thus we can individuate a total order of hyperplanes of simultaneity in it. In order to give a name to fragments in the frame-theoretic conception we postulate that by uttering Baptism" one also names the fragment 'F_{e_0}, I_0', where I_0 is an arbitrary frame, and the hyperplane that is 'present' in the fragment is the one in which e_0 is contained.[9] All other frames get labelled analogously. The result is a bit of redundancy, since for any couple of events e_n and e_m that are simultaneous in a frame I_x, the labels 'F_{e_n}, I_x' and 'F_{e_m}, I_x' will refer to the same fragment; but that is innocuous.

Fine considers only those two options, and favours the second one because he takes the first one to rely on a symmetry between space and time that is somewhat against the spirit of tense realism (2005: 305). The frame-theoretic conception is, as Fine puts it, 'quite remarkable':

> The usual view is that [special relativity] shows space-time to be Minkowskian rather than Newtonian; physical processes are to be seen as taking place within a physical space-time with the structure of Minkowskian rather than Newtonian space-time. But the present view is that what [special relativity] shows to be mistaken is not that space-time is Newtonian but that there is a single space-time. Thus we should picture physical processes as taking place within a plurality of physical space-times, each of them enjoying a common ontology of space-time locations and each of them Newtonian in structure, and yet differing in the spatial and temporal relationships that hold among the space-time locations.
>
> Fine 2005: 306

This frame-theoretic conception of relativistic fragmentalism has been criticized. Roughly, the problem is the following. We can 'translate' the spatial and temporal distances that hold relative to a given frame of reference to those that hold relative to any other. Technically, the translations are possible because the Lorenz transformations hold. Such equations are part of special relativity and are implicit in the Minkowskian structure of space-time. But what are the facts that correspond to those transformations in the frame-theoretic conception, given that each fragment only encodes information about Newtonian structures? Is it legitimate for the frame-theoretic conception to 'inflate' the fragments so to encode also information about the Minkovskian structure? Was not the whole point to call the conception 'remarkable' that it substitutes the idea of a fundamental unique Minkowskian space-time structure with a plurality of

Newtonian ones?[10] We will not engage in this discussion here, because we have a more general worry. The problem with the frame-theoretic conception is that frames of reference are *conventional*, in the sense that the choice between them is arbitrary (from a metaphysical point of view, there may be good pragmatic reasons to choose it, of course). Even if we can think of a frame of reference as somehow given by the body on which it is centred (sometime called 'the observer'), this is just a heuristic to make easier to grasp what kind of spatial and temporal distances hold in the corresponding systems of coordinates. For instance (the example is Newtonian to keep it simple), if we consider a train passing by a station at constant speed, we can talk of the frame of reference of the train and the frame of reference of the station, to distinguish a system of coordinates according to which a certain passenger has been in the same place for the whole trip, and a system of coordinated according to which the same passenger has moved at constant speed for all the trip. However, the truth behind the heuristic is that frames of reference are mere mathematical constructions that do not necessarily capture anything of physical significance. We can define frames of reference that do not correspond to any body moving at a constant motion.[11] But why should reality be fragmented along the lines of conventional options after all? In the next section, we defend a third option, which exploits the treatment of causation in Flow Fragmentalism, in particular of the relation of causal connectivity $<_{psc}$ (see p. 115) to go around the problem of conventionality.

4.3 Relativistic Flow Fragmentalism

The third conception of relativistic fragmentalism is based on the idea that the facts that compose each fragment encode the point of view of a given event along a certain causal chain, or more generally a time like curve, in the space-time manifold.[12] While certain claims about events are true in certain frames and false in others, other claims are *frame invariant*; that is, they are such that their truth status does not vary across frames. Importantly, $because_{C.A.}^{m}$-claims (see p. 109) are *not* frame invariant, since the temporal (and spatial) distance between two events c and e that stand in a causal relation does vary across frames. However, $causes_{ps}$-claims are frame invariant, and thus if an instance of ⌜ϕ $causes_{ps}$ ψ⌝ is true in a frame of reference, it is true with respect to *any* frame of reference. It follows that also true claims of the form ⌜$\phi <_{psc} \psi$⌝ are frame invariant (see p. 115). This is not surprising since the relation of causal connectivity $<_{psc}$ is the counterpart of the *time- or light-like separation* relation in a non-fragmentalist, block universe context. Therefore, while we can say that for any two events e_x, e_y if $e_x <_{psC} e_y$, then $e_x < e_y$, the converse is not guaranteed, since while $<_{psC}$ is frame invariant, the temporal order between events < is not.

Frame invariant features are good candidates for building a notion of relativistic fragment that is not conventional in the above sense, precisely because they are not dependent on an arbitrary choice. However, there is an immediate problem in relying on $<_{psC}$ in doing this. Facts about $<_{psC}$-connections are not invariant in their metric aspect. Even if it is true that if two events are $<_{psC}$-connected in a frame, then they are so connected in every frame, their absolute temporal distance will generally vary across frames. The solution is taking something a little bit more complex as a starting point. First, for ease of exposition, let us make the simplifying assumption that within each fragment the ontology is eternalist (contrary to what we have allowed in section 1.2.3), namely that all the point-like events named by convention $\mathfrak{F}^{\mathfrak{R}}$ exist.

The idea is the following. Call $\mathbb{C}$ the set of all events labelled by convention $\mathfrak{F}^{\mathfrak{R}}$. We can define on it a set $\mathbb{H} = \{h_0, h_1, \ldots\}$ of maximal chains of $<_{psC}$-connected events, which we will call *relativistic pseudo-histories* (or RP-histories, for short) of $\mathbb{C}$. RP-histories are different from the pseudo-histories that we have used to make sense of the indeterminacy of the future (see p. 81). Pseudo-histories are chains of *fragments*, while RP-histories are chains of events. Therefore, RP-histories are *not* spatially maximal like pseudo-histories are. Indeed, given that the events in question are point-like, they are spatially minimal. More generally, the facts about a RP-history will be local rather than global, and because of that, they are frame invariant also in their metric aspect. For instance, consider a RP-history h_0 in which we have events e_1 and e_2, such that $e_1 <_{ps} e_2$. It will be characterized by facts such as that e_1 happens in it, and that it is after (or in the future of) e_2. And those facts are not frame-variant: if it is the case in one frame that event e_1 is in h_0, then that is so relative to every frame. But take another event e_3 that is *not* on h_0. No fact about h_0, not even a relational one, involves e_3. From 'the point of view of' h_0, we cannot say, for instance, that e_3 happens three meters in a certain direction from where e_1 happens. This is so, because facts about things not on h_0 are generally not frame invariant, and what 'happens' to e_3 relatively to h_0 will be generally unsettled unless we fix a frame of reference. This holds also for temporal relations involving events not on h_0. More precisely, if e_3 is space-like separated from an event e_1 on h_0,[13] then not even the temporal order between them will be frame invariant. It may be that in certain frames $e_1 < e_3$ and in others $e_3 < e_1$ or they are simultaneous. While if e_3 is a time-like and light-like separated event not on h_0, the temporal order relative to the events on h_0 is frame invariant. For instance, if e_3 is time-like separated from e_1, then $e_1 < e_3$ relative to one frame, and that will be the case relative to all frames.

However, *metric* facts about temporal (and spatial) distances between events on h_0 and events that are not on h_0 will be always frame-relative, regardless of the kind of separation in question. And this is a crucial difference between facts concerning those events and facts concerning events *on the same RP-history*. For the temporal metric facts concerning events on the same RP-history *are* frame invariant. If two events are k units of time apart from each other with respect to the path that separates them along a given RP-history, then they are so temporally separated no matter what frame of reference we are considering. This is not surprising, given that RP-histories are the counterpart of (maximal) causal paths in the standard framework, and the so-called *proper time* of an object following a causal path is frame invariant in special relativity.

We can exploit this last feature of RP-histories to define a notion of fragment that is not dependent on conventional partitions, and it is based on a relativistic understanding of tense. According to the RP-history based conception, rather than having fragments that correspond to pairs of a reference frame and one of its hyperplane selected as the present time – as in the frame-theoretic version – fragments correspond to pairs of a RP-history and one of its events. A relativistic fragment in this third conception is a collection of facts that are *tensed* in the sense of encoding the perspective from an event on a succession of events – rather than the perspective of a time on a succession of times. Given that temporal distances between events on the same RP-history h_0, relative to h_0 are frame invariant, once we have 'fixed' an event e_0 in it as its perspectival centre, also the metric tensed facts relative to the couple $\langle h_0, e_0 \rangle$ will be frame invariant. For instance, if e_3 is k units of time after e_0, it is frame invariant not only that relative to h_0 e_3 is k units of time after e_0, but also that relative to $\langle h_0, e_0 \rangle$ it will be the case in k units of time that e_3 happens.

It should be clear that we have now all it takes to define relativistic fragments in a way that does not involve conventional elements. In the RP-history based conception, fragments are collections of tensed facts that do not 'partition' reality according to frames of reference, but according to frame-*in*variant elements: RP-histories. In harmony with the RP-history based conception, we name the fragments not through a frame and a time, but through a pseudo-history h_x and an event e_y in it (F_{h_x, e_y}). A relativistic fragment according to Flow Fragmentalism can be thus characterized along the definition below.

Relativistic Fragment$_{FF}$ A relativistic fragment F_{h_x, e_y} is the collection of tensed facts that ϕ such that it is frame invariant that it is the case that ϕ relative to $\langle h_{x, e_y} \rangle$

In order to formulate the theory we need an object language that is richer than $\mathcal{L}^{+\odot}$. Let us call $\mathcal{L}^{\Re}$ a language that is like $\mathcal{L}^{+\odot}$ but instead of the 'old' $\odot_{F_n}$ operators, contains 'within fragment' operators indexed to the relativistic version of fragments that we have introduced above. $\mathcal{L}^{\Re}$, thus, contains sentences of the form $\ulcorner \odot_{F_{h_x, e_y}} \phi \urcorner$. If ϕ is an atomic claim formalizing a present tense sentence, $\odot_{F_{h_x, e_y}} \phi$ is true if and only if the fact that ϕ is in F_{h_x, e_y}. More complex cases, in particular cases with future and past tense operators, require more elaboration and can be put aside here.

Each RP-history based fragment has its 'local present'. We can thus group the fragments in classes of fragments that share the same RP-history, but differ in the event at their centre. Within each class we can order the fragments according to the pseudo-temporal relation $<_{ps}$. For every RP-history h_k we can thus define an ordered sequence of fragments $F_{h_k, e_1}, F_{h_k, e_2}, \ldots$, which we call $R <_{ps}$-sequence, as follows.

$R <_{ps}$-sequence An $R <_{ps}$-sequence of a RP-history h_k is a sequence of fragments (ordered by $<_{ps}$) such that, for every pair of events e_x and e_y within fragment F_{h_k, e_x}, event e_x is present, and event $e_y < e_x$ if and only if $F_{h_k, e_y} <_{ps} F_{h_k, e_x}$

The fact that *each* event along a RP-history is a perspectival centre of a fragment along a $R <_{ps}$-sequence is a consequence of the relativistic counterpart of the principle of Neutrality (cf. p. 127). Whereas in the non-relativistic case each time along the temporal dimension is the perspectival centre of a corresponding fragment, in the relativistic case each event along a RP-history is a perspectival centre of a corresponding fragment. However, while in the pre-relativistic case each fragment has a centre on a global perspective, in the RP-history based case the perspective is restricted to a causal path and what is frame invariant with respect to it.[14] The various sequences of fragments that share the same RP-history, thus, can partially overlap and can criss-cross one another at more than one point. Let us see what exactly are the consequences of this fact.

4.3.1 Crossing paths

As we have just pointed out, in the non-relativistic version of Flow Fragmentalism, the fragments are both temporally and *spatially* maximal. In each fragment we find presently obtaining facts not only about any time in the past and the future, but also any location in space. This feature makes them suitable to play the role of semantic points of evaluation, akin to possible worlds in more traditional semantic frameworks. In the RP-history based conception of fragments, that is not the case. Given that within each fragment there are locations in space and in time about which no fact obtains, as semantic points of evaluations for propositions, stories are 'gappy'. More precisely, for each fragment $F_{h_x,\, e_y}$, any claim about things that do not happen along the RP-history h_x is indeterminate. Apart from some non-metric information in the time- and light-like separation case (see p. 123–4), from the point of view of a fragment $F_{h_x,\, e_y}$, we cannot say of an event that is spatially far away from any of the events on h_x when or where it happens. More generally, there is no guarantee that any two RP-histories will be 'synchronized'. RP-histories can overlap, and many of them will do it in various points, but in general there will not be facts of the matter about the temporal distance of two *distinct* events on two different RP-histories.[15]

However, it is always possible to say *relative to a certain RP-history and an event on it* what facts obtain. This is particularly interesting in the case of crossing paths, namely when two RP-histories overlap on at least one event. In such cases, even if the two RP-histories, h_1 and h_2 say, share an event e_0 as perspectival centre, they do not share the same 'local present'. This is so, because the fragment in which the event e_0 is present in the $R <_{ps}$-sequence corresponding to h_1, namely $F_{h_1,\, e_0}$, is different from the fragment in which e_0 is present in the $R <_{ps}$-sequence corresponding to h_2, namely $F_{h_2,\, e_0}$. Although there are no facts about events in h_2 other than e_0 in $F_{h_1,\, e_0}$ (assuming h_1 and h_2 cross paths only once), we can always state what is the case within $F_{h_2,\, e_0}$, even if we are located in $F_{h_1,\, e_0}$. Relativistic neutrality goes not only up and down along RP-histories, but also sideways across RP-histories, as it were.

It is important to notice that, analogously to the non-relativistic case (cf. section 1.1.3), by allowing sentences of the form ⌜$\odot_{F_{h_x,\, e_y}} \phi$⌝ we are *not* thereby introducing a further kind of fact. As there are not 'indexed' facts in the pre-relativistic case, there are also no facts that are 'indexed' to a history (and an event on it) in the relativistic one. For instance, by stating that $\odot_{F_{h_m,\, e_n}} \phi$, we are not expressing a fact. Although it may be tempting to think of this expression as analogous with the tenseless expression of an internally relative fact (cf. section 0.4), such as the fact that *Socrates is sitting at t*, one should resist the temptation. We are simply *stating* something of the (tensed) fact that ϕ; namely we are stating that it obtains within the fragment that we have labelled $F_{h_m,\, e_n}$.

The fact that RP-history based fragments are local, but the non-standard framework permits of a form of Neutrality among them, brings in certain advantages. Think of the twin paradox, as a scenario in which two paths cross each other more than once. Martha and Nicole are two twins that have lived all their lives very close to each other, so that we can say that they have shared a RP-history up to a certain event e_1, which is the departure of Nicole for an intergalactic trip to Alpha Centauri and back. Fig. 6 shows the so-called worldlines of Martha and Nicole, roughly the sequence of $<_{ps}$-related events that form their respective lives. Each worldline of an object individuates a class of RP-histories, those corresponding to all those histories that contain the worldline. Among the events constituting the lives of Martha and Nicole, Fig. 6 shows e_1, the moment of the departure of Nicole; e_2, the event of Nicole's reaching the midway point of her exciting trip, Alpha Centauri; and e_3, her reunion with the beloved sister, Martha.

As the story goes, when Nicole left the twins were both twenty-five years old, but when they reunite in e_3 Nicole is only twenty-nine, while Martha is forty-five. In the flow fragmentalist account, we should say that even if they occupy roughly the same spatiotemporal location of e_3 they do not share a fragment. If we call h_{Martha} the RP-history that includes all of Martha's life (i.e. worldline) and an arbitrary continuation before her birth and after her death, and *mutatis mutandis* we do the same for h_{Nicole}, we can say that Martha is in F_{h_{Martha}, e_3} while Nicole is in F_{h_{Nicole}, e_3}. Although, considering e_3 as perspectival centre, there are no facts about Nicole's journey to Alpha Centauri obtaining within Martha's fragment, and there are no facts about Martha's life on Earth on Nicole's, Martha can state what

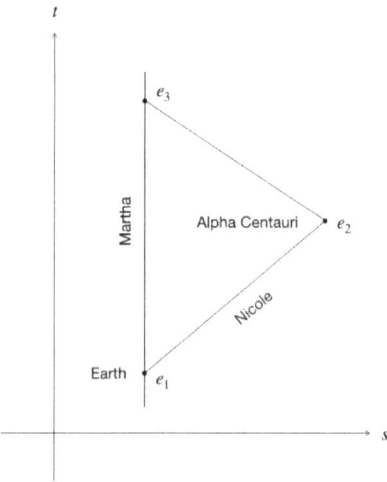

Figure 6 Twin paradox scenario.

was the case relative to Nicole's path and vice versa. For instance, Martha can truly say that last time they met it was sixteen years ago, although Nicole has lived only for four years since then, and Nicole can truly say that last time they met it was four years ago, although Martha has lived for sixteen years since then. Note, moreover, that although the two fragments centred on e_3 disagree on many 'historical' facts like the two just mentioned, they overlap in all the present-tensed facts, such as the fact that Martha's clock disagrees with Nicole's clock, and the facts concerning the age-status (wrinkles, white hair, memories, etc) of their bodies.

It is difficult to see how one can get this result in the frame-theoretic conception of relativistic fragmentalism. Even if there is an *inertial* frame of reference in which relative to e_3 last time that Nicole met Martha was four years ago, it is plausibly not one that tracks anything *physically significant* for Nicole (or Martha). It is only relative to Nicole's worldline (and the event of the sororal reunion), namely it is only with respect to Nicole's proper time that it makes sense to say that relative to e_3, they last met four years ago. The same goes for Martha's life and the fact that she has not met her sister for sixteen years, at least if she has not inhabited an inertial frame for the whole time. This is a consequence of the fact that RP-history based fragments cut reality according to frame-invariant directives, as it were, as the proper time of an object along its worldline, which is what a RP-history mimics.

Finally, a defendant of the frame-theoretic conception could counter-object by making a *tu quoque* point. Perhaps our theory is better at capturing facts about diverging worldlines, but it leaves entirely ungrounded facts about the spatial and temporal relations between space-like separated events, in the sense that there is no RP-history based fragment within which such facts obtain. This is correct. Indeed, such facts are not frame-invariant, not even if we specify a RP-history. It is merely relative to *frames* that we can establish the spatial and temporal distances in question. But, as we have stressed, the choice of a frame of reference is *conventional* in a relativistic setting. It seems therefore to us that it is a good result that according to our theory there is no ground for such facts, beside conventional decisions. We will finish this chapter by discussing how to make sense of our explanation of the flow in a relativistic setting.

4.3.2 Relativistic flow

When we have provided the core tenet of the theory of passage that we are defending in this book, we have done so in the background of a Newtonian, non-relativistic context and convention $\mathfrak{F}$. To repeat, the idea is to describe the 'harmonic behaviour' of the tensed facts throughout the fragments in terms of explanatory links across them. The past- and future-tensed facts within each fragment, the facts that are about temporal locations that are not the present of the fragment in question are explanatorily dependent on the present-tensed facts that we find in other fragments. And those links are the push (from the past) and the pull (from the future) that *constitute* the flow of time (cf. section 1.1.4.5). Formally, the thesis is that for any x and $n \neq 0$ and some ϕ, Fragmentalist Flow (repeated below) holds.

Fragmentalist Flow $\odot_{F_x} TENSE_n \phi$ because $\odot_{F_{(n+x)}} \phi$

Once we move to a relativistic context and convention $\mathfrak{F}^{\mathfrak{R}}$, those pushes and pulls can no longer be *global*. It cannot be that past- and future-tensed facts obtaining at a time are explanatorily dependent on present-tensed facts that obtain at different times simply because facts no longer obtain *at a time* in this context. More precisely, the fragments F_{h_x, e_y} labelled by convention $\mathfrak{F}^{\mathfrak{R}}$ are collections of facts that are about the events along a given relativistic pseudo-history h_x and their tensed status depends on their distance, along h_n, from the 'present' of the fragment e_y. The explanatory links are thus *restricted* to the events of each relativistic pseudo-history. The thesis of the fragmentalist flow in its relativistic version can be expressed as follows: for any h_x, and numbers y and $n \neq 0$, and some ϕ, Fragmentalist Flow$_R$ below holds.

Fragmentalist Flow$_R$ $\odot_{F_{h_x, e_y}} TENSE_n \phi$ because $\odot_{F_{h_x, e_{(y+n)}}} \phi$ [16]

In a universe that is relativistic and contains robust passage, the flow of time is given by the fact that from the perspective of each event relative to a relativistic pseudo-history, there is a push from the past and a pull from the future that explain how reality is updated. And such an update is no longer global, as in the non-relativistic case, but relative to time-like spatiotemporal paths. Quite clearly, the relativistic, local version of the flow invites a reductive reading of the temporal flow in terms of local causal connectivity, along the lines suggested above (cf. p. 115). We will leave the suggestion for further work, and finish the chapter by explaining how we can drop the simplifying assumption that we have made, to the effect that each fragment's ontology is an eternalist one (cf. p. 124).

Whether the flow fragmentalist endorses a causal theory or not, there is a problem with the idea of a relativistic and local *pseudo*-temporal order. The point came out already when we quoted Fine (2005) stating that the various fragments 'enjoy . . . a common ontology of space-time locations' (p. 306). Fine there was discussing the frame-theoretic version of relativistic fragmentalism, but why should one think that it is any different for the RP-history based version? Of course, if the point is simply that facts about the various temporal and spatial locations constitute reality in an absolute manner, we are not denying it. But the idea here seems to be that within each fragment, the same facts about the existence of the various locations in space and time obtain. This claim clashes against the idea that we should leave open the option according to which the ontology within each fragment is limited by the facts about simple existence concerning the entities that are located at its perspectival centre (cf. section 1.2.3). In a relativistic setting, in the case of the RP-history based conception, the perspectival centre is an event along a given causal chain of events, while in the case of the frame-theoretic version, it is the hyperplane of simultaneity that is 'present' within the fragment.

We do not deny that a version of Flow Fragmentalism that has an eternalist ontology within each fragment is a very 'natural' option in a relativistic setting. This is why making the simplifying assumption that each fragment has an eternalist ontology has facilitated the exposition enormously. If we follow this route, we can define the various $R <_{ps}$-sequences as we did above in terms of the temporal relation < between events on a given RP-history (p. 126). However, the eternalist option is not forced upon the flow fragmentalist. Alternatively, one can 'inflate' the ideological commitment of the theory.

Let us begin by considering RP-histories as primitive. For each h_n, we have a sequence of events related by $<_{ps}$ (and thus by < in the same way; cf. p. 124). Let us now take the various collections of facts that correspond to each event in h_x according to the definition Relativistic Fragment$_{FF}$ above. We now have two ways of individuating the $R <_{ps}$-sequence of fragments corresponding to h_n. One is to use the order of the events in h_x, as we did above. Another is to look at the 'at least' facts in each of the $F_{hn, \, ey}$ fragments (where h_n is constant), and define the order on the basis of their overlap, along the lines of section 2.2.2. It is obvious that in both cases, we need the information that the events along the RP-history constitute a time-like curve in a Minkowski space-time to be encoded in the fragments. However, we do not need this information to be encoded in the spatiotemporal relations between events of space-time. In the non-relativistic case, fragments are collections of tensed facts that play both the role of temporal location (by encoding information about the perspectival centre of the facts) and the role of temporal perspective (by encoding information about how other locations are from the point of view of that centre). The tense anti-realist's commitment to a temporal dimension constituted by temporal locations and external relations between them is traded for a commitment to metric tensed facts and global collections thereof. In the relativistic case, we need something more, because the collections in question (the fragments) are no longer global, and thus we need the information of how they partition the global space somehow encoded in the fragments themselves. In other words, we need a further commitment to pluralities of metric tensed facts that correspond to frame-invariant RP-histories. And given that, once we drop the simplifying assumption, we cannot individuate the RP-histories in terms of the temporal or causal relations between events, we need to take the collections of fragments that correspond to them as primitively individuated. The most natural option in the context of Flow Fragmentalism is to take the various $\odot_{F_{h_x, e_y}}$ as what does the job. As part of the official idiom of the theory, such operators allow us to make metaphysically cogent claims. Even though we do *not* take them as expressing facts of a certain kind (facts 'indexed' to histories), we take them as stating something about the facts involved that cannot be reduced to anything more fundamental. Namely, we take claims of the form $\ulcorner \odot_{F_{h_x, e_y}} \phi \urcorner$ to state that the fact that ϕ is about a certain local partition of tensed facts, that is, the pseudo-history h_x and the event e_y in it.

5

Time Travel

Time travel is a fairly recent, yet well-established topic of philosophical interest. Making sense of time travel scenarios is a good test for a view on the nature of time. First, certain types of time travel seem to be nomologically (although not technologically) possible, and thus a metaphysics that rules them out a priori may be charged of being too remote from empirical sciences to be of interest.[1] Second, even if other types of time travel pertain exclusively to science fiction, a philosophical reflection about time should still be able to say something interesting about such 'thought experiments'.[2] At any rate, Flow Fragmentalism, as we have seen at the end of Chapter 3, is committed to the claim that the temporal flow and the causal flow can (at least at the level of metaphysical possibility) part company. If so, Flow Fragmentalism allows for backwards causation, namely causal chains that run against the direction of the flow of time. But backwards causation is, or it is strictly connected to, time travel. Therefore, an account of time travel should be part of the flow fragmentalist's grand view on the nature of time. In this chapter, we will provide one.

In section 5.1, we discuss the case of Novikovian time travel, which is illustrative and can easily be accommodated in the flow fragmentalist universe. In section 5.2, we move to the non-Novikovian scenarios, in which, as a consequence of the time travel, the past is changed. We will see that they are problematic in particular with respect to how the flow fragmentalist construcs the flow of time. In section 5.3, we propose a solution, which comes with a cost: articulating what we call a 'tracking role' for times, beside their more customary location and perspective roles. In section 5.4, we discuss the standard view of non-Novikovian time travel, and argue that also standard positions have to accept a tracking role for times.

5.1 Novikovian time travel

What is time travel in a flow fragmentalist framework? Recall the two explanatory links to which Flow Fragmentalism is committed in order to account for the flow of time and causal successions, respectively. First, we have the link expressed by the 'because' connective in the account of the fragmentalist flow (p. 40).

Fragmentalist Flow $\odot_{F_x} TENSE_n \phi$ because $\odot_{F_{(n+x)}} \phi$

Roughly, Fragmentalist Flow says that if now the fact that – say – tomorrow I will go to the beach obtains, it is so because in the future reality will contain the fact that I am going to the beach. And crucially, it says so in the context of Neutrality, the thesis according to which *no* fragment is privileged. As we have put it, each fragment receives a push from the 'past ones' and a pull from the 'future ones'. Scare quotes are due because the fragments are not ordered through the ordinary earlier/later relation, but through the pseudo-temporal relation $<_{ps}$ that expresses the structure of their partial overlap (see section 2.2.2).

Second, we have the causal link expressed by '*because*$_C$' (p. 106), which is used in causal explanations involving events that happen in different fragments, such as in (semi-formal) claims like (1) below.

(1) $\odot_{F_m} e_E$ is happening *because*$_C$ $\odot_{F_n} e_C$ is happening

In the previous chapter, we have assumed that $n < m$, namely that the fragment in which the cause is presently happening is 'after' the fragment where the effect is presently happening. If we drop that assumption, backwards time travel becomes possible. In the jargon of the view, time travel happens when $F_x <_{ps} F_y$, and fragment F_y contains causes whose effects are in F_x.

This idea squares with the general philosophical understanding of time travel. According to David Lewis (1976), who initiates the philosophical tradition of time travel in analytic philosophy, time travel requires a 'discrepancy between time and time' (p. 145). More precisely, a discrepancy between *external time* and the *personal time* of the traveller. Roughly, external time is just the global succession of times, and personal time is the local succession of events that constitute the worldline (the life) of the traveller. In the flow fragmentalist framework, we can identify external time with the succession of fragments as ordered by $<_{ps}$, and personal time as the succession of events, located in different fragments, that constitute the causal history of the life of the traveller, namely that compose the life of the traveller and are linked by *because*$_C$-connections.[3] Normally, namely when time travel does not happen, external time and the various personal times are one and the same. If an event e_x comes after an event e_y in external time, that is, if e_x is future with respect to e_y, things are so in every personal time, and if the two events are separated by n time units in external time, things are so in every personal time. We have then time travel every time that this is no longer the case, namely if there is a discrepancy between external time and the personal time of the traveller. Putting on the side time travel towards the future, a backwards time travel scenario is one in which the personal time of the traveller goes in the opposite direction than external time. For instance, the event departure to the past is in fragment F_m, the event arrival into the past is in fragment F_n, the two events are such that the first happens *because*$_C$ the second happens, and yet $F_m <_{ps} F_n$.

One thing that could happen if causal links can go backwards with respect to the flow of time is... not much. This is the case if only Novikovian (or Ludovician, as it is sometimes called) time travel is possible.[4] Roughly, a time travel scenario is Novikovian if we can tell the story of how it happened in a way that is coherent in a 'normal' block universe. In other words, Novikovian coherence requires that the time traveller will be doing, in the future of her personal time, *exactly* what happened in the past of external time, and more generally the events that happen as a consequence of the trip to the past have to be among the ones that happened in that very past. The traveller has then partly affected the past, in the sense that it is among the causes of what happened then, but she has not *changed* the past.[5] Suppose Dr Who activates the time machine in 2024 to go back to Piccadilly Circus in 1960. It is very tempting to reason as follows. Surely in 1960 Dr Who was not in Piccadilly Circus. Therefore, by activating the time machine he must have created a 'second' 1960. But we do not *need* to arrive at that conclusion, *if* a time machine popped out of thin air in Piccadilly Circus in 1960 in the first place! Novikovian time travel is metaphysically (and arguably also nomologically) possible without fancy business – apart from backwards causation.

In a flow fragmentalist framework, Novikovian time travel is as unproblematic as it is in an eternalist block universe. What we need to have backwards causation is to drop the assumption that the fragment in which the event cause e_C happens is always earlier, in the pseudo-temporal order, than the fragment in which the event effect e_E happens. Let us see more closely how we can represent explicitly a time travel scenario in Flow Fragmentalism. The representation that we develop in this section contains, in a sense, many redundancies, but it will become clear when we pass from the Novikovian to the non-Novikovian case that they constitute necessary detours. In order to keep the exposition as linear as possible, we will make two simplifying assumptions, which we drop later on. First, we assume that within each fragment eternalism is true (cf. section 1.2.3). Second, we assume that the pseudo-temporal order of fragment given by $<_{ps}$ is primitive; that is, it is not derived from the overlap among fragments (cf. section 2.2.2).

Now, recall the distinction between the *location*-role and the *perspective*-role of times that we made since the Introduction (p. 11). A fragment is the collection of tensed facts that 'tells' us how the temporal dimension, that is, the order of temporal locations, is like from a particular perspectival centre. When we say that within fragment F_0 the fact that *Petunia ate bell peppers yesterday* obtains, we are stating how a temporal location (t_{-1}, say) is like from the temporal perspective centred on the present of the fragment F_0 (t_0, say). More precisely, we are saying something about (i) the *content profile* of t_{-1}, namely that it contains the event of a guinea pig eating, and (ii) the *tense* profile that t_{-1} has from the perspective of t_0, namely that of being one day in the past. In general, the content profile of a temporal location (in a given fragment) is constituted by the entities that are located at it, and the properties in the qualitative profile of the facts (cf. p. 53–4) in which they are involved. The tense profile of a temporal location is the A-property that it exemplifies. Note that the content profile of a temporal location t_x at least partially depends on the causal links in which the entities located at t_x enter. Think again of the example of Petunia eating lettuce. The fact that the eating event is part of the content of that temporal location is a consequence of certain causal antecedents, such as Petunia becoming hungry, and me getting the vegetable out of the fridge and near her. To the contrary, the tense profile of a temporal location depends only on its position relative to the time that is present within the fragment.

Let us introduce a way to represent graphically the content and tense profiles of the series of temporal locations that constitute the temporal dimension in each fragment. Firstly, we need to coordinate talk of fragments, perspectives, and locations. We will call F_x the collection of tensed facts that gives us the content and tense profiles of the temporal dimension and in which t_x is present. What we call F_x, we also call perspective x, or the perspective centred on t_x. We can represent the content and tense profile of each location in the temporal dimension as they are in the various fragments ordered by $<_{ps}$ through the combination of a perspective coordinate and a location coordinate $\langle x, y \rangle$, as in Fig. 7.[6] The numbers on the horizontal axes give us the number x of the perspective that is represented in the corresponding vertical line, which is thus a representation of the tensed facts in fragment F_x. The numbers on the vertical axis give us the index y of the content profile of a temporal location t_y. Thus, the corresponding horizontal line tells us how that location is from the standpoint of the various perspectives.

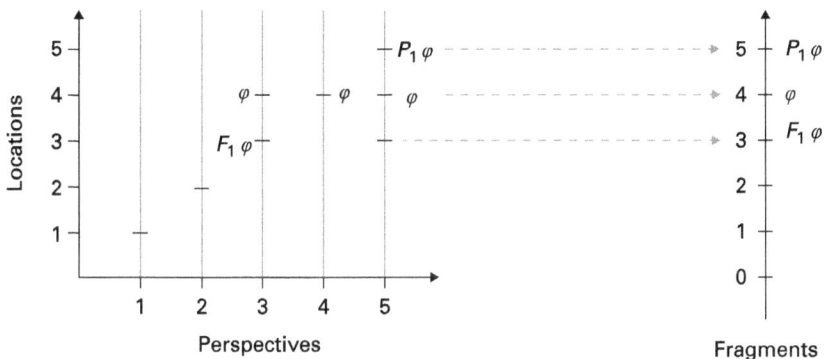

Figure 7 An 'expanded' representation of fragments though a system of (perspective, location) coordinates, and its 'compressed' version as a sequence of fragments.

This 'expanded' representation of the fragments through a system of coordinates is redundant in two ways. First, in the representation of the facts that constitute a given fragment that we have along the vertical lines, writing ϕ at coordinate $\langle 3, 4 \rangle$ is merely a *notational variant* of writing $F_1 \phi$ at coordinate $\langle 3, 3 \rangle$. Both represent the future-tensed fact that ϕ will be the case in one unit of time, which obtains within fragment F_3 (or from the perspective of t_3). To the contrary, writing ϕ at $\langle 4, 4 \rangle$ is *not* a notational variant of writing $F_1 \phi$ at coordinate $\langle 3, 3 \rangle$, since it is a way to say that the present-tensed fact that ϕ obtains within fragment F_4 (or from the perspective of t_4). Second, the content profile of a temporal location does *not* change across fragments. Therefore, the horizontal lines represent the same content many times over. One way to see this double redundancy is to notice that the expanded representation of the temporal dimension that we have on the left in Fig. 7 can be 'compressed' in the sequence of fragments that is represented on the right in the same picture.

In order to accommodate a Novikovian time travel story as the one of Dr Who going back to London, 1960 and doing exactly what he did, we just need two things. First, the fragment centred on the time in 1960 in which the Tardis (Dr Who's time machine) pops out of thin air in Piccadilly Circus has a content profile that is partially caused by events that are in the future, namely that are located at times that are perspectives of 'later' fragments – such as the turning on of the time machine in 2024, as in the (semi-formal) explanation (2). (Remember that the content profile of a temporal location t_x depends, at least in part, on the causal links that involve the entities that are located at t_x.)

(2) $\odot_{F_{1960}}$ The Tardis appears in Piccadilly Circus *because*$_C$ $\odot_{F_{2024}}$ Dr Who activates the Tardis

Second, that the tense profile of 1960 and 2024 'behaves' in accordance with the explanation of the flow that we have given, namely with Fragmentalist Flow above. This means that how the temporal location 2024 is from the perspective of 1960 and how the temporal location 2024 is from the perspective of 1960 has to 'harmonize', as in the (semi-formal) explanations (3) and (4) below.

(3) $\odot_{F_{1960}}$ It will be the case in sixty-four years that Dr Who activates the Tardis because $\odot_{F_{2024}}$ It is the case that Dr Who activates the Tardis

(4) $\odot_{F_{2024}}$ It was the case sixty-four years ago that the Tardis appears in Piccadilly Square because $\odot_{F_{1960}}$ It is the case that that the Tardis appears in Piccadilly Square

It is easy to see that in the expanded representation of fragments this would require merely that certain causal links go 'downwards' in a direction that is opposite to that of the flow encoded in the explanatory links of claims such as (3) and (4). But as long as the tensed profile of the facts along the pseudo-temporal order of fragments is 'harmonic', the picture is basically the same as the one in which *no* time travel happens at all. Fig. 8 shows the relevant facts and links in the case of a Novikovian time travel. Dr Who leaves with Tardis in $\langle 4, 4 \rangle$, which we can assume is some day in 2024, and arrives in London in $\langle 3, 3 \rangle$, which we can assume is some day in 1960. Those two events are described by ϕ an ψ respectively.[7] Accordingly, we have that within the fragment of the perspective 3,

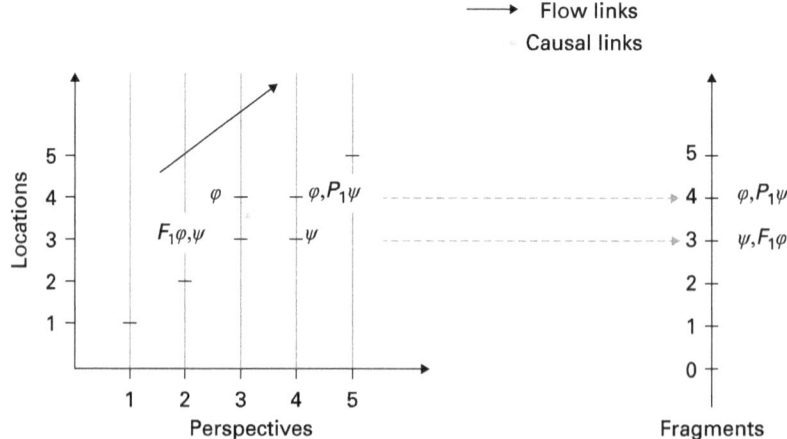

Figure 8 Novikovian time travel.

in which Tardis arrives in Piccadilly Circus, the fact that the Doctor will live in sixty-four years obtains, and within the fragment of the perspective 4, in which the Doctor leaves, the fact that sixty-four years before Tardis arrived in Piccadilly Circle obtains.

Novikovian time travel is all nice and clean,[8] and it can be fun too.[9] But what if the Tardis was *not* in Piccadilly Circus in 1960 and Dr Who nonetheless activates the time machine in 2024? Then we *do* need fancy metaphysical business and a 'second' 1960 of some sort to be around. In order to accommodate non-Novikovian time travel scenario we (and it is a universal 'we'; it is not restricted to flow fragmentalists) have to tweak the structure of the temporal dimension. Let us see how the flow fragmentalist can do it.

5.2 Changing the past: the problem

On a first thought, it may seem that in order to accommodate non-Novikovian time travel it suffices to give a more liberal interpretation of the two roles – location and perspective – that times can play. What we need is to allow for the possibility that what happens at a temporal location t_x from the perspective of a time t_y is *different* from what happens at the same location t_x from a different temporal perspective t_k.[10] In a non-Novikovian scenario, the content profile of a temporal location t_x changes across temporal perspectives as its tense profile normally does. Maybe from the perspective of 2021, in 1912 the *Titanic* sank. But if someone builds a time machine and in 2050 goes back to 1912 and manages to avoid the collision with the iceberg, from the perspective of times after 2050, in 1912 the *Titanic* did not sink. We will argue that being more liberal with respect to what can change in the content of a temporal location from the perspective of another time *means* to accept a further role for times. In order to see why, let us begin with a more elaborate example.

In the Episode 'Time Squared' of *Star Trek: The Next Generation*,[11] Captain Picard and his crew are exploring a region of space with their starship *Enterprise* when they find a shuttle adrift in space. Inside the shuttle there is a comatose individual who looks very much like Picard himself. For reasons that will be apparent soon, let us call him *Future Picard* to distinguish him from his 'twin', the perfectly conscious *Present Picard*. After a discussion between Present Picard and the chief medical officer of the ship, Dr Pulaski, Future Picard is confined to the infirmary where he remains unconscious. Two members of the crew, Gordie La Forge and Commander Data, analyse the shuttle and its logs, and discover that is from six hours in the future. They also discover that it has left the *Enterprise* in its journey towards the past just before the *Enterprise* got destroyed by an energy vortex. The crew begins to discuss what to do. They decide to go ahead as planned, but they end up caught in a mysterious energy vortex. While Present Picard debates with the others what to do, in the infirmary Future Picard regains consciousness, escapes and reaches the shuttle. Warned by Dr Pulaski, Present Picard runs to the cargo bay and confronts Future Picard, who wants to take the shuttle into the vortex again, as he did six hours before. Present Picard wants to try another course of action, because he thinks his 'twin' is not lucid. Present Picard attempts to stop him, and in the altercation, Future Picard is killed. Present Picard decides to take the whole *Enterprise*, and not just the shuttle into the vortex. His guess was correct. By entering the vortex with the starship, Present Picard changes the past. The *Enterprise* exits the vortex intact, while the shuttle and the corpse of Future Picard vanish in thin air.

We can summarize the events as shown in the episode as follows.

1. Future Picard is found comatose in a shuttle adrift in space.
2. Geordie and Data discover that the shuttle is from six hours in the future, and that it has left the *Enterprise* just before it got destroyed by an energy vortex.
3. The *Enterprise* gets caught into an energy vortex.
4. Future Picard wakes up and tries to enter the vortex with the shuttle.
5. Present Picard kills Future Picard and takes the *Enterprise* into the vortex.
6. The past is changed: Future Picard and the shuttle disappear and the *Enterprise* exits the vortex intact.

If we take the moment in which the *Enterprise* enters the vortex as a turning point in the narrative, we can distinguish a 'former' past and a 'new' past. Although the details about the 'former' past are unclear, we know that in it the *Enterprise* was destroyed, while in the 'new' past it is not. We can draw a diagram of the story as in Fig. 9. The fact that the *Enterprise* is destroyed by the vortex is expressed by ϕ, which obtains at $\langle 3, 3 \rangle$. The fact that Picard enters the vortex in a shuttle is expressed by ψ, which obtains at $\langle 4, 4 \rangle$. As the backwards causal link indicates, the latter fact has as effect that the *Enterprise* is *not* destroyed. And thus, while at $\langle 4, 3 \rangle$ ϕ 'still' holds, at $\langle 5, 3 \rangle$ $\neg \phi$ holds. The past from the perspective of 3 and from the perspective of 5 is *different*. In particular, the content profile of the temporal location t_3 has changed from containing the destruction of the *Enterprise* to having the *Enterprise* ready for the next adventure.

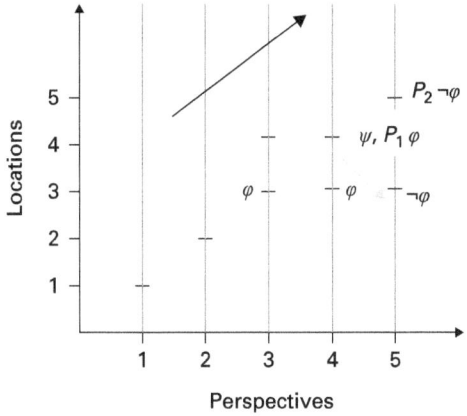

Figure 9 Non-Novikovian time travel. First attempt.

Now, it seems that we can tell the story by only appealing to the perspective and the location coordinates. So in which sense is a *further* role for times required? This is our reply. First, the perspective role has been 'enriched' by moving from the Novikovian to the non-Novikovian case, and in a sense that is enough to acknowledge that the perspective parameter, as originally intended, is no longer sufficient. In a non-Novikovian scenario, the perspective coordinate tells us not only how the tense profiles of the locations are, but also what theirs content profiles are. It tells us not only how distant from the centre of the perspective the various past and future events are, but also *what* those events are from the perspective of the time in question. As a consequence, the location coordinate in the representation of the content of a fragment *is no longer redundant*, and we can no longer 'compact' the succession of vertical lines along the x axis of the diagram in a sequence of fragments. Fig. 10 illustrates that, by showing how the content of a temporal location does not remain constant along the y axis. Compacting the diagram in a sequence of fragments is impossible without either losing information or ending up with incoherent fragments.

Second, we think there are good reasons to explicitly assign a further parameter to the piece of information concerning how the content profiles of the locations are, rather than inflate the prospective parameter, which keeps thus being limited to the piece of information concerning how the tense profiles of the locations in the temporal dimension are. The main reason to make room for an explicit further parameter is a desideratum that we think tense realist accounts of time travel should respect. In the end of this section, we will spell out the

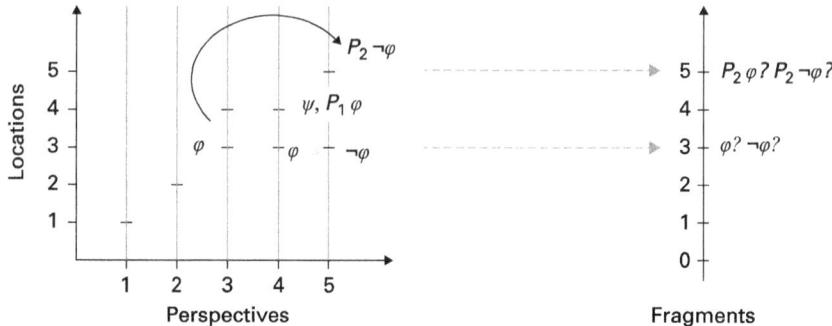

Figure 10 The problem with the first attempt: incoherent fragments.

desideratum, and argue that for the flow fragmentalist is particularly important to respect it. In the next section, we will explain how to respect it through the introduction of what we will call the tracking parameter, and a suitable metaphysical interpretation of it.

In a nutshell, the desideratum is not to allow for pasts that *have never been present*. There is an obvious reading of the diagrams in which we have summarized the Star Trek episodes above in which this is the case, and thus the desideratum is not respected. Although there is a perspective, namely 5, in which at the temporal location t_3 the *Enterprise* exited the vortex safe and sound, there is *no* temporal perspective in which such an event is present. The perspective from t_3 itself (namely perspective 3) is one in which the *Enterprise* is destroyed at t_3.

This reading is almost forced upon us, if we only make use of the location and the perspective parameter in representing non-Novikovian scenarios. Before spelling out this point in more detail, let us ask why it would be bad, for a metaphysics underlying an account of time travel, to accept that the past could never be present. We do not think there are conclusive arguments in favour of the desideratum, but we will give some general reason for it, and see why it is crucial for the non-standard tense realist, and the flow fragmentalist in particular, to comply with it.

One way to see why a past that has never been present is problematic is to think of what the mental activities of their inhabitants would be. There is a well-known issue of 'zombies in the past' for a metaphysics that combines a non-presentist ontology and an objective present. Very roughly, if mental episodes outside the objective present are conscious as the ones happening in the objective present, then it is very likely that *we* are living in the past. It is easy to see that we have just opened a can of epistemological worms.[12] One can prevent the worry by saying that people that exist *now* in the past are not conscious: in the past there are actions and brain activity, but not consciousness.[13] Notice that those 'zombies in the past' are not the usual philosophical zombies. The latter are supposed to be creatures that never had consciousness (although, if they are lucky they may end up in a thought experiment in which they have a conscious twin). They are different from horror movie zombies, who are unconscious human flesh-eating creatures that are supposed to *have been conscious* when alive. The 'zombies in the past' are somewhat more similar to the horror movie zombies, not in the flesh-eating habit, but in having been conscious when the past was present and they were thus inhabiting the present. But if the past in question is one that has *never* been present, then the zombies that inhabit it never enjoyed consciousness. They are what we may call *super-zombies*; they are not just 'zombies in the past', but also like philosophical zombies in never having been conscious at all. If what 'Time Squared' shows us is a past that never was present, Present Picard is actually a super-zombie (and thus the moniker is a bit of a misnomer). There is a present, for instance $\langle 5,5 \rangle$, in which Picard *remembers* seeing himself arriving from the future, and then engaging in a discussion with Dr Pulaski, but he never consciously experienced anything of it, since his past version is a super-zombie.

One way to avoid super-zombies is to follow the way out that the tense realist has: presentism.[14] Consider the ersatz version of presentism for simplicity. In that framework, the past is not inhabited by concrete zombies, since there is no past at all. There are only, in the present, ersatz past times, which are not past times at all, but abstract entities *representing the past*. Whatever the merit of this solution (or other presentist variants) for the problem, we do not find it very convincing in the case of non-Novikovian scenarios. It is strange to have ersatz times (or other presently existing surrogates) to represent *the past*, when they do not have any specific connection with the content profile of what happened. Consider presentism in a non-time travel (or Novikovian) scenario. The ersatz times (or other surrogates) have metaphysical significance in virtue of their having been present: they encode how reality *was*. But a past that has never been present in the non-Novikovian scenario has not the same metaphysical import. Someone activating a time machine in this framework is like someone writing down how things could have gone but have not. By activating the time machine the traveller creates certain representations (or other surrogates) that do not have the same role of encoding information about what happened, as the ersatz times have in the non-time travel (and Novikovian) case. Perhaps the presentist can insist that the *present* has changed because of the time travel. It is *now* (but was not before) the case that the past is such and such (while it was thus and thus), as the content of the ersatz times witnesses. It seems to us that such a reply is just another way to state the problem, and leaves us without an explanation.

At any rate, let us see why the non-standard tense realist, and the flow fragmentalist in particular, should be worried about a past that never was present. Note that for the tense *anti*-realist the problem does not take off the ground. For them, there is no distinction between an *alleged unique objective present* and past and future times. The problem disappears because the tense anti-realist, by embracing tenseless facts as fundamental, denies that there is an objective present, and thus a fortiori a unique objective present. But also the non-standard tense realist denies *that last bit*, even though they do not deny the reality of tense. Indeed, one of the motivating ideas for going non-standard is to combine irreducible tensed facts and the denial of a unique objective present. Each time is the centre of its own perspective, and enjoys objective presentness within it. If it turns out that there are locations that never 'make it' to being the centre of a perspective anyway, we may well just stick to a standard view, or move to the anti-realist side.

And the situation for the flow fragmentalist is even more pressing. By creating a past that never was present, it looks like we are undermining the flow fragmentalist explanation of the flow of time. The fact that the *Enterprise* exited the vortex intact has not been 'pushed' into existence by anything. To see the point, consider that writing down $\neg\phi$ at $\langle 5, 3\rangle$ is nothing more than a notational variant of writing down $P_2\neg\phi$ at $\langle 5, 5\rangle$. And now remember how we explained the flow of time in terms of exemplifications of Fragmentalist Flow, repeated below.

Fragmentalist Flow $\odot_{Fx} TENSE_n \phi$ because $\odot_{F(n+x)} \phi$

Clearly, we do not obtain a true instance of the scheme if we substitute ϕ with $\neg\phi$ (in the intended meaning given above). Simply because at $\langle 3, 3\rangle$ the *Enterprise* is destroyed and whatever exactly the truth-conditions for a 'because' claim may be, they require that the explanans be true.[15] Look at Fig. 10 again, which illustrates this.

How bad is this for Flow Fragmentalism? One may be tempted by a dismissive attitude. After all, strictly speaking it is *not* true that the non-Novikovian scenarios are incompatible with our official formulation of the theory. In section 1.1.4.5, by introducing Fragmentalist Flow, we claimed that the thesis is that for any x and $n \neq 0$, and *some* ϕ, the exemplification of the scheme gives true propositions. Thus we do not need that *all* past- or future-tensed facts get pushed or pulled into existence by their past or future versions, but only that at least *some* of them do. And maybe the ones that are the effects of a backwards time travel are *not* among those. The only ground for their existence is causal, and resides entirely in the 'weird' causal links that that time travel generated. This dismissive attitude leads quite naturally to the idea of a 'purified' flow, in which no qualitative fact about the content of the temporal locations is involved in the pushes and pulls that underlie the flow of time. Only pure tensed facts, the ones about the tensed profile of the *temporal locations themselves*, are explanatory of the flow. That means that in the scheme Fragmentalist Flow only sentences of the form $\ulcorner t_x$ is present$\urcorner$, $\ulcorner t_x$ is past$_{15}\urcorner$, $\ulcorner t_x$ is future$_3\urcorner$, ... lead to true instances. The content profiles of the temporal locations, whether they contain an exploding *Enterprise* or a pristine one, for instance, is entirely due to the causal relations in which they enter. And if they enter into anomalous causal relations like the ones entailed by non-Novikovian scenarios, and therefore are different in different fragments, so be it.

This interpretation of the flow, as in general the dismissive attitude towards the problem that non-Novikovian scenarios raise for the explanation of the flow in Flow Fragmentalism, does *not* eliminate the fact that there are content profiles that are never at the centre of a perspective, namely that there are pasts that were never present. It is true that if we purify the flow, the fact that t_3 was two units of time in the past, which obtains within the fragment of perspective 5, gets pushed into existence by the fact that t_3 is present, which obtains within the fragment of perspective 3. However, many qualitative events that are located at t_3 from the perspective of t_5 (including brain activities, if any) have come into existence as mere past shadows. Therefore, even if there is a perspective from which t_3 is present, there is no perspective from which t_3 is present *and* such events occupy t_3.[16] Let us see then how our official account of the non-Novikovian case solves the problem of the past that never was present and that of explaining the flow in the non-Novikovian case head-on and in one and the same move.

5.3 Changing the past: the solution

The idea is to 'square' the perspectives and make thus explicit the extra work that the perspective coordinate does in non-Novikovian time travel. In other words, we have to accept the idea of a perspective on a perspective. That is, the temporal dimension (the order of temporal locations) is not just so and so from the perspective of a time t_x. Rather: the temporal dimension is so and so from the perspective of a time t_y as seen from the perspective of (a possibly different time) t_x. The idea is more natural than it may seem at first. Let us explain it by unpacking step by step the sentence that we just stated. There are two perspectives involved in it, one embedded in the other: the perspective from t_x is the more internal perspective in the embedding, while the perspective from t_y is the more external one. We can think of them as two distinct parameters. The parameter of the internal perspective, the one centred on t_x tells us what is the *content* profile of the temporal dimension from that perspective. The parameter of the most external perspective, the one from t_y, tells us what is the tense profile of *that* temporal dimension, the one whose content profile has been individuated by the first parameter. We can keep on calling the two parameters 'perspectives' if we wish, but the first one is clearly doing a job quite different from that of the second one. While the latter's job is to give the tense profile of the temporal dimension, which is precisely the perspective role as we have specified in discussing the non-Novikovian cases, the former's job is the extra bit that the non-Novikovian case requires: it tells us how the temporal dimension has changed its content (possibly as a consequence of a backward causal connection).

By indexing the fragments not just to a perspective, but to a second temporal parameter, we give times a third role, beside the location and the perspective roles. Let us call it the *tracking* role. If a temporal location has a certain content profile relative to a time in its tracking role, then it keeps on having it relative to the successive times *until* a time travel event that changes the past happens. For instance, the content profile of temporal location t_3 contains the event of the destruction of the *Enterprise*, relative to t_3 in its tracking role, and keeps on having it relative to t_4, when Future Picard leaves in the shuttle. However, relative to t_5, temporal location t_3 does not contain the destruction of the *Enterprise*, and this is so because t_5 has 'tracked' the change in the past. Relative to times later than t_5, temporal location t_3 will keep on containing an *Enterprise* coming out intact of an energy vortex, unless a non-Novikovian event changes the past again.[17]

In the Novikovian context, the fragments have one index, which corresponds to the perspective they encode. In the non-Novikovian context, we have two indices for each fragment: one for a time in its tracking role, and one for a time in its perspective role. Each *indexed fragment* is thus of the form $F_{x,y}$ – the first parameter, x, being the tracking parameter, and the second, y, being the

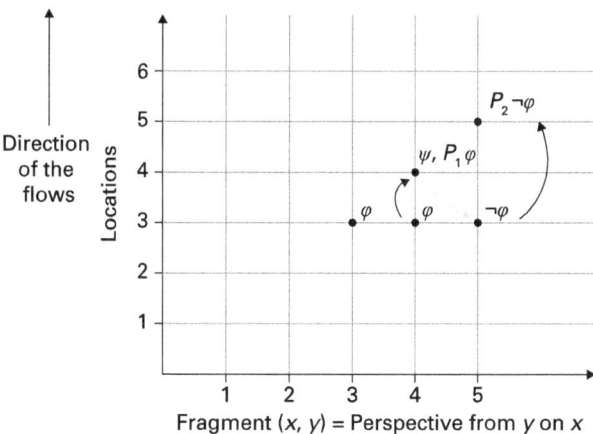

Figure 11 The tracking role solution.

perspective parameter. We can represent the indexed fragments as points of a diagram like that of Fig. 11. The horizontal lines give us the various 'versions' of the content profile of a given temporal location. The vertical lines are the pseudo-temporal sequences of fragments that have the same tracking parameter, and thus 'agree' on the content profile of the timeline.

By 'unpacking' the representation of the extra job that perspectives must play in non-Novikovian scenarios into a tracking and a perspective parameter, we can clarify the metaphysical interpretation that we give of the diagram in Fig. 11, and explain how the flow fragmentalist account of time travel solves the problem of the never present past, while sticking to the explanation of the passage of time that we gave in section 1.1.4.5.

By adding a further parameter we are in a position to relativize the explanation of the passage of time to all fragments that share the same tracking parameter, as in Fragmentalist Flow' below (where, as above, x is the tracking parameter and y is the perspective parameter).

Fragmentalist Flow' $\odot_{F_{x,y}} TENSE_n \phi$ because $\odot_{F_{x,(y+n)}} \phi$

We take the classes of explanatory claims that share the same tracking parameter x to be explanatory in the same sense in which the explanation of a unique flow in the non-time travel scenario is. This means that the points along the vertical lines have to be taken as sequences of *fragments*. And across those fragments only the *tense* profile of the various temporal locations changes, not their content profile. Therefore, there is no risk to have, say, the fact that $P_3 \phi$ in a certain fragment without also having the fact that ϕ in the relevant 'past' fragment along the vertical line.

However, while writing ϕ in a point along a given vertical line entails that n units up the same vertical line, we have to write $P_n \phi$, and *mutatis mutandis* for $F_n \phi$, what we have here are *not mere notational variants* of the description of the same fragment. Rather, they are the descriptions of two fragments through which the 'same flow' passes, namely two fragments linked by $<_{ps}$. Given that in this interpretation there are many flows along the various vertical lines, there is no risk of a past that never was present. Each point in the grid is the centre of a perspective, and the content profile of that location is present within that fragment, and past and future with respect to fragments down and up the vertical line, respectively. Notice also that we can express the causal links in the enriched language too. For instance, the causal path from the leaving of Future Picard in the shuttle to his arrival in the past is expressed by (5) below.

(5) $\odot_{F_{5,3}} \neg \phi \text{ because}_C \odot_{F_{4,4}} \psi$

Now, there is clearly an analogy here between the idea of having a tracking parameter, and the idea to index a temporal location to a *universe*, that we find both in certain versions of non-Novikovian time travel, and in certain interpretations of quantum mechanics.[18] After all, it is a crucial part of the tracking role to settle all the content profiles of a sequence of temporal locations, and this seems exactly what universes do, when they are understood as parameters. However, if the vertical lines are understood as universes, they are 'quasi-parallel' and not parallel universes. This is so, because the causal links that allow for time travel *connect* the various universes. Indeed, what makes the content of certain temporal locations vary across the horizontal lines is the presence of backward causal links that 'cut through' the vertical lines, as the one expressed by (5) above.

If the analogy is cogent, the flow fragmentalist is liable to the worry that what they are depicting here is not *really* time travel, but rather 'universe hopping', as it is sometimes put. The problem with the latter is that it is like going to an exotic country, an unusual form of tourism, as it were, headed towards parts of reality which are not normally accessible to us. Some of those parts may *look* very much like our past, and we may even *call* them different 'versions' of the past, but what they are *au fond* is just normally inaccessible areas of reality. Applied to Flow Fragmentalism, the worry is that by introducing a tracking parameter, we are just 'partitioning' the facts that constitute reality into classes that correspond to various universes.[19] And what we call time travel is just a movement from one partition to another. The 'universe hopping' problem is pressing for any form of non-Novikovian time travel that explicitly resorts to indexing temporal locations to allow for different 'versions' of a temporal location (e.g. one in which the *Enterprise* is destroyed, and one in which is pristine). When the underlying metaphysics is such that the indexing is merely a labelling of numerically distinct entities, the worry is very much justified. Think of a theory which uses Lewisian modal realism as a starting point, and allows for causal connections between the 'quasi-isolated' concrete possible worlds. By hopping from one universe to another, the traveller is 'visiting their past' merely in the sense that they are visiting a temporal location that is labelled by the same temporal coordinate (but a different universe coordinate) as the one in their own past.

However, not all versions of the idea are liable to this criticism in such a harsh form. In the flow fragmentalist picture, even if the various vertical lines in Fig. 11 in a sense represent different universes, each one with its non-standard flow, they are still universes that *share* their temporal locations.[20] What varies between them, if non-Novikovian time travel happens, is the *content* of each location. If the time traveller reaches different facts than the ones that happened in her past, this is not because she ended up in a different 'part' of the temporal dimension. Rather, she ends up at the same location, but its content profile is different. And this is not surprising, since she has triggered a change in the parameter[21] that tracks the changes due to non-Novikovian time travel events by engaging in... non-Novikovian time travel! We are aware that this reply is not entirely convincing, and it may sound as a mere restatement of the problem to someone who is not willing to consider non-Novikovian time travel as an option. We will come back to this point shortly, but first let us consider a more urgent worry.

The worry is that by indexing fragments to a further temporal parameter we are at the end of the day endorsing a form of external relativism, rather than fragmentalism, since now constitution seems to be relativized and not absolute after all.[22] The idea is that in the Novikovian or non-time travel version, a fact constitutes reality *absolutely*, when it obtains relative to the fragment of a perspective. In the non-Novikovian version, it looks like we should say that a fact constitutes reality *relative* to a time t_x in its tracking role, if it obtains relative to a fragment that is indexed to a perspective t_y and to t_x. And this is bad news since having an absolute notion of constitution is a distinguishing feature of fragmentalism in all its varieties, and at any rate of Flow Fragmentalism.

Our reply is that what the objection really shows is just that non-Novikovian cases require us to complicate the notion of *obtainment*. Flow fragmentalists embrace explicitly the primitive distinction between an absolute notion of constitution and an irreducibly relative notion of obtainment. Until Chapter 4 the relativization of obtainment was simply to a time as a perspective parameter. Once Non-Novikovian scenarios enter the scene, we need to 'square our perspectives' and factor in also a tracking parameter. But the relation between obtainment and constitution remains the same. It is still the case that a fact constitutes reality absolutely speaking when it obtains relative to a fragment. But now the relativization in question involves not just a perspective, but also an index for the contents of the temporal locations of the temporal dimension (i.e. a tracking parameter).

This reply allows us to explain how we can get rid of the simplifying assumptions that we made at the beginning, namely, that of considering only eternalist versions of Flow Fragmentalism, and that of considering the order $<_{ps}$ as primitive rather than given by the partial overlap among fragments (p. 135–6). We start from the second assumption because it is all but obvious how to drop it. If we consider separately each sequence of fragments along the vertical lines, we do not need to take $<_{ps}$ as primitive, but we can derive it from the overlap of 'at least' facts within the fragment *with the same tracking parameter* in a manner utterly analogous to the way we described in section 2.2.2.

How to drop the second assumption is more tricky. Before we introduced explicitly the tracking role, we heavily relied on the idea of a temporal location t_x having various content profiles depending on which temporal location t_y we were considering as perspective (in an 'inflated' sense). It seemed almost inevitable thus that the perspective from t_y contained the temporal location t_x whose (variable) content profile we were considering. But once we introduce explicitly the tracking role with a further parameter, it should be clear that we do not need facts about the simple existence of past locations (or entities in general) to obtain within each fragment. As in the non-time travel case, times are collections of tensed facts, and the temporal dimension is nothing over and above the overlap among times made up of metric 'at least' facts. You can think of it in these terms: Flow Fragmentalism accomplishes to implement *three* roles for times through only *two* indices. This is so because the location role, as we noted since Chapter 1 (section 1.2.3) is implicit in the metric of the tensed facts obtaining within each fragment. But then it is obvious that *once we accept the further commitment to a tracking role for times*, the temporal metric can play the part of the eternalist ontology as in the non-Novikovian case (indeed, as in the standard presentist case). As in the relativistic case (see p. 131), we trade an ontological commitment to temporal locations and the relationship thereof with an ideological commitment to the more complex $\odot_{F_{x,y}}$ operators.

5.4 Movable present and vacillating past

We now know what is the price to have non-Novikovian time travels in a fragmentalist universe: commitment to a tracking role for times. The question now is: how high is the price? We will not try to answer this question in absolute terms. Rather, we will see whether it is the case that also standard theories of time need to make room for a tracking parameter once non-Novikovian scenarios are taken into account. We will argue that yes, they do, and if so, the price is, at least comparatively, not so high to pay. The two theories that we will consider are examples of views that take tense realism seriously and are tailor-made to accommodate cases of changing the past: the movable objective present (MOP) and vacillating time.[23] We think the results generalize, although we will not attempt to show it here.

First, MOP. According to the view, when the time traveller, who at the moment of departure finds herself in the objective present (where else?) activates the time machine, she *thereby* moves the objective present to a past temporal location along the temporal dimension. In Fig. 12, we have again a schematic representation of the events of 'Time Squared', with the objective present following Picard's journey in the shuttle from location $\langle H_4, T_4 \rangle$ to location $\langle H_5, T_3 \rangle$ of the two-dimensional timeline.

MOP explicitly requires hyper-time.[24] And it is easy to see that the parameter connected to the hyper-time coordinate in MOP plays the same role as the one played by the tracking parameter in Flow Fragmentalism. In this picture, specifying a hyper-temporal coordinate $\langle H_x, T_y \rangle$ is to specify a temporal perspective (the one from t_y) on the temporal dimension *as specified by the*

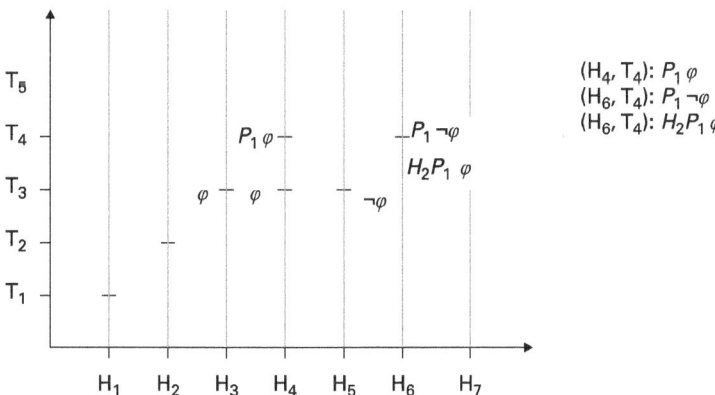

Figure 12 MOV and changing the past.

H-parameter. What the hyper-time does, thus, is to settle the content profile of a sequence of temporal locations, which is precisely the role of the tracking parameter in the theory that we have elaborated in the previous sections. Similarly, what the flow fragmentalist expresses with their $\odot_{F_{x,y}}$ operators, the MOPer can express with a combination of usual metric tense operators (F_x, P_x), which allow her to move vertically in two-dimensional time, and two metric hyper-tense operators (HF_x, HP_x), which allow her to move horizontally in two-dimensional time. For instance, when T_4 comes the 'first time', namely when $\langle H_4, T_4\rangle$ is present and Picard leaves for the past in a shuttle, the *Enterprise* has been destroyed one unit of time before. When T_4 comes for the 'second time', namely when $\langle H_6, T_3\rangle$ is present, we have that $P_1 \neg \phi$, namely, that the *Enterprise* was not destroyed, and $H_2 P_1 \phi$, namely that in the 'old' timeline the *Enterprise* was destroyed. Thanks to the hyper-tense operator, we can move not only 'vertically' along the temporal locations of a given version of the timeline, but also 'horizontally' along its different versions. And again it is the sensitivity of the H_n operator to a tracking parameter that makes this possible.

The difference between Flow Fragmentalism and MOP is that the former is a *non*-standard form of tense realism. Therefore, according to it, how reality is like is given by the totality of fragments or perspectives on the temporal dimension, whereas the latter is a standard form of tense realism. Therefore, how reality is like, according to it, is how reality *presently* is. Although according to the theory reality was and will be, and hyper-was and hyper-will be, in possibly different ways.

Second, vacillating time theory.[25] Whereas in MOP the present 'follows' the time traveller, according to vacillating time theory, the objective present follows its 'natural' path, even after a time travel departure event. Fig. 13 shows how the vacillating time universe behaves in the 'Time Squared' story. The movement of the present is represented by the diagonal with identical coordinates, that is, the succession $\langle 1, 1\rangle$, $\langle 2, 2\rangle$, etc. At $\langle 4, 4\rangle$ Future Picard leaves for the past. After that, at $\langle 5, 5\rangle$ the past is changed, as it is showed by the fact that at $\langle 5, 3\rangle$ the *Enterprise* is not destroyed, even though at $\langle 3, 3\rangle$ it is.

Since the present moves *independently* of time travel and its changing effects on the past, vacillating time (in its tense version) clearly admits pasts that never were present. Consider again $\langle 5, 3\rangle$ in the diagram, the 'new past' in which the Present Picard meets Future Picard and the *Enterprise* is not destroyed. The only 'counterpart' of it that ever was present is $\langle 3, 3\rangle$; but when $\langle 3, 3\rangle$ was present, the *Enterprise* was destroyed by the energy vortex. Note that the problem for vacillating time theory arises from the fact that it is a standard form of tense

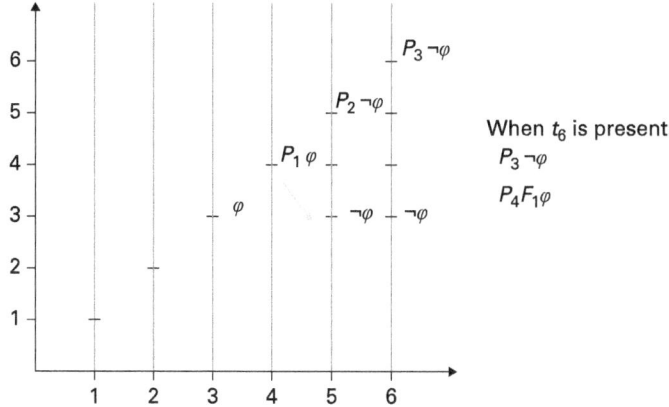

Figure 13 Vacillating past.

realism, rather than a non-standard one. In non-standard forms such as Flow Fragmentalism, every time is the perspectival centre of at least one fragment. Indeed, the idea behind the introduction of a tracking role for time was precisely allowing that times may be perspectival centres for more than one fragment, and have different content in different fragments, if non-Novikovian time travel happens. But according to vacillating time theory, there is only one present time and it flows inexorably towards the future regardless of whether non-Novikovian time travels happen. Thus, given that neither the present follows the traveller as in MOP, nor is it the case that each time has 'its own' present, as in the non-standard picture, vacillating time theory is bound to never-present pasts in non-Novikovian scenarios.

But let us put aside the 'never-present past' problem, and ask whether the vacillator can accommodate non-Novikovian scenarios without relying on a tracking index. Perhaps the cost of never present pasts is worth paying if the theory comes with a simpler ideology than that of Flow Fragmentalism. In order to answer the question we need to go a bit more into its details. A crucial feature of the view is that it *distinguishes* itself from strategies that exploit indexing to hyper-times or indexing to universes. Roughly, vacillating time alleges to achieve the same results of those strategies by resorting to metric tense operators with 'unusual' truth-conditions.

Have a look again at Fig. 13, and see what happens when t_6 is present a bit after the past changing time travel happened. We have that $P_3 \neg \phi$; that is, three units of time in the past, it is the case that the *Enterprise* is not destroyed by entering an energy vortex. Now, how can we say by resorting merely to metric tense operators that the past has changed with respect to that, and that at a certain point the *Enterprise* was destroyed by an energy vortex? The 'trick' is made possible by giving to the tense operators truth-conditions that yield possibly different results for tensed sentences that 'lead' to the *same* temporal location. In metric tense logic, a sentence embedded in a formula of the form ⌜$P_n \alpha$⌝ and one embedded in a formula of the form ⌜$P_{(n+1)} F_1 \beta$⌝ have necessarily the same truth-value if $\alpha = \beta$, and necessarily opposite truth-values if $\alpha = \neg \beta$ (or the other way around). This is so because both sentences are 'about' the same temporal location, namely the time that is *n* units of time in the past. In vacillating time theory, different embeddings can 'lead' to different pasts (in cases where the past has changed). Look again at Fig. 13; we have that when t_6 is present, namely at location ⟨6, 6⟩, both $P_3 \neg \phi$ and $P_4 F_1 \phi$ are true. Despite being both about the same temporal location t_3, the second one reaches the content profile that t_3 had before the arrival of Picard from the future, while the first one reaches the content profile generated by the non-Novikovian time travel. If all this is done only by metric temporal operators, it looks like the vacillator can do without the tracking role, and obtain the same bounty. If so, maybe the never present past and its super-zombies is a price worth paying.

But fortunately for us, the vacillator cannot do without the tracking parameter, or so we argue. Let us see exactly how the 'unusual' truth-conditions work. The idea is to treat as two distinct primitives the relations of *later than* and the relation of *before than*. A non-Novikovian event of leaving for the past leaves the *later than* relation intact, but blocks the *before than* relation from the future, while reconnecting the time of the arrival in the 'new' past to the previous moment in the old past only through the *before than*, but not the *later than* relation. The result is that if from time 6 we go back three units, we find ourselves in the changed past where the *Enterprise* is not destroyed, that is, the rectangle tagged with 3' in Fig. 14. But if we go back four units, we end up in the 'previous' past, and given that the *later than* relation does not connect the old and the new past, if we have to go up one unit in the future, we end up in the rectangle labelled with 3 (and not 3'), which is the original past where the *Enterprise* is destroyed by the energy vortex.

The rectangles in Fig. 14 are called hyperplanes, or ersatzplanes in the presentist version. Certain erstazplanes, like 3 and 3' and 4 and 4' are 'coetaneous'. That is, they are versions of the same temporal location in cases in which its content profile has changed, as in the case of non-Novikovian time travel. Now it is crucial for the theory to have the means to distinguish between coetaneous ersatzplanes. Without distinguishing ersatzplane 3 from ersatzplane 3' we cannot

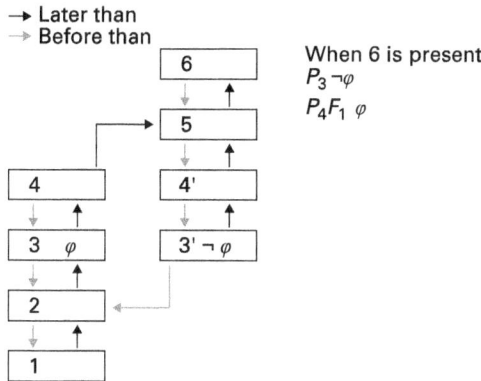

Figure 14 Vacillator's truth-conditions.

get the result that when 6 is present, three units ago the *Enterprise* is fine, but four units ago it would have been the case that *then* it is destroyed. More generally, in order to have enough *ersatzplane structure* to give truth-conditions in case of time travel, coetaneous ersatzplanes have to be indexed to a parameter that gives us the *correct* content profile of the temporal location. And only a parameter for *tracking* the changes – what stands 'before' and 'after' the past changing event – can do the trick.

In articulating the truth-conditions for metric tense operators that yield the desired results thus, the vacillating time theorist needs to add a parameter so that a time (an ersatzplane) can play not only the location and the perspective role, but also the tracking role. Now, one may object that there is a crucial difference between labelling coetaneous ersatzplanes with different content in order to distinguish them, and resorting to a parameter for the tracking role for time. The vacillating time theorist needs a *meta*-language enriched with indices for ersatzplanes, but in their object language only 'ordinary' metric tense operators show up, the language is not enriched by an extra index. In Flow Fragmentalism, once we enter the non-Novikovian world, the *object* language needs to be enriched, and we need a way to 'talk about' the tracking role of times, namely an extra index in the within operators. How significant is such a difference? We do not think that the difference should be valued much. However, someone may insist that while it is always legitimate to give a purely instrumentalist reading of the metalanguage of a theory (think of someone giving a semantic for a modal language in terms of possible worlds, but not buying into Lewis' modal realism), it requires specific philosophical reasons to do the same with respect to the object language of a theory that we take seriously (purely instrumentalist readings of physical theories of fermions, say, are possible, but not trivial to defend from a philosophical point of view).

We take the point. However, we do not think that the vacillating time theorist can avoid the problem by enriching their object language with some sort of ersatzplane indices *and* ending up with a theory that is equally expressive than Flow Fragmentalism. To see the point, we have to ask what happens to the 'in-between' pasts when more than one change of the *same* past happens (see Fig. 15). Consider this alternative ending of 'Time Squared'. After that the *Enterprise* has safely exited the energy vortex, it is detected by the Borg,[26] and as a consequence the whole Federation is enslaved. Resistance is futile, but Dr Pulaski manages to escape the hive mind and realizes that the only way to save the Alpha Quadrant is to go back in time and 'restore' the original timeline, in which the *Enterprise* is destroyed. She embarks a time machine, goes back to the moment Future Picard arrives from the future in a shuttle, and convinces her older self to kill Present Picard and let Future Picard get into the shuttle, enter the vortex and trigger the chain of events that leads to the destruction of the *Enterprise*. There is now, when hyperplane 7 is present, the 'newest' past, which looks almost like the first, original past and the 'in-between' past, where the *Enterprise* is not destroyed but the Borg rule. However, the truth-conditions of the vacillator cannot 'see' anything in between the newest past and the original past. Consider for instance the claim that four units of time ago the *Enterprise* was destroyed, $P_4 \varphi$. It is true when 7 is present. But what about the claim that five units of time ago, it would have been the case in one unit of time that the

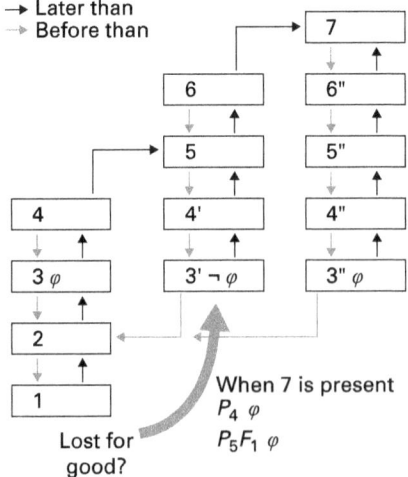

Figure 15 Whither the in-between past?

Enterprise is destroyed, $P_5 F_1 \phi$? If we go five ersatzplanes down, starting from ersatzplane 7 (that is, the present), we find ourselves in the original timeline and from there we cannot, by going up, reach the past in which the *Enterprise* is not destroyed. Hence, also $P_5 F_1 \phi$ is true, although in virtue of the facts in the original timeline, rather than in the 'restored' one as a consequence of Pulaski's heroism.

Without enriching the *object* language in a way that reflects the ersatz structure, the vacillator theorist cannot use combinations of tense operators to distinguish between the 'new' and the 'old' past. In the version of the theory that does not have an object language that contains indices for differentiating the various (content-wise distinct) ersatzplanes, information is lost for good as time goes by. In order to state what happens in the various 'in-between' pasts, if many changes happen, we need the tracking role to play a part not only in the structure which we exploit to give the truth-conditions, but also in the language that we use to make claims about the past, namely the object language of the theory. A metric parameter on a tense operator per se won't suffice. The moral is thus that the need for a tracking role for times is not a drawback of the fragmentalist approach. Rather, it is an inevitable cost of any framework in which non-Novikovian scenarios are accounted for.

Notes

Introduction

1 See, for instance, Correia and Rosenkranz (2011, 2012), Deng (2013), Merlo (2013), Tallant (2013), Lipman (2015, 2016, 2018), Savitt (2016), Ingthorsson (2016: Chap. 8), Loss (2017), De Florio and Frigerio (2017, 2019: Chap. 6), Iaquinto (2019), Torrengo and Iaquinto (2019, 2020), Fine (2020), Merlo (2022) and Eker (2022). See also Solomyak (2013, 2020).
2 See Lipman (2020), Slavov (2020), Hofweber and Lange (2017, 2020) and Iaquinto and Calosi (ms).
3 This application is presented in Simon (2018), and criticized in Iaquinto and Calosi (2021). See also Merriam (2022).
4 See Fine (2005: 285), Iaquinto (2020), and Zhan (2021). See also the account of change in Pickup (forthcoming), in which a conceptual machinery similar to that of fragmentalism is used.
5 We take inspiration for this methodology from Fine (2005)'s distinction between *what is really the case* and *what is merely the case*. Metaphysical cogency, as the former notion, is meant to be stricter than truth: 'the question concerns the fit, or lack of fit, between the tensed character of our representations and the character of reality itself. But fit is not simply a matter of truth. Both sides to the debate can agree to the truth of particular tensed statements (such as the statement that I am sitting). Fit in some deeper sense is involved; and the metaphysical concept of reality simply provides a way of codifying its presence' (p. 270). The idea of a metaphysically cogent description, one that carves nature at the joints, is articulated in Sider (2011) in slightly different terms, as the articulation of a *metaphysical semantics*. See also the methodology of an *ideal language* as formulated in Bergmann (1967).
6 Cf. footnote 38.
7 Another realist tradition, which begins with Stein (1991), and more recently can be individuated in Maudlin (2007), Norton (2010), Oaklander (2015) and Leininger (2018, 2021), sees ordinary passage as *inherent flow*, a mind-independent feature of time that differentiates it from space. We will be concerned only marginally with this other realist tradition.
8 See Russell (1903). The labels 'robust' and 'anaemic' are from Skow (2015).
9 We classify theories of anaemic passage as forms of anti-realism of the passage of time for ease of exposition. More precisely, they are forms of tense anti-realism.

Whether they count as forms of anti-realism of the passage depends on whether one takes ordinary passage to require the reality of tenses (cf. the realist tradition we just referred to in footnote 7 for examples of philosophers who disagree). There are also more radical forms of anti-realism, according to which not even anaemic passage is an aspect of reality. McTaggart (1908) and Gödel (1949), and possibly to a certain extent Kant (1781) can be seen as part of this crew of 'time anti-realists'. There is also a deflationist position, which does not take the debate to be substantive; see Dorato (2002), Savitt (2002) and Deng (2010, 2013).

10 One may wonder why capturing the passage is not sufficient for a metaphysical theory. In the next chapter, we will discuss this worry in connection with Fine (2005)'s 'frozen present objection' (cf. sections 1.1.4.1 and 1.1.4.4).

11 Merlo (2013) discusses the contrast between these two intuitions.

12 For the opposition between the A- and B-theory, aka tensed and tenseless theories of time, see Gale (1968) and Oaklander and Smith (1994).

13 Notice that the B-theorist is only committed to *downplay* (the metaphysical significance of) the first intuition, not to discard it. For instance, she can grant that the present is phenomenologically special, or has other psychologically significant characteristics. See Balashov (2015) and Torrengo and Cassaghi (2021) for a criticism.

14 On this point, see Spolaore and Torrengo (2019).

15 As Tallant and Ingram (2021) argue, it is impossible to find a formulation of presentism that satisfies all (self-recognized) presentists. There are also version of presentism that are not forms of tense realism, at least in the sense that they do not agree that there are substantive tensed *properties*. Tallant (2012, 2014)'s existence presentism is an example.

16 Different brands of the view support different ways of understanding the idea. Cf. Tooley (1997), Forrest (2006), Rosenkranz and Correia (2018) and Forbes (2016).

17 In the next chapter we will unravel the notion in more detail, and provide more precise definitions of standard and non-standard tense realism.

18 Unless *being present* is compatible with *being past*. See Tallant (2015) for a defence of this idea.

19 Of course, as soon as relativistic considerations are brought in, talk of 'the' present becomes ill-defined, if further assumption are made, and it is not a trivial matter how to elaborate relativistic extensions of the various positions. More on this in Chapter 4.

20 The vice versa means not that there are not other realist attempts to vindicate realism (for instance, the Stein-style idea of an inherent flow in the temporal relation; see footnote 7), but only that we do not count them as based on the standard framework.

21 Notice that we are not defending the methodological point of view according to which the most important theoretical virtue in metaphysics is to respect ordinary intuitions (or as many of them as possible). We are just noting that fragmentalism is

a metaphysics that somehow hosts the gist of both of them, and this is a precondition for an explanatory advantage that – we will argue – fragmentalism has over other forms of realism.
22 See Cameron (2015), Skow (2015) and Deasy (2015, 2021).
23 Cf. Sider (2011) and Deasy (2015). We do not think that the terminology is particularly cogent, but we will follow suit.
24 There are many ways to construe the idea that a persisting object *o* instantiates a property *P* relative to a time *t*. For instance in terms of a persisting *o* instantiating a corresponding time-indexed property P_t, or in terms of *o* having a temporal part located a *t* instantiating *P simpliciter*. See Haslanger (2003). Which option one chooses is immaterial to our point. Issues of persistence in the context of fragmentalism will be briefly discussed in section 1.2.3.1.
25 Cf. Prior (1958, 1968a).
26 Prior (1968a: 11), *verbatim*.
27 See Prior (1968a): 'This last change [in how far in the past a certain event is], of course, is a case of precisely that recession of events into the past that we are really talking about when we say that time flows or passes' (p. 9).
28 Although in a context that is not much sympathetic to (what we nowadays call) the moving spotlight theory, also Prior (1968a) seems to suggest that the passage of time is to be understood as a form of non-qualitative change: 'The flow of time, we would then say, is merely metaphorical, not only because what is meant by it isn't a genuine movement, but further because what is meant by it isn't a genuine change; but the force of the metaphor can still be explained – we use the metaphor because what we call the flow of time does fit [Priorian Flow]' (pp. 11–12). It seems to us that here Prior does not think that the passage of time is not a form of genuine change because it is not robust, but rather because it is not qualitative. Consider also how he goes on: 'On this view it might be that . . . my own growing older will not count as a change in the strict sense, though growing older is normally *accompanied* by genuine changes, and the phrase is commonly extended to cover these – increasing wisdom, bald patches and so on' (p. 12, italics in the original).
29 See Sider (2011) and Cameron (2015). Not everybody agrees with this interpretation of the classic view. Deasy (2015) argues that in C-MST, given that tensed *propositions* change truth-value absolutely (and not merely relative to times) as time goes by, then things undergo tensed qualitative change, and not mere at-at change. The point is not crucial for this introduction. Thus for ease of exposition we will rely on Sider's interpretation of C-MST.
30 The fact that the passage of time is a form of pure change in this tradition does *not* entail that pure change is possible *without* qualitative change. More broadly, that is an open question for both the A- and B-theorists. A-theorists may take pure change as a mere (although informative) abstraction from qualitative change (see e.g. Lowe

1998). And B-theorists may think that it is possible that there are lapses of time during which no qualitative change happens (see Shoemaker 1969).
31 Cambridge change is a change in the relations an entity stands with other entities that does not come with a difference in intrinsic properties. Typical examples are Xanthippe becoming a widow when Socrates dies, or me becoming farther away from the Moon as it revolves around the Earth.
32 See also Sullivan (2012) and Bacon (2018) for related views. Smith (2002) and Schlesinger (1991) can be seen as precursors.
33 See Skow (2015).
34 Cf. Cameron (2018).
35 Versions of the worry are in Fine (2005: 287), Frischhut (2013), Deng (2013) and Leininger (2015).
36 See Torrengo (2018) for more on this. There are of course differences: space 'splits up' in three, and has not (apparent) directionality, and the constraints that spatial and temporal distances put on causality are significantly different. However, it is difficult to see how all such differences could account for the idea that time flows, while space is static. Unless, of course, time does not really flow, but it only seems so (cf. Callender 2017).
37 We will come back to this point with a more serious tone in Chapter 1 (p. 38), where we will also argue that the standard framework cannot overcome the problem easily.
38 For ease of expression, authors discussing fragmentalism tend to define it in terms of facts. However, strictly speaking the fragmentalist is not committed to the existence of facts as a distinct ontological category. In Fine's formulation of the view, for instance, reference to facts can be avoided by means of a proper 'in reality' sentential operator (2005: 268).
39 Although we won't use this terminology, not to complicate things further, note that external relativism abides with what one might call weak global coherence, while the fragmentalist abides with strong local coherence.
40 See Loss (2018) and Torrengo and Iaquinto (2020). Lipman (2018) would probably disagree with the letter of what we claim for negation in a fragmentalist framework here. We will be more precise in Chapter 1.
41 This means that the logic of fragmentalism cannot be Priest's LP, the logic of paradox (1979).

1 Flow Fragmentalism

1 We have given a reformulation of the second version of the theses (p. 273), avoiding the distinction between composition and constitution that Fine makes, since it is immaterial to our main point. Presentness is not explicitly formulated in Fine.

2 Cf. Loss (2017), who reconstructs several arguments with the same structure.
3 See Fine (2005: 271, 273). We have taken more liberty in the reformulation of Neutrality than with Realism, Absolutism and Coherence, but nothing substantive hinges on this choice.
4 This holds also for some versions of fragmentalism, notably, Fine's one. See section 1.3.1.
5 Although it should not strike as problematic in terms of ontological burden. More on the point also in section 1.1.3.
6 As anticipated in footnote 38, the idea of recurring to an official idiom to avoid commitment to facts is also in Fine (2005). In this and the next sections, we will sketch some rules and truth-conditions in a rather informal way. We will have a more precise formulation, as a model theory, in section 2.3.
7 We do not claim, however, that fragmentalism per se is necessarily incompatible with the existence of negative facts.
8 Cf. Fine (2005): 'a thought commonly had by [standard] realists is that [passage] essentially consists in the successive possession of the property of being PRESENT or NOW; for time to pass from one moment to the next is for a property of presentness to pass from one moment to the next' (p. 286). Deasy (2015) offers an interesting argument to the conclusion that someone maintaining a moving spotlight view should avoid primitive tense operators, and opts for attributions of presentness in an otherwise tenseless environment. Although we remain neutral on the topic, and we will use tense operators to express Flow Fragmentalism, our point does not seem to us at odds with the gist of his view. On the notion of real tense in general, see Dyke (2013).
9 We touched upon the issue in section 0.4. Besides the references given there, see also Meyer (2005), Jhou (2021) and Eker (2022), and for replies Tallant (2013), Cameron (2015: Chap. 2), Ingram (2019) and Correia and Rosenkranz (2020, forthcoming).
10 See also this passage: 'For suppose we ask: given a complete tenseless description of reality, then what does [the realist] need to add to the description to render it complete by his own lights? The answer is that he need add nothing beyond the fact that a given time t is present, since everything else of tense-theoretic interest will follow from this fact and the tenseless facts. But then how could this solitary "dynamic" fact, in addition to the static facts that the anti-realist is willing to accept, be sufficient to account for the passage of time?' (p. 287). The scare quotes around 'dynamic' suggest that the fact is merely *intended* to be dynamic.
11 Besides, there are also many formal points connected to the issue which have been discussed at length. See, for instance, Correia and Rosenkranz (2020, forthcoming).
12 He is also unhappy with it because by introducing primitive tensed properties we lose the motivation for having an eternalist ontology. We will not dwell on this second motivation here, since it is internal to Cameron's project and whether it is a

good motivation depends on whether the reasons for accepting the existence of past and future entities are good as well. On the relation between passage and presentist vs. eternalist ontology we will say something in section 1.2.3.

13 Cameron also considers an alternative position, but rejects it precisely because it takes A-properties as primitive: 'One could say, e.g., that there are things, times, that have temporal distributional properties and ages just like ordinary objects like you and me, and that these temporal distributional properties describe times as being non-present, then non-present, then non-present, then ... etc ... then present, then non-present, then non-present, then ... etc. Then combined with its age, this will entail whether a time is present, has been present, or will be present. I don't want to go this route because I don't want the fundamental properties to be about presentness. I want an explanation of *what it is* to be present' (p. 188).

14 Cf. 'Past things continue to change as time progresses: Caesar is a certain age now, but will be a different age tomorrow. Things in the distant future will be different when they are in the not-so-distant future, and different again when they are present. A yet to be born sun has a certain age, will have a different age when it is born, and will have yet a different age when it dies. This change in the ages of things, combined with their having the temporal distributional property they always have, results in things changing with respect to their more mundane properties' (p. 186).

15 In summing up the basic tenet of his view, Cameron explicitly states: 'Every substance that exists simpliciter instantiates simpliciter an age. ... Substances change with respect to their ages. In fact, such change is constant: every substance has a different age property at every moment of its existence. If A has a certain age simpliciter, A has never previously had simpliciter, and never again will have simpliciter, that particular age' (p. 213).

16 One may counter-object that this rejoinder risks to overgeneralize. If I have a theory according to which change reduces to Swiss fondue, and you complain that change *isn't* Swiss fondue, it seems weird if I reply that this is just what in my theory change is, after all! We disagree. If your reply is that my theory does not work *merely* because change is not Swiss fondue, then your argument against my theory is bad, and it remains bad also if my theory is bad too (indeed, worse than yours). Therefore, there is no risk of *over*generalization, because arguments against theories according to which subject matter *X* is or reduce to *Y* based *merely* on the observation that *X* is not *Y* are *always* bad. If my 'crazy' reductive theory of change turns out to have more explanatory power (with respect to the relevant explananda) and connects better to the rest of science than your reassuring and intuitive theory, then I am more likely to be right than you. In the case of the Swiss fondue theory of change your counter-objection that change simply isn't Swiss fondue is convincing *not* because my theory is counterintuitive (if that were enough, then we should never have accepted the relativistic conception of simultaneity, for instance), but because my theory is very

bad under all respects: it does not have any explanatory power, and it does not connect at all with other sciences, to begin with. To repeat, there is no risk of overgeneralization, as long as it is clear that the legitimacy of my reductive theory relies on the general criteria for apprising theories (empirical adequacy, theoretical virtues and the like), and not simply on its capacity to resist a very weak objection.

17 A fortiori, then, the justification for the extra bit should come from theoretical virtues, rather than from sheer intuitions; even if intuitiveness is a theoretical virtue, few would argue that it is not defeasible, or that it is the only theoretical virtue.

18 This is roughly the idea behind Skow's MST-Time (2015), which we will discuss in more detail in section 1.3.4.

19 Notice that Skow grants that MST-Time does not 'give us' robust passage, but, correctly perhaps, insists that it is not *merely* a theory of anaemic passage either. One way to read this claim is that his view explains passage (in terms of variation of tensed properties across perspectives), but it does not capture robust passage. Sattig (2019a, 2019b) developed a similar insight in the context of our experience of temporal flow.

20 The reason why we put 'after' and 'before' in scare quotes will be discussed in section 1.2.4.

21 The characterization of the flow of time sketched above might prima facie recall Lowe (1987a, 1987b)'s, who distinguishes between an internal perspective on the temporal dimension and an external one. He proposes to think of our life as a space-time route, that is, an ordered sequence of the form $\langle (s_1, t_1), (s_2, t_2), \ldots, (s_n, t_n) \rangle$, where the first member of each couple is a point in space (a spatial perspective), while the second one is a point in time (a temporal perspective). Crucially, these routes should not be taken as descriptions of reality *sub specie aeternitatis* (see Lowe 1987b: 69), that is, as mere B-theoretical chains of space-time locations. Rather, they must be conceived as descriptions of 'what it would be like ("from the inside") to experience the world from perspectives other than here and now. In other words, we must understand what it would be to use the words "now" and "here" *correctly* at other times and places – times and places which I cannot now refer to other than by recourse to other indexical expressions' (p. 69, italics in the original). We agree that our distinction between a global perspective and the perspective of each time bears similarities with Lowe's distinction between a description of reality *sub specie aeternitatis* and a description 'from the inside'. Still, there is a crucial difference. Lowe's position is a standard approach in which Presentness and Coherence hold. Reality is taken to be coherent *sub specie aeternitatis* as much as it is coherent 'from the inside': it does not contain incompatible tended facts at all. Lowe's aim, indeed, is precisely to show that contrary to McTaggart (1908)'s argument, describing time by resorting to tensed notions yields no contradiction whatsoever. And this is so, crucially, because when it comes to what facts constitute reality, the perspective from

the present time *is* privileged – although what time we find at its centre constantly changes. Rather than a multiplicity of fragments reflecting a multiplicity of perspectives, there is always one perspective and many *hypothetical* perspectives. See Torrengo and Iaquinto (2019: 192–3).

22 We will discuss why we take this relation to be a *pseudo* B-relation in section 1.2.4.

23 Bear in mind that here we are using 'simple' and 'complex' in the technical sense described in section 1.1.3.

24 The clause reads: 'The truth-value of p, relative to fragment F_n in a model $\mathcal{M}$ is T iff the valuation function v, given F_n, assigns T to p.'

25 As we should expect, the truth-value of prefixed sentences does not vary across fragments. The presence of 'within' operators makes the logic for $\mathcal{L}^{+\odot}$ described here similar to a tensed hybrid logic (cf. Blackburn 2006).

26 To be sure the reader does not get misguided here, the square brackets serve to provide different versions of the principle. Presentist Flow is thus the conjunction of (i) if it will be the case that in reality a present-tensed fact obtains, it is so because in reality its future-tensed version obtains at present, and (ii) if it was the case that in reality a present-tensed fact obtains, it is so because in reality its past-tensed version obtains at present.

27 For instance, Sanson and Caplan (2010) and Tallant and Ingram (2015). One of us has criticized this strategy in print (Torrengo 2014; but see also the more moderate position in Andreoletti et al. 2020).

28 See the baptism convention in sections 1.2.2 and 3.3.2.

29 The view has been first mentioned, but not discussed in detail, in Fine (2005). It has been explored in Iaquinto (2020) and defended in Zhan (2021).

30 See also Fine (2006: 400).

31 In analogy with the temporal case, Modal Fragmentalism does not require a commitment to the existence of facts as a distinct category. Once again, we adopt a definition in terms of facts only for ease of expression.

32 The details of the view are discussed in Iaquinto (2020: § 4).

33 A view similar to this is discussed in Bricker (2001, 2006), with the important difference that he allows more than one world to be absolutely actual, to support the possibility of island universes.

34 See also our discussion of Fine below, section 1.3.1.

35 A similar point is made by Lipman (2018). See also Deng (2013), who says, commenting on standard tense realism: 'The reason this is not quite satisfactory is that the passage of time manifests itself more in a change between descriptions of temporal reality, than in the content of the descriptions themselves' (p. 26).

36 See Prior and Fine (1977).

37 Notice that Fine (2005) uses the notion of an orientation towards a perspectival centre to characterize the standard framework and the idea of a unique present, but

he also considers the notion as strictly connected to tenses in general, as it is clear in Fine (2005: 275–6).

38 See Fine (2005: 306); here Fine is talking about the relativization of these realities to frame-time in the context of the relativistic expansion of the non-standard framework.
39 One obvious option is to take temporal locations as concrete entities (events, say), and identify them with the centre of the various perspectives. But then, as Fine correctly notices, external relativism would collapse into internal relativism, namely tense anti-realism. Fine considers other options too, but they all lead to failure. Fine does not consider the possibility of identifying temporal perspectives as locations in supertime. On this option see section 1.3.4.
40 The idea of a revenge argument comes from philosophy of logic in the context of the liar paradox. The sentence 'This sentence is not true' is paradoxical, because if it is true, then we have to conclude that it is not true, and if it is not true, then we have to conclude that it is true. A proposed solution is to interpret the notion of truth in terms of a different notion, for instance assertability. The sentence is then not true after all, since it is not assertable. Paradox solved. However, a different paradox, which constitutes the basis of the revenge argument against the solution to the original paradox, can be easily created by explicitly resorting to the notion of assertability. Consider: 'This sentence is non-assertable.' The *locus classicus* on the subject is Kripke (1975). See also Murzi and Rossi (2020).
41 Remember that 'co-obtainment' in Flow Fragmentalism is simply taken to mean 'obtainment relative to the fragment with the same label'.
42 Also the growing block view has an ontology that changes over time; cf. Tooley (1997), Correia and Rosenkranz (2018) and Forbes (2016). We will not focus on this option here though.
43 In favour, see Ingram (2019). Against, Skow (2015: Chap. 3).
44 See Iaquinto (2019) and Torrengo and Iaquinto (2019, 2020).
45 As anticipated in the Introduction, in footnote 15, it is indeed unclear whether there is a core thesis that all such positions have in common (see Tallant and Ingram 2021).
46 Cf. Fine (2005: 299, n. 28): 'Presentists in my sense [*viz.* factive presentists] have sometimes been called "A-theorists" or "tensers", though there is no established terminology.'
47 It is somehow strange that Fine does not stress this fact, given that the chapter's focus is precisely non-standard tense realism.
48 Torrengo (2012) argues for this distinction in general. See also Correia and Rosenkranz (2018), who adopt a similar conceptual machinery.
49 Note that the non-standard presentist disagrees with the tense anti-realist in that according to the latter if the fact that *Socrates exists simpliciter* constitutes reality, then it obtains at every time, regardless of whether Socrates is there located or not.

50 Cf. also Skow (2015: 65–6) where he briefly comments on the analogue of the Barcan formula for a non-standard tense realist theory.
51 See, among others, Heller (1992), Lombard (1999) and Benovsky (2009).
52 See Quine (1960), Lewis (1983), Heller (1990), Oderberg (1993), Casati and Varzi (1999) and Sider (2001).
53 Whether this is a problem for perdurantism is obviously a matter of controversy. See Lombard (1986: 128) for a positive answer and Sider (2001: 212–16) for a negative one.
54 See Heller (1992).
55 See also Lowe (2012: 95).
56 The details of this view are discussed in Iaquinto (2019).
57 We will come back on the issue of external vs. internal relations in Chapter 3.
58 Note also that being a counterpart only requires intrinsic similarity between entities, and intrinsic similarity is clearly an internal relation. I am similar to all my counterparts only in virtue of me having certain properties and them having the properties that they have.
59 As argued at length in Torrengo (2008).
60 See footnote 21.
61 The notion of verification here is not an epistemic one, but it is rather close to that of truth-making. See our Torrengo and Iaquinto (2019), where we discuss at length the argument from truth and provide a solution in a flow fragmentalist framework.
62 Italics in the original. Those remarks would suit us as glosses to our notions, respectively, of 'obtaining within the same fragment' and 'obtaining in two different fragments'.
63 Simplification for co-obtainment holds only in the special case in which the operator embeds an atomic sentence. In that case, one has simplification with respect to that sentence: $p \circ \phi \vDash p$. See Lipman (2015: 3130).
64 As Simon himself points out, his objection also applies to what he calls smooth fragmentalism, a somehow 'softened' version of fragmentalism where the only cases of incompatibility that reality is able to host are 'those cases of metaphysical incompatibility that do not generate logical incompatibility – i.e. distinct determinates of a common determinable, like being scarlet (all over) and being crimson (all over)' (p. 129).
65 For specular reasons, we also have that an atomic sentence is always false if evaluated relative to a pair of fragments. As Lipman (2018) has it, 'contrary to passage facts, [atomic facts] do not obtain *insofar as* matters pass' (p. 113).
66 See section 1.1.4. The point is extensively argued in Torrengo (2018). See also Dyke (2021: 52).
67 A diminished notion of tenses, in which they are merely perspectival and indexical representational tools is, of course, also coherent (and it is possibly a more general

one, applicable to anything that can be understood as a 'dimension' of reality. See Torrengo 2011). We are just claiming that it is not the notion employed in Flow Fragmentalism.

68 Notice that the idea of considering a cross-temporal relation as primitively dynamic has been explored also within the B-theoretic framework. See, on this, Maudlin (2007), who Lipman quotes, but also Deng (2010) and Leininger (2018, 2021).

69 How come they are not the same world then? The question has been asked in the literature. See Bricker (2001).

70 For more details on subvaluationism, see Varzi (1997) and Cobreros (2013).

71 Note that in his 2015 book, though, he explores non-standard versions of tense realism and defends a 'block universe' view.

72 Skow's supertime here is not a 'hyper-time', *viz.* a second dimension of time, as the one sometimes discussed in the framework of time travel scenarios (see Meiland 1974 and van Inwagen 2010). Rather, it bears similarity to Schleisinger (1991)'s modal notion of 'meta-time'. However, in his 2015 book, he uses the term for something closer to a further temporal dimension.

73 Already Williams (1951) points out a similar problem for the view that he attributes to McTaggart. Pooley (2013) dislikes the duplication of time because of the epistemic problems it gives rise to (see Braddon-Mitchell 2004).

74 'Now the idea that there is such a thing as supertime is crazy. It is just insane' (Skow 2015: 47).

75 Another alternative is to introduce irreducible super-tense operators. We will put that on the side, as Skow himself does not find this option very promising.

76 Skow (2015: 67) himself takes his proposal to be akin to external relativism.

2 Open Future

1 See, for instance, the references in Mariani and Torrengo (2022).

2 Of course, it is not trivial how to treat the semantics of definite descriptions in those situations, and we are not claiming that treating them as cases of indeterminate reference is the only, or the best, option. We are just using the example as an aid to intuitions.

3 In what follows, we will mainly talk about the presentist option, unless otherwise specified. But our remarks apply also to other non-eternalist ontologies.

4 Strictly speaking, a 'shrinking future' view would also make do. Cf. Casati and Torrengo (2011), Hudson (2014: Chap. 5), Norton (2015) and Lam (2021).

5 Barnes and Cameron (2009) and Cameron (2015) argue that branching fails to capture this and elaborate a model in which the future part of the universe is metaphysically indeterminate and yet unique.

6 See, for instance, Bourne (2006). In a similar vein, Le Poidevin (1991) observes that 'the extent to which the principle of bivalence is violated by statements about the past or future depends, for [the presentist], upon how much causal determinism he is prepared to allow.... In an indeterministic universe ... many statements about the future must ... lack a truth-value' (p. 38). To some extent, this position seems sympathetic to Markosian (2013: 137)'s one. He seems to think that within a presentist framework, if laws of nature turned out to be wildly indeterministic, it would be impossible to evaluate contingent truths about the past as true or false. And, we add, similar considerations could be easily applied to future contingent claims.

7 See Markosian (2013).

8 See Prior (1967: Chap. 7), Belnap et al. (2001: Chap. 6) and Øhrstrøm (2009).

9 Cf. Borghini and Torrengo (2012) for a defence of the thin red line option based on metaphysical considerations. See Torre (2011) for an overview.

10 Cf. Ciuni and Torrengo (2013).

11 See Bigelow (1996). Other options in the literature are adopting primitively tensed relations (Brogaard 2006, 2013), or embracing the haecceitist version of presentism (Keller 2004, Ingram 2016, 2018), which defines past and future entities as uninstantiated thisnesses. Still another option is to embrace a form of ersatzer presentism. The ersatzer takes times to be maximal abstract objects, that is, abstract representations of a given state of the world (see Bourne 2006 and Crisp 2007).

12 To be more precise, there are not *irreducible* weak future facts. One may well admit that as the strong future facts ground facts about future contingent truths, they also ground weak future facts.

13 Unless they simply stipulate that even if there is an actual future, the semantic for the tense language is not bivalent. But that seems highly ad hoc.

14 There are ways to salvage bivalence without appealing to the thin red line (cf. Barnes and Cameron 2009). According to those views, it is a fact that future contingents have now determined truth-values, although it is not (yet) determined which ones. For these options of course our rationale does not hold.

15 The idea of such a metaphysical 'pruning' has been explored in McCall (1994). Cameron (2015) argues that this topological change is not enough to account for the flow of time, but rather than adopting a growing block ontology, he argues for a view in which the future exists, but it is metaphysically undetermined, whereas the past is metaphysically determined. Mariani and Torrengo (2021) explore a similar picture, but in a context that is sympathetic towards the B-theory, and on the ground of the so-called dynamic models of quantum mechanics (whereas in Mariani and Torrengo (2022) a dynamic version is assessed).

16 The dialectical situation in the literature is a bit messy, since often philosophers *claim* that certain indeterministic physical theories, quantum mechanics or quantum

cosmology typically, support or suggest both an open future and a fundamental dynamism in reality. See for instance Lucas (1998). Forrest (2004) combines the growing block non-eternalist ontology with nomological indeterminism.

17 Is also constitution bound to be history-relative at bottom for the anti-realist who accepts topological openness? No, it may be that constituting reality relative to a history can be explained in terms of absolute constitution of a fact that is both time- and history-indexed, such as the fact that *Cleopatra is defeating Caesar at time t_x in history h_y*.

18 Can A-theoretic eternalism in its standard form (*viz.* the moving spotlight view) accept future facts in the strong sense? Cameron (2015: 64–8) argues that doing so would lead to a form of McTaggartesque paradox. As long as we stay within a standard framework, we agree that the answer is no.

19 As for instance in Bricker (2006)'s version of actualism, that combines modal realism with a primitive property of *vim* that only the actual world possesses.

20 See Thomason (1970).

21 We will use for pseudo-histories the same labels that we have used so far for histories, since there should be no problem of ambiguity.

22 In section 2.2.2 we will also discuss a, crucial for our account, vertical overlap between the fragments in the various pseudo-histories.

23 As we said in section 1.1.4.5, we employ the operator '$TENSE_n$' to express a distance of n units from the present. When n is negative, '$TENSE_n$' reads 'it was the case n units of time ago that'. When n is positive, the operator reads 'it will be the case in n units of time that'.

24 This entailment can be formally accounted for by means of a unary operator '$AT\ LEAST_n$', to be read as 'at least n units of time ago'. The background logic here is more complex than the one presented in the previous chapter. For all the details, the formal-minded reader can refer to the appendix (2.3) at the end of this chapter.

25 As we have underlined in the previous section, every past fact that we find in a given fragment is past in the weak sense, that is, it is nothing but a presently obtaining past-tensed fact (and analogously for future facts). The same goes for the 'at least' facts: they are past in a weak sense.

26 The motto has not to be taken literally, in terms of the number of facts involved. Rather it is the metric in the at least facts that gives us the order. Here we are considering only the discrete case for simplicity.

27 To keep things simple, we assume that F_1 and F_2 are the only 'future' fragments directly connected to F_0. Analogously, we assume that in the immediate 'future' of both F_1 and F_2 there are no more than two fragments.

28 See Varzi (2007).

29 See Koymans (1990) for details.

30 In the sense of Di Maio and Zanardo (1994: 269–73).

31 See Spolaore and Gallina (2020: § 2) for an example of synchronized metric tree structure.

3 Causation

1. Note that intrinsic facts can be relational, in the sense of being relations between the *parts* of the entity involved. Indeed, (i) may be seen as expressing relations between the part of my niece (or her body), roughly, a distance relation between the top of her head and the bottom of her toes. And the same can be said of (ii), *mutatis mutandis*.
2. The point is partly terminological. If one wish to count them as external, some terminological adjustments in what follows would then be in order.
3. Hence, virtually any view apart from those that accept a radically open or indeterminate past (cf. Lukasiewicz 1970: 127–8, Markosian 1995, and Bourne 2006: 47–50). Notice though that presentists have the related problem of the existence of singular propositions about entities that do not exist any longer (cf. p. 101).
4. See also Torrengo (2008, 2010), who argues that irreducible cross-temporality is a problem even for standard tense realists (presentists and non-presentists alike).
5. If one is a substantivist with respect to space, maybe the relation involves only indirectly my niece and me, in virtue of our being located at certain regions. However, the spatial relation between those regions would be an external relation in the sense relevant here.
6. Cf. Keller (2004) and Markosian (2004).
7. As we saw in section 1.3.2, Lipman (2018)'s version of fragmentalism is different, since it allows for at least one relation that is cross-fragment, that is, the relation of *passing into*.
8. Cf. Mumford and Anjum (2011).
9. Cartwright (1983) takes them to be approximate descriptions of causal powers.
10. See Goodman (1954).
11. More generally, the presentist has the problem of finding some alternative to space-time regions that are temporally extended. Cf. Brogaard (2007), who uses 'span' operators to achieve something similar.
12. Cf. De Clercq (2006), and Crisp (2005).
13. As Sider (1999) notes, an Armstrong-like conception may be problematic insofar as uninstantiated universals do not exist. We bracket this worry, as few others that the attentive readers may have here. On primitivism of the laws, see Maudlin (2007) and Carroll (1994).
14. Does that mean that cross-temporal individual causal claims are true, rather than quasi-true, for the presentist? Perhaps. After all, if the cross-temporal claim does not

express an external relation, then what it expresses is reducible to facts that (modulo worries about singularist causation below) can be accepted by the presentist. This is a thorny question that hinges on one's meta-ontology (or, more generally, on methodological considerations). Luckily we do not need to answer it, since the flow fragmentalist version of the strategy can unproblematically take cross-temporal claims about individual causation as true and if you believe that the presentist can do the same, there are just few terminological adjustments that you have to make.

15 Do they need to be irreducible? Not really, they just do not have to be reducible to the laws. They may be, for instance, derivative on primitive powers of basic entities.
16 The idea dates back to Prior (1968c, 1969), who treated the relation of temporal succession in terms of sentential connectives. See Torrengo (2008: 147). The treatment here is very loosely based on Sider (1999)'s.
17 Cf. several passages in Prior (1968b). See also Prior (1971).
18 For instance, Bigelow (1996) takes causation to be a relation between Lucretian properties, and Ingram (2019) a relation between presently existing thisnesses. See also Brogaard (2006)'s strategy, which is to adopt primitive cross-tensed relations and construe them as not entailing existence.
19 Note that a presentist could embed the whole statement into a past-tense operator. This is the original strategy suggested in Sider (1999), which is probably more faithful to Prior's. However, also in this case it would be ultimately about the present, since the whole past-tensed fact is still obtaining in the present.
20 Cf. Merlo (2013) and Fine (2020).
21 Note also that pattern facts remain stable across the fragments. More precisely, they remain stable across pseudo-histories (see p. 81) and thus stable on the actual course of events, the invisible thin red line. A bit trickier to say what happens if Humean Supervenience is not true, but we do not see why the facts concerning universals on which the laws are grounded should vary through fragments. The same goes for primitivism about laws.
22 As stated, we are making the simplifying assumption that there is only one event per couple of coordinates. If we drop this assumption, for the convention to work we will have to assume that we have some independent way to individuate events that are co-located at the same coordinates, and add a third parameter n_x with a name for each event. So that by snapping the fingers we label $e_{(t_0, s_0, n_0)}$.
23 See Reichenbach (1956: Part 2), Grünbaum (1974: Chap. 7), and Sklar (1974: 318–47).

4 Relativity

1. It is a legitimate attitude to bracket the complications that arise from considering relativistic settings, when formulating a metaphysics of time. Recent examples of this attitudes are Cameron (2015) and Ingram (2019).
2. Cf. Zimmerman (2011) and Markosian (2004).
3. Recent contributions in metaphysics of time that explicitly elaborate relativistic versions of their theories are Skow (2015) and Correia and Rosenkranz (2018). The main reason why we think it is bad to deflate special relativity and at the same time accepting an absolute, non-frame independent relation of simultaneity is that by doing so we seem compelled to conclude that the universe *conspires* against the possibility of discovering empirically which events are absolutely simultaneous with the one we currently experience.
4. In principle, we could treat simultaneity differently, as a genuine temporal relation. However, unless Newtonian space-time is fundamental, there are no good reasons to do so, as it will be clear from what follows. Notice also that once we have a metric version of the earlier/later relation, it is natural to treat simultaneity as a special case of it, the one in which the metric parameter (expressing the temporal distance) is set to zero.
5. We are not here considering the complications due to general relativity and quantum gravity.
6. Non-vacuously in the sense that a temporal relation between two events can hold relative to one frame of reference but not relative to another. Notice that we do not say that the relativization must be fundamental or 'irreducible', since once we consider metric facts, the fact that relative to a certain frame of reference a certain temporal relation holds between two events can be reduced to absolute facts about the space-time interval.
7. As we will see in the last section, this simplification will create a glitch, and we will have to drop it to be precise when we formulate our theory of a relativistic flow (see footnote 16).
8. Cf. Mermin (2009), for instance.
9. Notice that once we have (arbitrarily) selected one frame, e_0 will be contained only in *one* hyperplane of simultaneity.
10. See Hofweber and Lange (2017, 2020) and Iaquinto and Calosi (ms). The view is also discussed in Slavov (2020). For a defence of frame-theoretic relativistic fragmentalism, see Lipman (2020).
11. To be fair, while more or less everybody agrees that systems of coordinates are conventional, not everybody agrees that inertial frames of reference are so; see Di Salle (2020).

12 Fine (2005: 303) considers this option briefly, but only in the context of criticizing *standard* tense realism for not allowing the formulation of a convincing relativistic notion of tense. See also Clifton and Hogarth (1995) – mentioned by Fine too – for certain similarities with our view.
13 On the notion of time-like, light-like, and space-like separation see, for instance, Mermin (2009). Causal connectivity coincides with being either time-like or light-like separated.
14 Notice that the frame-theoretic conception is closer to the non-relativistic case in this respect, since even if the perspectival centre of a frame-theoretic fragment is relative to a frame of reference, it is nonetheless global: it comprises facts concerning the whole temporal dimension, although from the point of view, as it were, of the selected frame.
15 No branching in the sense that they are all 'in' the invisible thin red line (see Chapter 2). Bringing together branching future and relativity is not something that will engage us in the present book. For an attempt (not in a fragmentalist setting), see Belnap (1992) and Belnap et al. (2021).
16 There is a bit of dust under the carpet here with respect to the interaction between the metric index n and the index y. As the attentive reader may recall, indices like y are supposed to be shorthands for quadruples of Minkowskian coordinates (see p. 120). Fixing things precisely would require convoluted and boring specifications. Intuitively, we can construct a metric for each RP-history, because we know that the events in h_x are totally ordered by $<_{psC}$ and the metric of the tense operators is defined on *that* order. Hence, it is possible to label the events in each history in a way such that the metric parameter n of the tense operator '$TENSE_n$' makes us shift along h_x accordingly.

5 Time Travel

1 Cf. Earman (1995: Chap. 6) and Smeenk and Wüthrich (2011). There are philosophers who explicitly argue against the metaphysical possibility of time travel. See, for instance, Mellor (1998) for an argument within a tense anti-realist framework, and Markosian (2020) for an argument within a tense realist one.
2 Of course not any random thought experiment is necessarily a good experiment for any philosophical reflection, but time travel seems to have the right features of taking temporal notions to the limit.
3 For simplicity we consider cases in which the traveller is a person, but the idea, with some adjustments, can be expanded to other entities (cf. Wassermann 2018) and also to the case in which the backward causal link is not part of the life of anything (e.g. when information is sent to the past).

4 The first term comes from Igor Dmitriyevich Novikov, a physicist who in the early 1980s studied the consistency constraints in general relativity for closed timelike curves (i.e. paths to the past). The second term is in honour of the philosopher David Lewis.
5 On the distinction between *affecting* the past and *changing* the past, see Casati and Varzi (2001).
6 To accommodate the symbols more easily in the figures, we will use 'F_n' as we have used so far '$WILL_n$', namely as for what informally we would express with 'it will be the case, n units of time in the future, that', and 'P_n' as we have used so far 'WAS_n', namely as for what informally we would express with 'it was the case, n units of time in the past, that'. We are positive that the ambiguity between the symbol for the future tense operator and the label for fragments won't create confusion.
7 We are here using Greek letters as signposts for specific sentences. In the previous chapters, we used them, more standardly, as meta-variables. We do this here mainly for graphical clarity.
8 To the best of our knowledge, there is no good argument against Novikovian time travel. On this point see e.g. Dowe (2000).
9 For good science fiction that depict Novikovian scenarios, see: any time travel story by R. A. Heinlein (e.g. the novel *The Door Into Summer*, 1956), several episodes of the series *Red Dwarf* (1988–present), and movies such as *Bill and Ted's Excellent Adventure* (Stephen Herek, 1989), *Twelve Monkeys* (Terry Gilliam, 1995), *Los Cronocrimines* (Nacho Vigalondo, 2007), *Interstellar* (Christopher Nolan, 2014) and *Predestination* (Michael and Peter Spierig, 2014, based on a short story by Heinlein).
10 More precisely: $t_y \neq t_k$, but it is not ruled out that either t_y or t_k is identical with t_x.
11 Season 2, Episode 13; first aired in 1989.
12 This is the 'how do we know that we are in the present?' problem (cf. Braddon-Mitchell 2004).
13 See Forrest (2004).
14 Bourne (2002) uses the problem of the zombie in the past (or more precisely, the problem of how we can know that we are in the objective present) as a reason to endorse presentism. Braddon-Mitchell (2004) also thinks that the presentist does not suffer from the problem. However, Cameron (2015) disagrees.
15 Notice that even if we allow for something weaker than truth, for instance empirical adequacy, in the style of van Fraassen (1980), it is likely that we find ourselves in the same position, given that the *qualitative* profile in question is one that has been changed by changing the past.
16 Besides, the idea of a purified flow forces us to individuate the temporal locations independently of the facts that obtain at the fragment centred on each of them, and thus it runs into at least some of the problems that the external relativist, as opposed to the fragmentalist, is bound to face (cf. p. 45).

17 If you are familiar with Asimov's *The End of Eternity* (1955), you can think of the tracking role as what tells us how 'our' temporal dimension looks like from the point of view of the inhabitants of Eternity.
18 Cf. Wasserman (2018) and Saunders et al. (2010).
19 More precisely, into classes of classes, since each universe corresponds to a sequence of fragments sharing the same tracking parameter.
20 The idea bears some analogy with the idea of a five-dimensional manifold of Lockwood (2005). And even if it is A-theoretic, it does not have the problems raised by Abruzzese (2001). We do not discuss here the 'slicing problem' for universe hopping (cf. Effingham 2012).
21 To dispel a possible ambiguity. The tracking parameter is a parameter of fragments, which expresses the time that has the tracking role for that fragment. We sometimes talk of the tracking parameter of a temporal location to indicate the content profile of the temporal location in the fragments that have that tracking parameter.
22 Thanks to Nikk Effingham for raising this objection.
23 Vacillating time is a theory that comes also in a tenseless version, but in what follows we are restricting ourselves to the tensed version only.
24 See Bernstein (2014) and Wasserman (2018).
25 Recently defended by Effingham (2020, 2021).
26 If you are not familiar with the Star Trek universe: the Borg are a collective, and try to assimilate any technologically advanced civilization they encounter by reducing them to 'drones' connected to a hive mind. They are the arch-enemies of the Federation (the 'good guys'), and their mantra is 'resistance is futile'. They normally inhabit the Delta Quadrant of our galaxy, but occasionally attempt to conquer the Alpha Quadrant where most of the planets of the Federation are.

References

Abruzzese, J. (2001), 'On Using the Multiverse to Avoid the Paradoxes of Time Travel', *Analysis*, 61: 36–8.

Andreoletti, G., J. Tallant and T. Giuliano (2020), 'Purely Theoretical Explanations', *Philosophia*, 49: 133–54.

Bacon, A. (2018), 'Tense and Relativity', *Noûs*, 52: 667–96.

Balashov, Y. (2015), 'Experiencing the Present', *Epistemology and Philosophy of Science*, 54: 61–73.

Barnes, E. and R. Cameron (2009), 'The Open Future: Bivalence, Determinism and Ontology', *Philosophical Studies*, 146: 291–309.

Belnap, N. (1992), 'Branching Space-time', *Synthese*, 92: 385–434.

Belnap, N., T. Müller and T. Placek (2021), *Branching Space-times. Theory and Applications*, Oxford: Oxford University Press.

Belnap, N., M. Perloff and M. Xu (2001), *Facing the Future. Agents and Choices in Our Indeterminist World*, Oxford: Oxford University Press.

Benovsky, J. (2009), 'Presentism and Persistence', *Pacific Philosophical Quarterly*, 90: 291–309.

Bergmann, G. (1967), *Realism. A Critique of Brentano and Meinong*, Madison, WI: University of Wisconsin Press.

Bernstein, S. (2014), 'Time Travel and the Movable Present', in *Being, Freedom, and Method: Themes from the Philosophy of Peter van Inwagen*, Oxford: Oxford University Press.

Bigelow, J. (1996), 'Presentism and Properties', *Philosophical Perspectives*, 10: 35–52.

Blackburn, P. (2006), 'Arthur Prior and Hybrid Logic', *Synthese*, 150: 329–72.

Borghini, A. and G. Torrengo (2012), 'The Metaphysics of the Thin Red Line', in F. Correia and A. Iacona (eds.), *Around the Tree*, Berlin: Springer Verlag, pp. 105–25.

Bourne, C. (2002), 'When am I? A Tense Time for Some Tense Theorists?', *Australasian Journal of Philosophy*, 80: 359–71.

Bourne, C. (2006), *A Future for Presentism*, Oxford: Oxford University Press.

Braddon-Mitchell, D. (2004), 'How Do We Know it is Now Now?', *Analysis*, 64: 199–203.

Bricker, P. (2001), 'Island Universes and the Analysis of Modality', in G. Preyer and F. Siebelt (eds.), *Reality and Humean Supervenience: Essays on the Philosophy of David Lewis*, Lanham, MD: Rowman & Littlefield, pp. 27–55.

Bricker, P. (2006), 'Absolute Actuality and the Plurality of Worlds', *Philosophical Perspectives*, 20: 41–76.

Brogaard, B. (2000), 'Presentist Four-dimensionalism', *The Monist*, 83: 341–54.

Brogaard, B. (2006), 'Tensed Relations', *Analysis*, 66: 194–202.
Brogaard, B. (2007), 'Span Operators', *Analysis*, 67: 72–9.
Brogaard, B. (2013), 'Presentism, Primitivism and Cross-temporal Relations: Lessons from Holistic Ersatzism and Dynamic Semantics', in R. Ciuni, K. Miller and G. Torrengo (eds.), *New Papers on the Present: Focus on Presentism*, Munich: Philosophia Verlag, pp. 253–77.
Callender, C. (2017), *What Makes Time Special?* Oxford: Oxford University Press.
Cameron, R. P. (2015), *The Moving Spotlight: An Essay on Time and Ontology*, Oxford: Oxford University Press.
Cameron, R. P. (2018), 'Skow, Objective Becoming and the Moving Spotlight', *Analysis*, 78: 97–108.
Carroll, J. (1994), *Laws of Nature*, Cambridge: Cambridge University Press.
Cartwright, N. (1983), *How the Laws of Physics Lie*, Oxford: Clarendon Press.
Casati R. and G. Torrengo (2011), 'The Not so Incredible Shrinking Future', *Analysis*, 71: 240–4.
Casati, R. and A. Varzi (1999), *Parts and Places*, Cambridge, MA: MIT Press.
Casati, R. and A. Varzi (2001), 'That Useless Time Machine', *Philosophy*, 76: 581–3.
Ciuni, R. and G. Torrengo (2013), 'Presentism and Cross-temporal Relations', in R. Ciuni, K. Miller and G. Torrengo (eds.), *New Papers on the Present: Focus on Presentism*, Munich: Philosophia Verlag, pp. 212–52.
Clifton, R. and M. Hogarth (1995), 'The Definability of Objective Becoming in Minkowski Space-Time', *Synthese*, 203: 355–87.
Cobreros, P. (2013), 'Vagueness: Subvaluationism', *Philosophy Compass*, 8: 472–85.
Correia, F. and S. Rosenkranz (2011), *As Time Goes By. Eternal Facts in an Ageing Universe*, Paderborn: Mentis.
Correia, F. and S. Rosenkranz (2012), 'Eternal Facts in an Ageing Universe', *Australasian Journal of Philosophy*, 90: 307–20.
Correia, F. and S. Rosenkranz (2018), *Nothing to Come: A Defence of the Growing Block Theory of Time*, Berlin: Springer Verlag.
Correia, F. and S. Rosenkranz (2020), 'Unfreezing the Spotlight: Tense Realism and Temporal Passage', *Analysis*, 80: 21–30.
Correia, F. and S. Rosenkranz (forthcoming), 'From Tense Realism to Realism about Temporal Passage: Reply to Nihel Jhou', *Analysis*.
Crisp, T. (2005), 'Presentism and 'Cross-time' Relations', *American Philosophical Quarterly*, 42: 5–17.
Crisp, T. (2007), 'Presentism and the Grounding Objection', *Noûs*, 41: 90–109.
Deasy, D. (2015), 'The Moving Spotlight Theory', *Philosophical Studies*, 172: 2073–89.
Deasy, D. (2018), 'Philosophical Arguments Against the A-theory', *Pacific Philosophical Quarterly*, 99: 270–92.
Deasy, D. (2021), 'The Modal Moving Spotlight Theory', *Mind*, online first.
De Clercq, R. (2006), 'Presentism and the Problem of Cross-time Relations', *Philosophy and Phenomenological Research*, 72: 386–402.

De Florio, C. and A. Frigerio (2017), 'A Note on Eternity', *Topoi*, 36: 685–692.

De Florio, C. and A. Frigerio (2019), *Divine Omniscience and Human Free Will. A Logical and Metaphysical Analysis*, London: Palgrave Macmillan.

Deng, N. (2010), '"Beyond A- and B-Time" Reconsidered', *Philosophia*, 38: 741–53.

Deng, N. (2013), 'Fine's McTaggart, Temporal Passage, and the A versus B-debate', *Ratio*, 26: 19–34.

Di Maio, M. C. and A. Zanardo (1994), 'Synchronized Histories in Prior-Thomason Representation of Branching Time', in D. Gabbay and H. Ohlbach (eds.), *Proceedings of the First International Conference on Temporal Logic*, Dordrecht: Springer, pp. 265–82.

Di Salle, R. (2020), 'Space and Time: Inertial Frames', in E. N. Zalta (ed.), *The Standford Encyclopedia of Philosophy*, https://plato.stanford.edu/archives/win2020/entries/spacetime-iframes.

Dorato, M. (2002), 'On Becoming, Cosmic Time and Rotating Universes', *Royal Institute of Philosophy Supplement*, 50: 253–76.

Dowe, P. (2000), 'The Case for Time Travel', *Philosophy*, 75: 441–51.

Dyke, H. (2003), 'Tensed Meaning: A Tenseless Account', *Journal of Philosophical Research*, 27: 67–83.

Dyke, H. (2013), 'Time and Tense', in H. Dyke and A. Bardon (eds), *A Companion to the Philosophy of Time*, Oxford: Wiley-Blackwell, pp. 328–44.

Dyke, H. (2021), *Time*, Cambridge: Cambridge University Press.

Earman, J. (1995), *Bangs, Crunches, Whimpers and Shrieks: Singularities and Acausalities in Relativistic Spacetimes*, Oxford: Oxford University Press.

Effingham, N. (2012), 'An Unwelcome Consequence of the Multiverse Thesis', *Synthese*, 184: 375–86.

Effingham, N. (2020), *Time Travel: Probability and Impossibility*, Oxford: Oxford University Press.

Effingham, N. (2021), 'Vacillating Time: A Metaphysics for Time Travel and Geachianism', *Synthese*, 99: 7159–80.

Eker, B. (2022), 'The A-theory of Time, Temporal Passage, and Comprehensiveness', *Synthese*, online first.

Fine, K. (2005), 'Tense and Reality', in K. Fine, *Modality and Tense*, Oxford: Oxford University Press, pp. 261–320.

Fine, K. (2006), 'The Reality of Tense', *Synthese*, 150: 399–414.

Fine, K. (2020), 'Comments on Philip Percival's "Beyond Reality?"', in M. Dumitru (ed.), *Metaphysics, Meaning, and Modality: Themes from Kit Fine*, Oxford: Oxford University Press, pp. 403–11.

Forbes, G. A. (2016), 'The Growing Block's Past Problems', *Philosophical Studies*, 173: 699–709.

Forrest, P. (2004), 'The Real but Dead Past: A Reply to Braddon-Mitchell', *Analysis*, 64: 358–62.

Forrest, P. (2006), 'Uniform Grounding of Truth and the Growing Block Theory: A Reply to Heathwood', *Analysis*, 66: 161–3.

Frischhut, A. (2013), *The Experience of Temporal Passage*, PhD Thesis, University of Glasgow.

Gale, R. M. (1968), *The Language of Time*, London: Routledge and Kegan Paul.

Gödel, K. (1949), 'A Remark About the Relationship Between Relativity Theory and Idealistic Philosophy', in P. A. Schilpp (ed.), *Albert Einstein: Philosopher-Scientist*, La Salle IL: Open Court, pp. 557–62.

Goodman, N. (1954), *New Riddle of Induction in Fact, Fiction and Forecast*, London: University of London, Athlone Press.

Grünbaum, A. (1974), *Philosophical Problems of Space and Time*, Boston: D. Reidel Publishing.

Haslanger, S. (2003), 'Persistence Through Time', in M. J. Loux and D. Zimmerman (eds.), *The Oxford Handbook of Metaphysics*, Oxford: Oxford University Press, 315–56.

Heller, M. (1990), *The Ontology of Physical Objects: Four-Dimensional Hunks of Matter*, Cambridge: Cambridge University Press.

Heller, M. (1992), 'Things Change', *Philosophy and Phenomenological Research*, 52: 695–704.

Hofweber, T. and M. Lange (2017), 'Fine's Fragmentalist Interpretation of Special Relativity', *Noûs*, 51: 871–83.

Hofweber, T. and M. Lange (2020), 'Fragmentalism and Special Relativity', *Theorema*, 39: 5–15.

Hudson, H. (2014), *The Fall and Hypertime*, Oxford: Oxford University Press.

Iaquinto, S. (2019), 'Fragmentalist Presentist Perdurantism', *Philosophia*, 47: 693–703.

Iaquinto, S. (2020), 'Modal Fragmentalism', *The Philosophical Quarterly*, 70: 570–87.

Iaquinto, S. and C. Calosi (2021), 'Is The World a Heap of Quantum Fragments?', *Philosophical Studies*, 178: 2009–19.

Iaquinto, S. and C. Calosi (ms), 'Is the World a Heap of Relativistic Fragments?'.

Ingram, D. (2016), 'The Virtues of Thisness Presentism', *Philosophical Studies*, 173: 2867–88.

Ingram, D. (2018), 'Thisnesses, Propositions, and Truth', *Pacific Philosophical Quarterly*, 99: 442–63.

Ingram, D. (2019), *Thisness Presentism: An Essay on Time, Truth, and Ontology*, Oxford: Routledge.

Ingthorsson, R.D. (2016), *McTaggart's Paradox*, Oxford: Routledge.

Jhou, N. H. (2021), 'The Moving Spotlighter's Way of "Unfreezing the Spotlight"', *Analysis*, 81: 439–47.

Kant, I. (1781), *Critique of Pure Reason*, translation by N. Kemp-Smith (1929), London: MacMillan.

Keller, S. (2004), 'Presentism and Truthmaking', in D. Zimmerman (ed.), *Oxford Studies in Metaphysics, Volume 1*, Oxford: Oxford University Press, pp. 83–104.

Koymans, R. (1990), 'Specifying Real-time Properties with Metric Temporal Logic', *Real-Time Systems*, 2(4): 255–99.

Kripke, S. (1975), 'Outline of a Theory of Truth', *The Journal of Philosophy*, 72: 690–716.

Lam, D. (2021), 'The Phenomenology and Metaphysics of the Open Future', *Philosophical Studies*, 178: 3895–3921.

Leininger, L. (2015), 'Presentism and the Myth of Passage', *Australasian Journal of Philosophy*, 93: 724–39.

Leininger, L. (2018), 'Objective Becoming: In Search of A-ness', *Analysis*, 78: 108–17.

Leininger, L. (2021), 'Temporal B-Coming: Passage without Presentness', *Australasian Journal of Philosophy*, 99: 130–47.

Le Poidevin, R. (1991), *Change, Cause and Contradiction: A Defence of the Tenseless Theory of Time*, London: Macmillan.

Lewis, D. (1976), 'The Paradoxes of Time Travel', *American Philosophical Quarterly*, 13: 145–52.

Lewis, D. (1983), *Philosophical Papers*, Oxford: Oxford University Press.

Lewis, D. (1986), *On the Plurality of Worlds*, Oxford: Blackwell.

Lipman, M. (2015), 'On Fine's Fragmentalism', *Philosophical Studies*, 172: 3119–33.

Lipman, M. (2016), 'Perspectival Variance and Worldly Fragmentation', *Australasian Journal of Philosophy*, 94: 42–57.

Lipman, M. (2018), 'A Passage Theory of Time.' In K. Bennet and D. Zimmermann (eds.), *Oxford Studies in Metaphysics, Volume 11*, Oxford: Oxford University Press, pp. 95–122.

Lipman, M. (2020), 'On the Fragmentalist Interpretation of Special Relativity', *Philosophical Studies*, 177: 21–37.

Lockwood, M. (2005), *The Labyrinth of Time*, Oxford: Oxford University Press.

Lombard, L. (1986), *Events: A Metaphysical Study*, London: Routledge and Kegan Paul.

Lombard, L. (1999), 'On the Alleged Incompatibility of Presentism and Temporal Parts', *Philosophia*, 27: 253–60.

Loss, R. (2017), 'Fine's McTaggart: Reloaded', *Manuscrito*, 40: 209–39.

Lowe, E. J. (1987a), 'Reply to Le Poidevin and Mellor', *Mind*, 96: 539–42.

Lowe, E. J. (1987b), 'The Indexical Fallacy in McTaggart's Proof of the Unreality of Time', *Mind*, 96: 62–70.

Lowe, E. J. (1998), *The Possibility of Metaphysics: Substance, Identity, and Time*, Oxford: Clarendon Press.

Lowe, E. J. (2010), 'Ontological Dependence', in E. N. Zalta (ed.), *The Standford Encyclopedia of Philosophy*, http://plato.stanford.edu/archives/spr2010/entries/dependence-ontological.

Lowe, E. J. (2012), 'Against Monism', in P. Goff (ed.), *Spinoza on Monism*, London: Palgrave Macmillan, pp. 92–122.

Lucas, J. R. (1998), 'Transcendental Tense II', *Aristotelian Society Supplementary*, 72: 29–43.

Lukasiewicz, J. (1970), *Selected Works*, Amsterdam: North Holland.

Mariani, C. and G. Torrengo (2021), 'The Indeterminate Present and the Open Future', *Synthese*, 199: 3923–44.

Mariani, C. and G. Torrengo (2022), 'The Metaphysics of Passage in Dynamical Reduction Models of Quantum Mechanism', in A. Santelli (ed.), *Ockhamism and*

Philosophy of Time: Semantic and Metaphysical Issues Concerning Future Contingents, Berlin: Springer Verlag, pp. 147–72.

Markosian, N. (1995), 'The Open Past', *Philosophical Studies*, 79: 95–105.

Markosian, N. (2004), 'A Defense of Presentism', in D. Zimmerman (ed.), *Oxford Studies in Metaphysics, Volume 1*, Oxford: Oxford University Press, pp. 47–82.

Markosian, N. (2013), 'The Truth About the Past and the Future', in F. Correia and A. Iacona (eds.), *Around the Tree*, Berlin: Springer Verlag, pp. 127–42.

Markosian, N. (2020), 'The Dynamic Theory of Time and Time Travel to the Past', *Disputatio*, 12: 137–65.

Maudlin, T. (2007), 'On the Passing of Time', in *The Metaphysics within Physics*, Oxford: Oxford University Press, pp. 104–42.

McCall, S. (1994), *A Model of the Universe*, Oxford: Oxford University Press.

McTaggart, J. M. E. (1908), 'The Unreality of Time', *Mind*, 17: 457–573. Reprinted in R. Le Poidevin and M. McBeath (eds.) (1993), *The Philosophy of Time*, Oxford: Oxford University Press, pp. 23–34.

Meiland, J. W. (1974), 'A Two-dimensional Passage Model of Time for Time Travel', *Philosophical Studies*, 26: 153–73.

Mellor, D. H. (1998), *Real Time II*, London: Routledge.

Merlo, G. (2013), 'Specialness and Egalitarianism', *Thought*, 2: 248–57.

Merlo, G. (2022), 'Fragmentalism We can Believe in', *The Philosophical Quarterly*, online first.

Mermin, D. N. (2009), *It's About Time: Understanding Einstein's Relativity*, Princeton, NJ: Princeton University Press.

Merriam, P. (2022), 'A Theory of the Big Bang in McTaggart's Time', *Axiomathes*, online first.

Meyer, U. (2005), 'The Presentist's Dilemma', *Philosophical Studies*, 122: 213–25.

Mumford, S. and R. L. Anjum (2011), *Getting Causes from Powers*, Oxford: Oxford University Press.

Murzi, J. and L. Rossi (2020), 'Generalized Revenge', *Australasian Journal of Philosophy*, 98: 153–77.

Norton, J. D. (2010), 'Time Really Passes', *Humana.Mente*, 4: 23–34.

Norton, J. D. (2015), 'The Burning Fuse Model of Unbecoming in Time', *Studies in History and Philosophy of Modern Physics*, 52: 103–5.

Oaklander, L. N. (2015), 'Temporal Phenomena, Ontology and the R-Theory', *Metaphysica*, 16: 253–69.

Oaklander, L. N. and Q. Smith (eds.) (1994). *The New Theory of Time*, New Heaven, CT: Yale University Press.

Oderberg, D. S. (1993), *The Metaphysics of Identity over Time*, London: MacMillan.

Øhrstrøm, P. (2009), 'In Defense of the Thin Red Line', *Humana.mente*, 8: 17–32.

Pickup, M. (forthcoming), 'The Situationalist Account of Change', in *Oxford Studies in Metaphysics*, Oxford: Oxford University Press.

Pooley, O. (2013), 'Relativity, the Open Future, and the Passage of Time', *Proceedings of the Aristotelian Society*, 113: 321–63.

Priest, G. (1979), 'The Logic of Paradox', *Journal of Philosophical Logic*, 8: 219–41.
Priest, G. (1987), 'Tense, Tense and Tense', *Analysis*, 47: 184–7.
Prior, A. N. (1958), 'Time after Time', *Mind*, 67: 244–6.
Prior, A. N. (1967), *Past, Present, and Future*, Oxford: Oxford University Press.
Prior, A. N. (1968a), 'Changes in Events and Changes in Things', in A. N. Prior (1968b), *Papers on Time and Tense*, Oxford: Oxford University Press, pp. 1–14.
Prior, A. N. (1968b), *Papers on Time and Tense*, Oxford: Oxford University Press.
Prior, A. N. (1968c), 'Stratified Metric Tense Logic', in A. N. Prior (1968b), *Papers on Time and Tense*, Oxford: Oxford University Press, pp. 88–97.
Prior, A. N. (1969), 'Tensed Propositions as Predicates', *American Philosophical Quarterly*, 6: 290–7. Also in P. Alse et al. (eds.) (2003), *A.N. Prior, Papers on Time and Tense. New Edition*, Oxford: Oxford University Press, pp. 195–212.
Prior, A. N. (1971), *Objects of Thought*, Oxford: Oxford University Press.
Prior, A. N. and K. Fine (1977), *Worlds, Times and Selves*, London: Duckworth.
Quine, W. V. O. (1960), *Word and Object*, Cambridge, MA: MIT Press.
Reichenbach, H. (1956), *The Direction of Time*, Berkeley and Los Angeles: University of California Press.
Russell, B. (1903), *The Principles of Mathematics*, Cambridge: Cambridge University Press.
Sanson, D. and B. Caplan (2010), 'The Way Things Were', *Philosophy and Phenomenological Research*, 81: 24–39.
Sattig, T. (2019a), 'XIII – The Flow of Time in Experience', *Proceedings of the Aristotelian Society*, 119: 275–93.
Sattig, T. (2019b), 'The Sense of Temporal Flow: A Higher-order Account', *Philosophical Studies*, 176: 3041–59.
Saunders, S., J. Barrett, A. Kent and D. Wallace (2010), *Many Worlds? Everett, Quantum Theory, & Reality*, Oxford: Oxford University Press.
Savitt, S. (2002), 'On Absolute Becoming and the Myth of Passage', in C. Callender (ed.), *Time, Reality and Experience*, Cambridge: Cambridge University Press, pp. 153–68.
Savitt, S. (2016), 'Kit Fine on Tense and Reality', *Manuscrito*, 39: 75–99.
Schleisinger, G. N. (1991), 'E Pur Si Muove', *The Philosophical Quarterly*, 41: 427–41.
Shoemaker S. (1969), 'Time Without Change', *Journal of Philosophy*, 66: 363–81.
Sider T. (1999), 'Presentism and Ontological Commitment', *The Journal of Philosophy*, 96: 325–47.
Sider, T. (2001), *Four-Dimensionalism. An Ontology of Persistence and Time*, Oxford: Oxford University Press.
Sider, T. (2011), *Writing the Book of the World*, Oxford: Oxford University Press.
Simon, J. (2018), 'Fragmenting the Wave Function, in K. Bennett and D. Zimmerman (eds.), *Oxford Studies in Metaphysics, Volume 11*, Oxford: Oxford University Press, pp. 123–45.
Sklar, L. (1974), *Space, Time, and Spacetime*, Berkeley and Los Angeles: University of California Press.

Skow, B. (2009), 'Relativity and the Moving Spotlight', *Journal of Philosophy*, 106: 666–78.
Skow, B. (2012), 'Why Does Time Pass?', *Noûs*, 46: 223–42.
Skow, B. (2015), *Objective Becoming*, Oxford: Oxford University Press.
Slavov, M. (2020), 'Eternalism and Perspectival Realism about the "Now"', *Foundations of Physics*, 50: 1398–1410.
Smeenk, C. and C. Wüthrich (2011), 'Time Travel and Time Machines', in C. Callender (ed.), *The Oxford Handbook of Philosophy of Time*, Oxford: Oxford University Press, pp. 577–630.
Smith, Q. (2002), 'Time and Degrees of Existence', in C. Callender (ed.), *Time, Reality and Experience*, Cambridge: Cambridge University Press.
Solomyak, O. (2013), 'Actuality and the Amodal Perspective', *Philosophical Studies*, 164: 15–40.
Solomyak, O. (2020), 'Temporal Ontology and the Metaphysics of Perspectives', *Erkenntnis*, 85: 431–53.
Spolaore, G. and F. Gallina (2020), 'The Actual Future is Open', *Erkenntnis*, 85: 99–119.
Spolaore, G. and G. Torrengo (2019), 'The Moving Spotlight', *Inquiry*, 64: 754–71.
Stein, H. (1991), 'On Relativity Theory and the Openness of the Future', *Philosophy of Science*, 58: 147–67.
Sullivan, M. (2012), 'The Minimal A-theory', *Philosophical Studies*, 158: 149–74.
Tallant, J. (2012), '(Existence) Presentism and the A-theory', *Analysis*, 72: 673–81.
Tallant, J. (2013), 'A Heterodox Presentism: Kit Fine's Theory', in R. Ciuni, K. Miller and G. Torrengo (eds.), *New Papers on the Present*, Munchen: Philosophia Verlag, pp. 281–306.
Tallant, J. (2014), 'Defining Existence Presentism', *Erkenntnis*, 79: 479–501.
Tallant, J. (2015), 'The New A-theory of Time', *Inquiry*, 58: 537–62.
Tallant, J. (2018), 'Presentism, Persistence and Trans-temporal Dependence', *Philosophical Studies*, 175: 2209–20.
Tallant, J. and D. Ingram (2015), 'Nefarious Presentism', *The Philosophical Quarterly*, 65: 355–71.
Tallant, J. and D. Ingram (2021), 'The Rotten Core of Presentism', *Synthese*, 199: 3969–91.
Thomason, R. H. (1970), 'Indeterminist Time and Truth Value Gap', *Theoria*, 34: 264–81.
Tooley, M. (1997), *Time, Tense and Causation*, Oxford: Oxford University Press.
Torre, S. (2011), 'The Open Future', *Philosophy Compass*, 6: 360–73.
Torrengo, G. (2008), *Time and Cross-temporal Relations*, Mimesis: Milan.
Torrengo, G. (2010), 'Time, Context, and Cross-temporal Claims', *Philosophia*, 38: 281–96.
Torrengo, G. (2011), 'The Modal Dimension', *Humana.Mente*, 19: 105–20.
Torrengo, G. (2012), 'Time and Simple Existence', *Metaphysica*, 13: 125–30.
Torrengo, G. (2014), 'Ostrich Presentism', *Philosophical Studies*, 170: 255–76.
Torrengo, G. (2018), 'Perspectival Tenses and Dynamic Tenses', *Erkenntnis*, 83: 1045–61.
Torrengo, G. and D. Cassaghi (2021), 'The Ways of Presentness', *Erkenntnis*, online first.
Torrengo, G. and S. Iaquinto (2019), 'Flow Fragmentalism', *Theoria*, 85: 185–201.

Torrengo, G. and S. Iaquinto (2020), 'The Invisible Thin Red Line', *Pacific Philosophical Quarterly*, 101: 354–82.
van Fraassen, B. (1980), *The Scientific Image*, Oxford: Oxford University Press.
van Inwagen, P. (2010), 'Changing the Past', in D. Zimmerman (ed.), *Oxford Studies in Metaphysics, Volume 5*, Oxford: Oxford University Press, pp. 3–28.
Varzi, A. (1997), 'Inconsistency without Contradiction', *Notre Dame Journal of Formal Logic*, 38: 621–39.
Varzi, A. (2007), 'Supervaluationism and Its Logics', *Mind*, 116: 633–76.
Wasserman, R. (2018), *Paradoxes of Time Travel*, Oxford: Oxford University Press.
Williams, D. C. (1951), 'The Myth of Passage', *The Journal of Philosophy*, 48: 457–72.
Williamson, T. (2002), 'Necessary Existents', in A. O'Hear (ed.), *Logic, Thought and Language*, Cambridge: Cambridge University Press, pp. 233–51.
Zhan, Y. (2021), 'A Case for Modal Fragmentalism', *Philosophia*, 49: 1309–28.
Zimmerman, D. (2011), 'Presentism and the Space-time Manifold', in C. Callender (ed.), *The Oxford Handbook of Philosophy of Time*, Oxford: Oxford University Press, pp. 163–244.

Index

absolutism 20–21, 41, 48, 58, 93, 109
A-MSTs 11–12, 28
anaemic passage 4, 68, 77, 159–60n.9
Angela Merkel (example) 29, 99
anti-realism,
   and bivalence 84
   the Block view 119
   causation 99
   introduction 4–5
   tense 26–27, 44, 49, 56, 58
   time travel 144
   time in universe/multiverse 78–79, 90, 92
Aristotle (example) 13
articulated moving spotlight theory 11–12, 28, 30
assumptions 15–17
A-theory 1, 5–7, 9–11, 25, 31–34, 41, 67, 78, 164–65n.16, 171n.18

Baptism 47, 112, 120, 122
Basic Principle 37
Belnap, N. 92
bivalence 70–71, 73, 75, 78–79, 84, 90, 170nn.6, 13–14
block view 1, 7, 48, 119
branching 69, 72, 74, 83–84, 89, 169n.5
Bricker, P. 42, 80, 166n.33, 171n.19
Brogaard, B. 51–52
brute facts 73–74
B-theory 5, 7–9, 33, 67–68, 77, 79, 119, 160n.13

Cambridge changes 10, 162n.31
Cameron, R. P. 11, 28–33, 163–164nn.12–15
causation,
   cross-temporal facts 97–101, 103–4, 172nn.3, 5
   deflationist Humeanism 101–3, 105
   fragmentalist 108–13, 173n.21
   temporal/causal successions 113–15, 173nn.21–2

   ways of fragmented 103–13, 173nn.15, 18
causes 113
Cleopatra (example) 29–31, 99
C-MST 7–10, 12, 161–62nn.24, 27, 29–30
coherence 20–21, 41, 83, 93
content stability 58
co-obtainment 15, 17, 22–23, 46, 57, 60–65, 167n.41, 168n.63
co-obtainment/passage theory (Lipman) 60–65, 168n.65
Correia, F. 11
counterparts 54, 105, 119, 123–26, 152, 168n.58
crossing paths 126–29
cross-temporality 55, 64, 99–100, 104–7, 110–12, 169n.68, 172–73nn.4, 14

Deasy, D. 27, 163n.11
deflationist view 101–3
Deng, Natalja 31
dialetheias 16
dinosaurs extinct (example) 87–89
disjunctions 84–85
Dr Who (example) 135, 137–39

Einstein, Albert 117
ersatzplanes *see* hyperplanes
ersatz times 143–44
eternalism 47, 49, 71, 76–77, 80, 84, 105, 136, 150
eternalist block universe 135
events 111–12, 124
existence entailing 101
external relations 99–101, 132
external relativism 13–15, 20, 45–46, 56, 64, 92–93, 149, 162n.39
external time 134–35

Factive Presentism 48–49
false beliefs 5
Fine, Kit,

anti-realism 25, 27, 31, 163nn.8, 10
fragmentalism 109, 130–31
fragmentalism/external relativism 46, 166–67n.37
Fragmentalist Flow* 39
frozen present problem 63
introduction 1–2, 4, 13–14, 16, 159n.5
original insights of 55–60
presentism 48, 162n.1, 167nn.46–7
relativistic fragmentalism 117, 119, 121–23, 175n.12
standard realism 41
tense realism 85
time/fragmentalist picture 86
fragment labelling 45–47
frame-dependent simultaneity 117
frames of reference 123, 174n.11
frame-theoretic conception 121–23, 129, 131
Frischhut, Akiko 31

global change 1–17, 10, 19, 35, 40, 56–57, 76, 93, 132
growing block view 1, 6

H-parameter 152
Hume, David 102, 105, 109–10
hyperplanes 121–22, 131, 154–56, 174n.9

identity dependence 52–53
indeterminism 70–71, 73, 76–77
individual causation 100–105, 109
instantiation 103, 105, 110
internal relativism 13–14
intrinsic facts 98, 172n.1
invisible thin red line (ITRL) *see* red lines, thin
Ismael, Jenann (example) 48

Joanna (example) 98
Jonathan hungry (example) 86–87
Josephine (example) 98

Lennon, John (example) 11–12
Lewis, David 98, 134
Lewisian modal realism 149, 155
Lipman, M. 16–17, 23, 45, 60–65, 166n.35
local passage 115
Lorenz transformations 122

Loss, R. 23, 65–66
Lowe, E. J. 52
Lucretian properties 75, 77
Ludovician time *see* time travel, Novikovian

McTaggart, J. M. E. 20, 55
Mars (example) 29
Martha and Nicole (example) 128–29
Minkowskian manifold 120–22, 131
modal case 1, 41–42, 54
Modal Fragmentalism 1, 41–43, 166n.31
model theory 64, 93–95
MOP (movable objective present) 151–53
moving spotlight theory 1, 6–10, 28, 31, 38, 66–67
MST-supertime *see* supertime
MST-time 66–68, 169n.75
multiverse 78–80, 90–91
Munchausen, Baron 13, 38

neutrality,
    flow fragmentalism 19–21, 40–42, 44, 47, 49, 54, 56, 59
    open future 93
    relativity 119, 126, 128
'never-present past' problem 153
Newtonian manifold 120, 122, 130
nomic (general) causation 102, 104, 108
nomological determinism 73
nomological facts 105, 110
nomological indeterminism 70, 73, 76–77
non-contradiction law 65
non-eternalism 49, 70
non-external relations 99, 106
non-standard framework 12–15, 33, 38, 56, 59, 66
non-standard tense realism 20–21, 54–55, 59, 65, 84, 93, 144
NOW 66–67

obtainment 53, 55, 57–58, 66, 83, 149–50
obtainment-constitution 22, 24, 37, 42–44, 46, 66
official idiom 2, 23–25, 159n.5, 163nn.6–7
Ontic Presentism 48–50
ontological openness 73–76, 80
original insights 55–60

passage theory 60–65
perdurantism 51–53
personal time 134–35
Petunia (guinea pig) 15–16, 29, 54, 136
pluralism 21–23, 40
Pooley, O. 67, 90–93
presentism,
    and anti-realism 80
    and Cameron's position 31
    and causality 100–101, 103–8, 110, 173n.19
    and flow fragmentalism 20–21, 38–39, 47–50
    introduction 1, 4, 6–8, 159n.7, 160nn.15, 19
    open future 74–76, 170nn.11, 13
    and tense realism/anti-realism 54, 56, 60, 92, 143–44
    and topological openness 77
presentist four dimensionalism 51
primitivism 26, 30–32, 34, 41
Prior, Arthur N. 3, 8, 34, 40, 64, 84
Priorian flow 8–9, 34–35, 45, 161n.28
pseudo-B relations 36, 81, 84, 87
pseudo-histories 81–82, 91–92, 124, 132
pseudo-temporal order 38, 85, 114–15, 130, 135–36

quasi-supervenience base 104
quasi-truths 104–6, 108

Raspe, R. E. 13
reality X 2–3
real tense 4, 25–26, 69
red lines,
    absence of 79
    thick 74–76, 78–80
    thin 74–75, 78–80, 84, 89–93
reductionism 33–34, 43, 45, 66, 68, 134nn.17, 19
reductive analysis 98, 100, 105–6
relative link 58
relativistic flow 129–32
relativity,
    introduction 115, 117, 174nn.1, 3–4, 6
    relativistic flow fragmentalism 123–32, 175nn.13–14
    solipsism/frame-theoretic conception 119–23

Special Theory of 1
time/space/space-time 117–19
revenge argument 46, 167n.40
robust passage,
    causation 103
    flow fragmentalism 27, 29, 34–35, 45, 47, 66, 68
    introduction 3–4, 6–7
    open future 69–73, 76–77, 84
robust realism 103
Rosenkranz, S. 11
RP-histories 124–28, 131–32, 175n.15
'rule of coherence' 54
Russell, Bertrand 4

semantics 8, 36, 44, 57–60, 73, 94–95, 107, 127, 155
sentential connectives 106–8, 173n.16
Sider, Ted 104–5, 172n.13
Simon, J. 62, 168n.64
simple existence 83–84
singular causation 101, 104, 106
singular propositions 107, 113
Skow, Brad 31, 66–68
Socrates (example),
    flow fragmentalism 20–24, 41, 47, 49, 51, 53, 58, 61, 65
    introduction 14
    open future 74–75, 77–78
    relativity 127
Socrates exists simpliciter 49, 167n.49
spatial relations 103, 105, 110, 119–20, 131
spatio-temporal manifold 120, 130
Special Theory of Relativity 1
standard framework 4–15, 81, 84, 121
standard realism 41
standard tense realism 19, 21, 45, 54, 76, 119
Star Trek (example) 139–44, 146, 148–49, 151–57, 177n.26
strong global coherence 6
subvaluationism 65–66
supertime 66–68, 169n.72
super-zombies 143, 154
syntactic rules 93–94

Tallant, J. 52, 86–87
temporal dimension 37, 50, 146

temporal distributional properties 29–30
temporal locations 8–9, 11–12, 55, 118, 131–32, 145
temporal order 8, 10, 19, 53, 76, 81, 84–86, 113–15, 124–25
temporal perspectives 11, 46, 66, 90, 101, 167n.39
temporal relations 103, 119–20
TENSE 83, 171n.23
tense anti-realism 49, 54, 65, 77–78, 80, 97, 119, 144
tensed facts 21, 55–59, 63–64, 77–78, 87, 121, 168–69n.67, 171n.25
tenseless facts 7, 14, 55, 58, 77
tense realism 56, 68, 77, 80, 117, 122, 151–52
Thrasymachus (example) 20
time,
  causal theory of 115
  debate on passage 3–7, 160n.20
  explanation of passage 1, 25, 30, 33–36, 76, 165n.21
  external 134–35
  Minkowskian structure of space-time 122, 131
  Newtonian 112, 114, 121
  in universe/multiverse 78
time travel,
  changing the past problem 139–45
  changing the past solution 145–50
  explanation 133, 175nn.1–2
  hyper-time 152
  movable present/vacillating past 151–57, 177n.21
  non-Novikovian 133, 135, 139, 141–46, 148–49, 151, 153–57, 176nn.15–17
  Novikovian 133–39, 146, 149, 175n.3, 176n.6
  vacillating time 151–54, 156, 177n.23
Titanic (example) 139
topological openness 76–80, 170n.15, 171n.17
tracking roles 133, 146–48, 150–51, 155, 177nn.17, 21
truth 36–37, 44, 57, 74, 85, 95, 97, 99, 123, 166n.24–5
truth-conditions 81, 90, 113–14, 155
truth-values 58, 73, 76–77, 79

über-reality 16, 57–58
universe(s) 78–80, 90–91, 105, 135, 148–49, 177n.20
update test 43–45

verification 58, 168n.61
viewpoints *see* temporal perspectives

weak future facts 75, 170n.12
Williamson, T. 11
worldline 128–29
worldly absolutism 41
worldly neutrality 41–42
worldly realism 41

'zombies in the past' 142–43, 176n.14

www.ingramcontent.com/pod-product-compliance
Lightning Source LLC
Chambersburg PA
CBHW061830300426
44115CB00013B/2321